CLIMATE CHANGE AND AGRO-EDAPHIC SYSTEM

ENV BOOKS SERIES

CLIMATE CHANGE AND AGRO-EDAPHIC SYSTEM

Editors

Dr. Alka Chauhan
Society for Environment, Health
Awareness of Nutrition & Toxicology (SEHAT)
B-225/5D, Top Floor, Subhash Gali, Road No. 7, Block B
Ashok Nagar, Shahdara, Delhi - 110 093
(India)

&

Dr. Pawan Kumar 'Bharti'
Society for Environment, Health
Awareness of Nutrition & Toxicology (SEHAT)
B-225/5D, Top Floor, Subhash Gali, Road No. 7, Block B
Ashok Nagar, Shahdara
Delhi-110093
(India)

Foreword by

M.S. Swaminathan
Founder Chairman
Ex-Member of Parliament (Rajya Sabha)

DPH

DISCOVERY PUBLISHING HOUSE PVT. LTD.
INDIA

Published by:
Namit Wasan
DISCOVERY PUBLISHING HOUSE PVT. LTD.
4383/4B, Ansari Road, Darya Ganj
New Delhi-110 002 (India)
Phone : +91-11-23279245; 23253475; 43596065
E-mail : discoverybooksindia@gmail.com
discoverypublishinghouse@gmail.com
namitwasan9@gmail.com
web : www.discoverypublishinggroup.com

First Edition: **2019**

ISBN: 978-93-86841-98-8

Climate Change and Agro-edaphic System

Printed at:
Infinity Imaging Systems
Delhi

FOREWORD

M.S. Swaminathan
Founder Chairman
Ex-Member of Parliament (Rajya Sabha)

I am very glad to know that a several books are being edited under the aegis of ENVBOOKS series Delhi, India on various sub-themes of Agriculture and environment like:

- Heavy Metals and Pesticides in Environment
- Heavy conservation and renewable sources Climate Change and Agriculture Production
- Geospatial Technology and Ecosystem Assessment
- Food Technology and Agriculture Advancement
- Vermicompost and Vermitechnology
- Pest Control and Management
- Plant Response to Environmental Stress
- Bioremediation and Biotechnology
- Noise and Air Pollution
- Risk and Disaster Management
- Agro-ecology and Environmental Biotechnology
- Water and Wastewater Management
- Soil Pollution and Lithosphere
- Earth Ecosystem and Pollution
- Microbial Ecology
- Waste Recycling and Product Development

I am very happy to learn that a number of editors and authors from different institutions and university of different nations are involved in editing these books. The books are the compendium of screened-in manuscripts received from different countries like UK, Canada, Egypt, Nigeria, Ghana, Ethiopia, China, South Africa, Japan, Guyana, PNG, Nepal, South America and various parts of India. I am feeling delighted in writing forward to these books and congratulate to Dr. Pawan Kumar 'Bharti', Editor-in-Chief and founder of ENVBOOKs series and of course his team for their tenacity and hard work in compiling these valuable compendiums.

I hope these books will be beneficial for academician, researchers, industrialist policy makes and students as study material and will work as reference for further research work.

M.S. Swaminathan

PREFACE

Climate change generally refers to changes in global weather conditions over a long-term timescale. It can be caused by natural processes, such as a change in the sun's strength, as well as by human activities—in particular, manmade emissions of GHGs that build up in the atmosphere and alter its chemical composition. On a global scale, climate is largely regulated by how much energy the Earth receives from the sun and how much energy it releases back to space. The global climate is also affected by other flows of energy within the climate system itself. These energy flows are regulated by the atmosphere (which provides gases, aerosols, clouds, and winds), the oceans (which help to distribute heat through currents), precipitation (in the form of rain, snow or ice), water (in the form of lakes and rivers), and land (which reflects or absorbs energy from the sun). Changes to any of these elements can affect the balance of the entire system, causing the climate to change.

Anthropogenic activities include the industrial emissions to the atmosphere, effluent discharge to streams and rivers, soil contamination by solid waste or industrial discharge and any man made undesirable and unwanted change into environmental components, which can alter the physical, chemical or biological characteristics of the environment. Generally, anthropogenic activities create environmental problems in the form of water pollution, soil pollution, and air pollution

The present book updates the subject content related to global climate change, global warming, green house gases, anthropogenic activities, IPCC, soil-plant-water interaction and impact of climate change on agriculture, microorganisms, air pollution.

Thanks are due to publisher and contributors from various institutions and universities.

The book will be helpful for the researchers, academia working in the field of global climate change, global warming, green house gases, anthropogenic activities, IPCC, soil-plant-water interaction and impact of climate change on agriculture, microorganisms, air pollution.

Editors
(envbooks@gmail.com)

CONTENTS

Foreword

Preface

1. Increasing Human Activities and Climate Change 1
   Dr. Pawan Kumar 'Bharti'
2. Climate Change Scenario in India and Evidences in the Indian Himalayan Region 20
   Bhavika Sharma, Shalini Singh Maurya and Jesmita Brahmacharimayum
3. Intergovernmental Panel on Climate Change with Special Reference to Health 50
   Prasann Kumar and Shweta Pathak
4. Air Pollution and Climatic Changes: *The Global and Regional Perspectives* 74
   Akash, Navneet and B.S Bhandari
5. Climate Change and its Causes: *A Moot for Discussion about Some Principle Issues* 103
   Prasann Kumar and Shweta Pathak
6. Soil Microorganisms and Climate Change 127
   P. Dhevagi and C.Ponniah
7. Climate Change and Indian Agriculture 147
   Alok Kumar Patra, Pulak Kumar Patra and Ranjan Kumar Patra
8. Phytoplankton to Combat Global Warming 163
   Noor El Deen A I E
9. Soil-Plant-Water Interactions in Varying Ecosystems: *Current Interactions and Future Predictions under Changed Climatic Conditions* 168
   Wenjun Ji, Asim Biswas
10. Egyptian Contribution to a Solution of Global Warming by Aquaculture in Qattara Depression: *A Simulation Study* 182
    A.I. Noor El Deen, Mona S. Zaki, M. Khafagy and M.S. Abd El Karim

Index 189

7. [illegible] ... [illegible]

8. [illegible] ... [illegible]

9. [illegible] ... [illegible]

10. [illegible] ... [illegible]

Climate Change and Agro-Edaphic System **Pages 1–19**
Edited by: Dr. Alka Chauhan & Dr. Pawan Kumar 'Bharti'
ISBN: 978-93-86841-98-8
Edition: 2019
Published by: Discovery Publishing House Pvt. Ltd., New Delhi (India)

1

Increasing Human Activities and Climate Change

[1]Dr. Pawan Kumar 'Bharti'

ABSTRACT

Researchers have studied that global climate change and stratospheric ozone layer depletion are inextricably linked. The latest studies predict that the major relationships between the two will cause ozone depletion to exacerbate climate change and climate change to exacerbate ozone depletion, with grave and potentially irreversible consequences for people and ecosystems. They are also agreed that the world is getting warmer. Globally, climate is largely regulated by how much energy the Earth receives from the sun and how much energy it releases back to space. The atmospheric composition, the ocean, precipitation, water and land, regulates these energy flows by their different roles. Changes to any of these elements can affect the balance of the entire system, causing change to climate. Atmospheric particles and Antarctica continent always play an important role to regulate the energy budget and climate of the planet. So, the increasing industrialization, emissions from automobiles and industries, release of heat radiation to atmosphere can harm environment & living organisms in the form of various diseases. The present paper highlights the anthropogenic activities and their effects on global environment. The role of Ozone layer, status of ozone layer depletion over Antarctica, green house effect, global warming, climate change and health effects, as the consequences of continuous and long term anthropogenic activities are described. Few legislative initiatives are also discussed, which is taken for the protection of ozone layer and to prevent global warming.

Key words: Human activities, Climate Change, Global warming, Ozone layer, Global Issues

Introduction

Earth is a unique and most probably the only planet in the universe that supports life in its biosphere. About 71 per cent of the Earth's surface is

[1] Antarctica Laboratory, R & D Division, Shriram Institute for Industrial Research, 19, University Road, Delhi-110 007, India.

covered with salt-water oceans, the remainder consisting of continents and islands. Earth is the only planet on which water can exist in liquid form on the surface and liquid water is extremely essential for life (Akimoto, 2003). Earth has been divided in the Northern and the Southern Hemispheres; the half of a planet is north of the equator and other half is south of the equator. The north contains about 90 per cent of its land area and most of its human population. The Arctic region lies in the north of the Arctic Circle. Entire Europe, North America, small parts of South America and entire Asia lies in it. Because of the Coriolis Effect, large-scale horizontal flows of air or water tend to form clockwise-turning spin north of the equator and ocean circulation patterns in the North Atlantic and North Pacific Oceans. The clockwise air circulation is characteristic of high-pressure weather cells in the Northern Hemisphere. Hurricanes and tropical storms caused because of highest low-pressure spin anti-clockwise in the Northern Hemisphere (Bharti and Kumar, 2012).

The Southern Hemisphere comprises the rest half of planet Earth, in the south of the equator, and includes Antarctica, Australia, parts of South America and parts of Africa, four oceans South Atlantic, Indian, South Pacific, and Southern and most of Oceania are part of it. Several islands off the Asian continental mainland are also in the Southern Hemisphere. Climates remain slightly milder, except in the Antarctica, which is colder than the Arctic. It has more oceans, less land, less population - a total of 10 to 12%, lower levels of industrialization, and smaller landmasses than the Northern Hemisphere. Air currents run mostly west-east, so pollution does not easily spread north or south makes it less polluted (Harris *et al.*, 2003).

Atmosphere

The Earth's atmosphere consists of 77 per cent nitrogen, 21 per cent oxygen, with traces of argon, carbon dioxide, and water (Akimoto, 2003). The tiny amount of carbon dioxide resident in the atmosphere is extremely important for the maintenance of the Earth's surface temperature via the greenhouse effect. Atmospheric circulation is the large-scale movement of air with ocean circulation that distributes heat on the surface of the Earth (Bharti and Gajananda, 2015). Scientists from all over the world have agreed that the world is getting warmer. By examining climate records, scientists have determined that the temperature of air on the surface of the Earth has warmed by approximately 0.6°C since the late 19th century (Venkataraman, 2005). In the 20th century, the Northern Hemisphere was the warmest of the past 1,000 years, with the 1990s being the warmest decade of the millennium. Furthermore, most experts agree that average global temperatures will rise by 1.4°C to 5.8°C over the next century (Harris *et al.*, 2003). These relatively small changes in average temperatures can have huge consequences.

Atmospheric air is contaminated with pollutants that are largely deteriorating and making it polluted. Sources of pollutant emission are natural, commercial, industrial, and residential. The natural sources of pollution are pollen, volcanoes and forest fires and agricultural remnants. Commercial activities include dry-cleaning operations, auto body shops, and automobile emissions. Industrial sources include fossil fuel-fired electric power plants and manufacturing facilities. Residential sources include home gas and oil burners and wood stoves (Pope, 2002).

Industrialization

Industrialization began in about CE 1750, further adding to the concentration of all major greenhouse gases. Their concentration has significantly increased in the atmosphere to such levels that are enough to bring about the changes in climate which are currently being experienced in the world. Between CE1000–1300, there was a period of relatively mild climate called the "Medieval Warm Period" when temperatures in the Northern Hemisphere were believed to be at least 0.8°C warmer than present times. A few centuries later, between CE 1450 and 1850, global temperatures were between 1.0 and 2.0°C cooler than today (McDonnell, 2000). Scientists believe that these two climatic shifts were caused by natural fluctuations in the sun's radiation and increased volcanic activity. These activities can interfere with the amount of energy absorbed on the Earth's surface and these may have also contributed to the cooling of temperatures on the Earth (Caldwell *et al.,* 2003). The Industrial Revolution took place in the late 18th and early 19th centuries in few countries of Western Europe and North America, beginning in Great Britain. This was the first industrialization in the world's history. The Industrial Revolution was the transition to new manufacturing processes in the period from about 1760 to sometime between 1820 and 1840. This transition included going from hand production methods to machines, new chemical manufacturing and iron production processes, improved efficiency of water power, the increasing use of steam power, the development of machine tools and the rise of the factory system. The First Industrial Revolution evolved into the Second Industrial Revolution in the transition years between 1840 and 1870, when technological and economic progress continued with the increasing adoption of steam transport (steam-powered railways, boats and ships), the large-scale manufacture of machine tools and the increasing use of machinery in steam-powered factories. The Second Industrial Revolution describes a later, somewhat less dramatic change, which came about in the late 19th century with the widespread availability of electric power, internal combustion engines, and assembly lines to the already industrialized nations. The lack of the industrial sector in a country is widely seen as a major handicap in improving a country's economy, and power, pushing many governments to encourage or enforce industrialization. Industrial process are releasing chemicals, particulate matter or biological materials that cause discomfort to humans or other living organisms and damages the natural environment, into the atmosphere that is essential to support life on planet Earth (Bharti, 2007).

Anthropogenic Activities

Anthropogenic activities include the industrial emissions to the atmosphere, effluent discharge to streams and rivers, soil contamination by solid waste or industrial discharge and any man made undesirable and unwanted change into environmental components, which can alter the physical, chemical or biological characteristics of the environment. Generally, anthropogenic activities create environmental problems in the form of water pollution, soil pollution, and air pollution (Bharti and Gajananda, 2013).Anthropogenic activities are mainly generating particulate matter, nitrogen oxides (NOx), sulphur dioxide (SO_2), and carbon monoxide (CO), carbon-dioxide (CO_2) as well as a range of organic gases and vapors of volatile organic compounds (VOCs) to the atmosphere. Ground-level ozone (O_3) concentration is a result of photochemical reaction between NOx and VOCs in the presence of heat and sunlight. All of these potentially toxic gases and substances are also major contributors to smog, and are together referred to as air pollutants (WHO, 2003). Aerosol (particles) introduced by anthropogenic activities and Antarctica continent always play an important role to regulate the energy budget and climate of the planet. Antarctica produced a very high quantity of Albedo and aerosols are important for reflection or absorption of radiation in atmosphere. Only these factors regulate the Global Climate, with global wind velocities in both hemispheres. The greatest threat to Antarctica is from global warming, caused by activities elsewhere on the planet.

Global Environmental Issues

The high degree of anthropogenic activities affects the environment and brings many changes in the environmental components like atmosphere, hydrosphere, and lithosphere (Bharti and Gajananda, 2015). In the recent past, few environmental issues became very hot even at the global level. Some of these are enumerated as follows:

Global Warming

The ability of a greenhouse gas to warm the Earth depends on its capacity to absorb heat as well as on its atmospheric lifetime when released into the atmosphere. Global warming potential (GWP) is the heat trapping potential per molecule of the gas compared to a molecule of carbon dioxide or CO_2 (which has a GWP of 1.0) over a 100-year timeframe. Methane has a GWP of 23, which means that over 100 years, each molecule of methane traps heat 23 times more effectively than CO_2. The atmospheric lifetime of a greenhouse gas refers to the length of time that a gas remains in the atmosphere and, hence, its ability to influence climate. Some gases have relatively short atmospheric lifetimes (e.g., 12 years for methane (CH_4)), while others (e.g., halo carbons) remain in the atmosphere and continue to absorb the sun's heat for hundreds or even thousands of years (UNEP, 2002). The greatest threat to Antarctica is from global warming, caused by activities elsewhere on the planet.

The main predicted impacts of global warming are as follows:

- Global sea levels could rise by more than 20 feet with the loss of shelf ice in Greenland and Antarctica, devastating coastal areas worldwide (Lovgren, 2004);
- The Arctic Ocean could be ice free in summer by 2050 (UNEP/GRID, 2001); and
- More than 35 per cent of all species on Earth could be driven to extinction by 2050 (Thomas, 2004).

Green House Effect

The natural greenhouse effect is that energy from the sun drives the Earth's climate. As the sun's energy reaches the Earth's surface, some of it is reflected back and some of it is absorbed. The absorbed energy warms the Earth. This heat is then radiated back out towards space as infrared energy. Certain chemical compounds in the Earth's atmosphere act as "greenhouse gases", absorbing the radiated infrared energy and thereby trapping some of the heat in the atmosphere. The greenhouse gases radiate this energy in all directions, including back to the Earth again. This energy is used in a number of processes, including heating the ground surface, melting ice and snow, evaporating water, and plant photosynthesis. Most importantly, this energy remains trapped within the climate system, warming the Earth's surface to an average of 14°C. This phenomenon, called the "natural greenhouse effect", keeps the Earth in a temperature range that allows life to thrive. Without it, the sun's heat would escape and the average temperature of the Earth would drop to –19°C (Fergusson, 2001). Human activities can disrupt the balance of the global climate system. Any changes in atmospheric greenhouse gas concentrations will affect the amount of energy stored in the atmosphere. For example, when the amount of carbon dioxide (CO_2)—a major greenhouse gas—is increased, more heat is trapped in the atmosphere (Cohen, 2000). This "enhanced greenhouse effect" causes the Earth's surface temperature to rise. Many gases in the atmosphere exhibit "greenhouse" properties. These include those gases occurring naturally in the atmosphere, such as CO_2, methane, nitrous oxide, and water vapour, as well as gases produced from human activities and referred to as halocarbons (i.e., chlorofluorocarbons [CFCs], hydrofluorocarbons [HFCs], perfluorocarbons [PFCs], and sulfur hexafluoride [SF6]) (Chestnut *et al.*, 1997). In January 2001, the Intergovernmental Panel on Climate Change (IPCC), comprising top scientists from around the world, concluded that "there is new and stronger evidence that most of the warming observed over the last 50 years is attributable to human activity". Humans are adding more and more greenhouse gases to the atmosphere, mainly through the burning or "combustion" of fossil fuels (i.e., petroleum, natural gas and coal) to transport people and goods, heat and cool buildings, generate electricity, and operate industries. Agricultural activities and manufacturing processes are also significant sources of some gases.

In addition, changes in land cover and land use for agriculture, urbanization, and road construction can affect the concentrations of greenhouse gases in the atmosphere. Land use change often involves the clearing of forests and vegetation. When these large swaths of vegetation are cleared, the area has considerably less capacity to absorb and store CO_2 through photosynthesis (the process by which green plants use energy from the sun to convert CO_2 into fuel for growth). In addition, if forests are removed by burning, the CO_2 stored in the tree wood is returned to the atmosphere. There are also natural activities that add greenhouse gases to the atmosphere. For example, natural sources of CO_2 include the respiration of people, animals and plants, volcanic eruptions, and gas emissions from the oceans (these vast water bodies are huge absorbers and storehouses of CO_2 and other gases). Together, these natural sources release about 550 billion tonnes of CO_2 each year, far outweighing the 30 billion tonnes released by human activity (McDonnell, 2000). While natural CO_2 removal processes, such as photosynthesis by plants, keep the large volume of natural releases in check, they cannot absorb the added emissions from human activity. Consequently, this gas is building up in the atmosphere. While international efforts are being made to reduce greenhouse gas emissions, these actions will not stop the occurrence of climate change, before the end of this century, at which time CO_2 levels are projected to double or possibly triple rom pre-industrial levels.

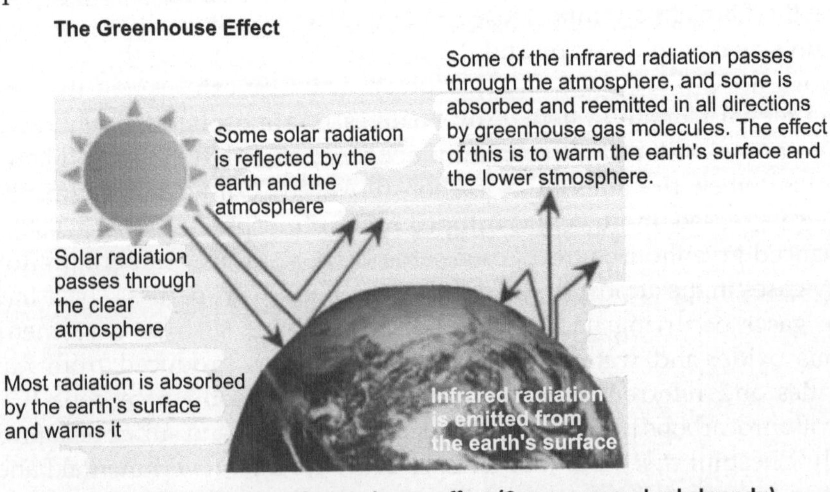

Fig. 1.1: A line diagram of green house effect (Source: ucmp.berkeley.edu)

Climate Change

Climate change generally refers to changes in global weather conditions over a long-term timescale. It can be caused by natural processes, such as a change in the sun's strength, as well as by human activities—in particular, manmade emissions of GHGs that build up in the atmosphere and alter its chemical composition (Environment Canada, 2005).On a global scale, climate is largely regulated by how much energy the Earth receives from the sun and how much energy it releases back to space. The global climate is also affected by other flows of energy within the climate system itself. These energy flows are regulated by the atmosphere (which provides gases, aerosols, clouds, and winds), the oceans (which help to distribute heat through currents), precipitation (in the form of rain, snow or ice), water (in the form of lakes and rivers), and land (which reflects or absorbs energy from the sun). Changes to any of these elements can affect the balance of the entire system, causing the climate to change. A good example of this is the weather phenomenon known as *El Niño*. Above-average Pacific Ocean water temperatures have affected the patterns of tropical rainfall from Indonesia all the way to the west coast of South America, a distance roughly equal to half of the world's circumference. These changes in tropical rainfall have, in turn, affected weather patterns around the globe. Climate change will significantly shift many aspects of weather, such as wind patterns, the amount and type of precipitation, and the severity and frequency of extreme weather events. It is influencing our way of life, the clothes we wear, eating habits, and choice of lifestyle and these changes could have far-reaching health, environmental, social, and economic consequences (Chauhan and Bharti, 2016). The World Health Organization (WHO) stated that "there is growing evidence that changes in the global climate will have profound effects on the health and well-being of citizens in countries throughout the world". Energy from the sun drives the Earth's weather and climate. Most of this energy is absorbed by the Earth's surface, causing it to warm, and some is re-emitted back to space (USEPA, 2006). Atmospheric greenhouse gases (GHGs), such as water vapour and carbon dioxide, trap some of the outgoing energy, retaining heat somewhat like the glass panels of a greenhouse. This natural "greenhouse effect" maintains the temperature and climate on Earth to support life as we know it (USEPA, 2006). However, due to the buildup of GHGs from human activities, including industrial processes, fossil fuel combustion and deforestation, the Earth is warming at an unprecedented rate. Temperatures at the Earth's surface increased by an estimated 1.4°F (0.8°C) between 1900 and 2005 (NASA, 2006a). The Earth was warmer in the late 20th century than it had been in the last 400 or possibly 1,000 years (Associated Press, 2006). The year 2005 was most likely one of the two warmest years on record since 1850 (WMO, 2005). Scientists expect that the average global surface temperature could rise 1–4.5°F (0.6–2.5°C) in the next fifty years, and 2.2–10°F (1.4–5.8°C) in the next century (USEPA, 2006).

These are the few predicted impacts of climate change:

- The glaciers of Greenland are melting twice as fast as they were five years ago and the ice sheets of Antarctica—the world's largest reservoir of fresh water—are also shrinking, according to a February 2006 report by NASA's Jet Propulsion Laboratory and the University of Kansas (NASA, 2006b);
- A WHO report in 2000 found that warming had caused malaria to spread from three districts in western Kenya to 13 and led to epidemics of the disease in Rwanda and Tanzania (Struck, 2006);
- Argentina's Upsala Glacier was once the biggest in South America, but it is now disappearing at a rate of 200 meters per year (BBC, 2005);
- The WHO concluded in 2005 that climate change already is claiming more than 150,000 lives each year, with causes ranging from heat waves to respiratory illness (Struck, 2006);
- Global warming accounted for around half of the extra hurricane-fueling warmth in the waters of the tropical North Atlantic in 2005, while natural cycles were only a minor factor (NCAR, 2006);

Ozone Depletion

Ozone depletion refers to the deterioration of the Earth's ozone layer located in the upper atmosphere known as the stratosphere. Chemicals (such as CFCs, halons, and methyl bromide) destroy ozone in the stratosphere, thus impairing the ozone layer's ability to shield UV radiation from the Earth's surface. The result is that the ozone layer becomes noticeably thinner and weaker, particularly in the Polar Regions. Any loss of ozone allows more UV radiation to reach the Earth's surface. This has significant impacts on human and environmental health, most notably increased incidence of skin cancer and cataracts (EIA, 2006). Life on Earth depends on the protection provided by the ozone layer. This thin layer of ozone molecules screens out nearly 99 per cent of harmful ultraviolet (UV) radiation from the sun (Rai and Mallik, 1998). Humans have severely depleted the ozone layer by releasing high quantities of chemicals that contain bromine, chlorine, and other ozone-depleting substances (ODS) into the atmosphere (UNEP, 2002). These chemicals react with sunlight in the upper atmosphere, or stratosphere, to destroy ozone, thus thinning the protective layer and allowing greater amounts of UV radiation to reach the Earth's surface. In 1985, scientists discovered severe thinning of the ozone layer over Antarctica due to human emissions of bromine and chlorine (UNEP, 2002). Satellite measurements have confirmed that an Antarctic ozone hole has reappeared each austral spring since its initial discovery. Although there is some variation from year to year, the ozone hole has generally grown larger and lasted longer each year. The 2005 ozone hole measured approximately 10 million square miles (25 million square kilometers) and was larger than the size of North America nearly equaling the all-time record set in 2000 (BAS, 2000 and NASA, 2006a). In 2005, the tip of South America and the Falkland Islands were also affected by the edges of the ozone hole between August and September. During these periods, ozone values dropped to more than 20 per cent below the normal value for that time of the year. By the end of September, ozone levels were down by over 30 per cent. The region was also affected by severe ozone depletion from October 7 to 10, when ozone amounts dropped 50 per cent below normal levels (NERC, 2006). Scientists recently were shocked to observe severe ozone loss over the Northern Hemisphere and now warn of the possible development of an Arctic ozone hole. In the winter of 2004–05, the scientific journal, *Nature* reported "the biggest ozone losses ever recorded over the Arctic" (Nature, 2005). Researchers observed a 30 per cent reduction in the ozone layer during the winter/early spring and measured a 50 per cent reduction in ozone at an altitude of 18 km (Gaurdian Unlimited, 2005). This follows measurements from the 1999–2000 winters, when the Arctic ozone layer lost over half of its ozone (NASA, 2002).Ozone layer thinning is not confined to Polar Regions; it is a global problem with serious worldwide implications. Current global average ozone levels are approximately 3 per cent below pre-1980 levels. In mid-latitudes, where most of the world's population resides, the ozone layer has thinned between 3–6 per cent from pre-1980 levels (UNEP, 2002). According to a recent report by European scientists, stratospheric ozone amounts over mainland Europe started to decline in the 1970s with larger decreases (between 5–10 per cent) occurring during the winter and spring seasons (EC, 2002). They also report that biologically active UV radiation has increased on the ground, in line with the reduced ozone amounts. Thinning of the ozone layer results in increases in the quantities of harmful UV radiation that reach the surface of the Earth (UNEP, 2002).

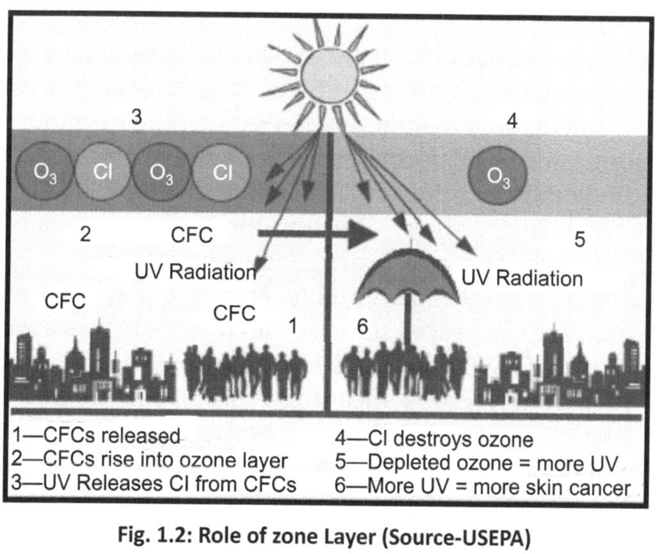

Fig. 1.2: Role of zone Layer (Source-USEPA)

Recent scientific research indicates that UV radiation is much more harmful to the eye and vision than had previously been suspected. Increased UV radiation from ozone depletion damages DNA in living systems, and increased exposure is likely to affect the immune system and reduce resistance to infection. Zooplankton and phytoplankton, the foundation of the ocean food chain, lack protection from UV-B radiation and thus are particularly sensitive to the effec of ozone depletion (UNEP, 2002).

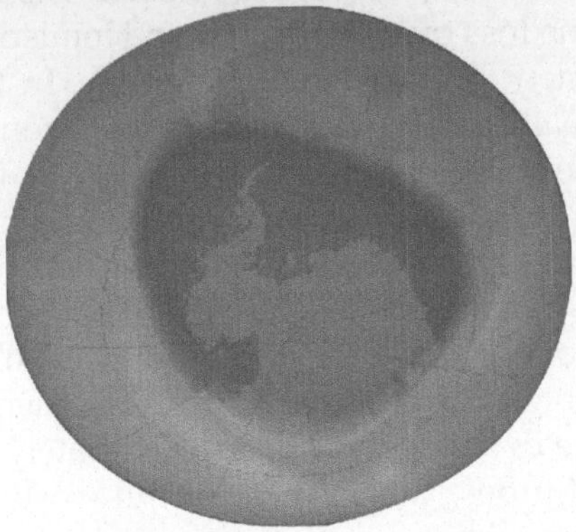

Fig. 1.3: The Antarctic Ozone hole (Source-NASA/GSFC)

Consequences

Globally, as a result of anthropogenic activities, there may be many predicted impacts of various environmental problems and climate change, to the entire world. This will be almost impossible to restore the ecological conditions at that time. A few long-term consequences are explained as follows:

Health Problems

Humans by way of several different routes will feel these effects. Most directly, health will be affected through temperature extremes of heat or cold that could result in illness and death. Extreme weather events, such as more frequent and intense rainstorms and windstorms, hurricanes and tornadoes, could result in death, injury, and other harmful effects. Climate change will also affect human health somewhat less directly by affecting the environment and ecosystems within which we live. These indirect effects will occur through insect and rodent-transmitted diseases (e.g., virus fever; Lyme disease, and Hantavirus Pulmonary Syndrome); increased smog and air pollution; waterborne and food-related illnesses (e.g., Giardiasis, E. coli infection, and shellfish poisoning); and stronger UV radiation, which is a leading cause of skin cancer and cataracts (Sheila *et al.*, 2005). The time frame for the emergence of these health impacts can range from immediately (e.g., a storm-related injury), to weeks or months (e.g., an insect-transmitted infection), to years and decades (e.g., UV-related malignancies).Some positive health effects may result from climate change as warmer winters could reduce cold-related deaths. However, the negative effects of climate change tend to far outweigh the positive effects. This primer deals primarily with the harmful, or potentially harmful, human health effects of climate change (Akimoto, 2003).

Temperature Variation

Extreme temperature events, by definition, are rare and usually associated with heat waves in the summer and cold spells in the winter. An extreme heat wave is a prolonged period of excessive daytime and nighttime heat, usually in association with high humidity and related to geographic location and time of year. In Canada, a heat wave is defined as three or more days of 32°C temperatures and beyond. With climate change, cold temperature extremes are expected to become less frequent, while heat waves will become more frequent. Record extremes in high temperatures are already occurring in some parts of the world, the most recent being heat waves that took place across Europe in the summer of 2003 and to which the WHO has attributed 20,000 deaths (WHO, 2003).Heat can kill by pushing the human body beyond its capability to keep cool. Under warm conditions, the body's internal thermostat makes the skin produce perspiration that evaporates and cools the body. However, in extreme heat and high humidity, this cooling process is slowed and the body must work harder to maintain a normal temperature. The clothed human body can handle most variations in weather, within certain limits. However, extreme changes in weather, such as heat waves, can cause adverse health effects, such as heat cramps, fainting, heat exhaustion, and heatstroke (Heat in combination with air pollution can also exacerbate respiratory and cardiovascular conditions). The magnitude of these health effects is difficult to predict and depends on a variety of factors, such as suddenness of heat onset, city planning for heat emergencies, and regional heat tolerance. In temperate climate cities, heat waves that occur early in the summer may be deadlier than those that occur later, mainly because people have not had time to acclimatize to the heat and, therefore, are more sensitive to hot weather stresses. The duration of the heat wave is also a significant factor. According to the American Red Cross, studies show that a significant rise in heat-related illnesses happens when excessive heat lasts more than two days. When the body is exposed to extreme or prolonged heat, one of its cooling mechanisms is to increase surface blood circulation, which requires the heart to pump faster and harder. Thus, groups susceptible to heat include the elderly and people with weak hearts or cardiac diseases. Studies have found that the risk for heat-related death increases sharply with age. Women over 85 years of age are most at risk of heat-related mortality. Increase in hospital visits for cardiovascular diseases and increase in deaths due to cardiovascular and respiratory diseases, have also been documented during heat waves, suggesting that heat exacerbates these conditions. Like the elderly, young children are at a high risk for heat-related illnesses. Both the very old and the very young tend to have more difficulty regulating body heat. In addition, they may be less able to move freely, resulting in less control over their situation (Venkataraman, 2005).

Local Weather

Weather becomes more extreme with climate change, largely because warming speeds up the water cycle (the process by which water vapour rises into the atmosphere and condenses as precipitation). In terms of weather, "extreme" often refers to severe events, such as hurricanes, tornadoes, ice storms, storm surges, floods, and drought. Warmer temperatures heat the Earth's surface, which leads to faster evaporation and hence, more moisture in the atmosphere. Increased moisture in the air means more water vapour will condense as precipitation. Therefore, as more heat and moisture is put into the atmosphere, precipitation-driven events, such as storms, floods, hurricanes, and tornadoes, will intensify in some parts of the world. Sea levels around the world will rise because increasing temperatures cause ocean seawater to expand as it warms (this "thermal expansion" is believed to have been a major influence on past changes in sea levels). Levels will also rise due to the melting of glaciers and ice caps, which will increase the volume of water in the world's oceans. This, in turn, will tend to lead to more storm surges along coastal regions. Land may become parched in some areas due to rapid evaporation of water from soils, lakes, and reservoirs. Interior regions, such as the Canadian Prairies, will become drier, with more prolonged periods of drought. This parching of soil can also lead to secondary effects, such as the development of unstable winds, tornadoes, and other powerful storms. According to the World Meteorological Organization (WMO), record extremes in weather and climate events, such as droughts, tornadoes, and high temperatures, continue to occur around the world. Recent scientific evidence indicates that, as global temperatures continue to warm due to climate change, the number and intensity of extreme events might increase. Changes in the pattern of inter-hemisphere wind paths especially on the equator, Walker circulation, Southern Oscillation, El-Nino, and La-Nina and their consequences are strong examples of local climate change.

Air Quality

The air we breathe is contaminated with pollutants that negatively impact human health. In general, these pollutants have many sources: natural (e.g., pollen, volcanoes, and forest fires), agricultural (e.g., methane, pesticides, and herbicides), commercial activities (e.g., dry-cleaning operations and auto body shops), industrial (e.g., fossil fuel-fired electric power plants and manufacturing facilities), transportation (e.g., truck and automobile emissions), and residential (e.g., home gas and oil burners and wood stoves) (Pope, 2002).Among the pollutants generated from these activities are nitrogen oxides (NOx), sulphur dioxide (SO_2), and carbon monoxide (CO), as well as a range of organic gases and vapours referred to as volatile organic compounds (VOCs). Ground-level ozone (O_3) is not emitted directly into the air from a specific source, but is created through a photochemical reaction between NOx and VOCs in the presence of heat and sunlight. Tiny particles, known as "particulate matter" (PM), are also generated from human activities, particularly fossil fuel combustion. All of these potentially toxic gases and substances are also major contributors to smog and are together referred to as air pollutants (Cohen, 2000).

Climate change could increase air pollution levels in several ways. First, changes in climate could affect local weather, and thereby local and regional pollution concentrations. Precipitation levels, cloud cover, water vapour levels, and wind speed and direction all affect how pollutants are dispersed and their specific concentrations. Some scientists have suggested that the formation of smog will increase with mean annual temperature increase as the smog precursors of NOx and VOCs react faster at higher temperatures and create more ground-level ozone. As a result, frequent and severe heat waves could translate into more frequent high-ozone-level days and air pollution advisories. Second, climate change will affect natural sources of air pollutant emissions, such as forest fires. Increased drought brought on by climate change could influence the occurrence of forest fires since they usually need dry conditions to start. When forests and other vegetation burn, particulate matter is released into the air along with CO, NOx, SO_2, and VOCs. If there are no winds to blow the pollutants away, the air can remain hazardous for weeks. If wind is present, the pollutants can be spread over a large region: in early July 2002, the northeastern part of the United States felt the effects of fires burning in northern Quebec, with elevated particulate matter concentrations recorded in many areas of New England and mid-Atlantic states.

Third, climate change could bring about an increase in man-made emissions. With higher temperatures, greater amounts of fossil fuels (e.g., coal) would be burned by power plants to satisfy increased air conditioning demands, thus, producing more greenhouse gases and smog-causing pollutants. Fourth, climate change will change the distribution and types of airborne allergens, such as pollen. Studies have shown that rising levels of CO_2 will bring about an increase in the production of pollen in some plants, producing more allergens and thereby making the situation worse for those people suffering from asthma, emphysema, and other respiratory illnesses (McDonnell, 2000). Changes in precipitation and temperature are also likely to influence the growth and distribution of allergen sources, such as ragweed. An accompanying increase in humidity would also mean a rise in the production of mould spores. There is already extensive evidence of the health effects that result from air pollution. The damaging effects of exposure to smog can range from eye, nose, and throat irritation to decreased lung function (a decrease in the ability to move air in and out of the lungs). Ground-level ozone can also aggravate respiratory and cardiac diseases and, in some cases, cause premature death. Studies have shown that, when smog level rises, there is an increase in the number of health problems faced by people, as well as increases in daily respiratory admissions to hospitals. Fine airborne particles, such as those found in smog, have damaging health effects because they are able to penetrate deep into the lungs, causing or worsening cardio-respiratory problems (Akimoto, 2003). With a warmer and wetter climate resulting in higher airborne concentrations of various pollens and spores in some regions, people suffering from allergies and respiratory disorders could suffer health impacts. People with asthma have bronchial tubes that can be easily inflamed, therefore particulate, which can irritate and inflame air passages, are likely to greatly affect this group. A number of studies have found a strong association between increases in the concentration of particulate matter and a rise in the number of associated health problems. These consequences are the main impacts of global phenomena of climate change and all these will be only due to the increasing anthropogenic activities in this industrialization era.

Legal Initiatives

There are many rules and regulations for the protection and conservation of the environment. A few of these were coined especially for greenhouse gases, ozone layer protection, and to prevent global warming and related environment issues. The main protocols are the Montreal and Kyoto protocols.

The Montreal Protocol

The Montreal Protocol on Substances that Deplete the Ozone Layer, a landmark agreement established in 1987, sets legally binding controls on the national production and consumption of ODS (Ozone Depleting Substances), with complete phase out as the final goal. Amendments to the Protocol were added at meetings in London (1990), Copenhagen (1992), Vienna (1995), Montreal (1997), and Beijing (1999).Widely considered the most successful international environmental agreement, the Montreal Protocol has done much to protect both the ozone layer and the global climate system. For example, atmospheric chlorine levels (the element in CFCs that depletes the ozone layer) are now decreasing due to Montreal Protocol controls on CFCs and other ODS. Many ODS and their substitutes are also known to be significant GHGs. These include CFCs, HCFCs, HFCs, and PFCs. However, regulatory control over these substances is split between the Montreal Protocol and the Kyoto Protocol. The Montreal Protocol has control over CFCs and HCFCs, whereas HFCs and PFCs are within the purview of the Kyoto Protocol. Given the overlap, both in the causes and effects of ozone depletion and climate change, and in the policy responses, it has become increasingly obvious that coordination between these two treaties is imperative.

Table 1.1: Summary of Montreal Protocol Control Measures (www.theozonehole.com)

Ozone Depleting Substances	Developed Countries	Developing Countries
Chlorofluorocarbons (CFCs)	Phased out end of 1995[a]	Total phase out by 2010
Halons	Phased out end of 1993	Total phase out by 2010
Carbon tetrachloride	Phased out end of 1995[a]	Total phase out by 2010
Methyl chloroform	Phased out end of 1995[a]	Total phase out by 2015
Hydrochlorofluorocarbons (HCFCs)	Freeze from beginning of 1996[b]; 35% reduction by 2004; 65% reduction by 2010; 90% reduction by 2015; Total phase out by 2020[c]	Freeze in 2016 at 2015 base level; Total phase out by 2040
Hydrobromofluorocarbons (HBFCs)	*Phased out end of 1995*	Phased out end of 1995
Methyl bromide	Freeze in 1995 at 1991 base level[d]; 25% reduction by 1999; 50% reduction by 2001; 70% reduction by 2000; Total phase out by 2005	Freeze in 2002 at average 1995-1998 base level; 20% reduction by 2005[e]; Total phase out by 2015

Notes:

[a] With the exception of a very small number of internationally agreed essential uses that are considered critical to human health and/or laboratory and analytical procedures.

[b] Based on 1989 HCFC consumption with an extra allowance (ODP weighted) equal to 2.8% of 1989 CFC consumption.

[c] Up to 0.5% of base level consumption can be used until 2030 for servicing existing equipment.

[d] All reductions include an exemption for pre-shipment and quarantine uses.

[e] Review in 2003 to decide on interim further reductions beyond 2005.

The Kyoto Protocol

The Kyoto Protocol is an amendment to the United Nations Framework Convention on Climate Change (UNFCCC). Countries that ratified it have agreed to reduce their emissions of carbon dioxide and five other GHGs (methane, nitrous oxide, sulfur hexafluoride, HFCs, and PFCs) through emissions trading. It is important to note that although HFCs and PFCs are replacements for some ozone-depleting substances, because of their high GWP, they are regulated under the Kyoto Protocol. They are, therefore, not regulated under the Montreal Protocol. The Protocol aims to reduce the collective emissions of developed country GHGs by 5.2 per cent from 1990 levels. This amounts to about 950 million mt of carbon dioxide equivalent (CO_2-eq) emissions of GHGs. The goal is to lower overall emissions of the six GHGs, calculated as an average over the five-year period of 2008–12. National targets range from 8 per cent reductions for the European Union and some others to 7 per cent for the US (which has yet to ratify the treaty), 6 per cent for Japan, 0 per cent for Russia, and permitted increases of 8 per cent for Australia and 10 per cent for Iceland (EIA, 2006). One mechanism for decreasing emissions under the Kyoto Protocol is emissions trading through the Clean Development Mechanism (CDM). The CDM enables companies in developed countries to receive credits for investing in emissions-reducing technology. The intention is to encourage investment in clean technologies, such as wind and solar power, and to reduce global emissions overall.

Table 1.2: Greenhouse Gases Trapped between Treaties (EIA, 2006)

Gas	Global Warming Potential (relative to CO_2)	Relationship to Montreal Protocol	Relationship to Kyoto Protocol
HCFC-22	1,700	Controlled under the Montreal Protocol, but promoted and funded as an alternative to CFCs	Not regulated despite its global warming impact.
HFC-23	11,700	Not regulated, but produced as a byproduct of HCFC-22, which is regulated under the Montreal Protocol.	Controlled for its global warming impact. Carbon Emissions Reduction credits can be earned for destruction of this chemical.
HFC-134a	1,300	Not regulated. Promoted as an alternative due to its low ozone depleting potential and despite its high global warming impact.	Controlled for its global warming impact

Recently, the positive solution of prolonged discussion COP21 (2015 Paris Climate Conference) meeting was also a mammoth step to handle the changing climate. The meet was held at Paris from 30 November to 11 December 2015 and concluded with a comparatively quite positive resolution. COP21 will for the first time in over 20 years of UN negotiations, aim to achieve a legally binding and universal agreement on climate, with the aim of keeping global warming below 2°C. It concludes that the developed country will provide financial assistance to developing/under developed nations to meet their growth/development requirements. In fact, it will always be one of the great decisions for Earth ecosystem.

Conclusion

Globally, climate is largely regulated by how much energy the Earth receives from the sun and how much energy it releases back to space. The global climate is also affected by other energy flows within the climate system itself. The atmosphere, ocean, precipitation, water, and land, regulates these energy flows by their different roles. Changes to any of these elements can affect the balance of the entire system, causing the change to climate. The entire world is running fast on the track of development and creating many environmental problems in the process. This is so because development and pollution are two sides of the same coin and no one is thinking about the global environment. Out of these environmental problems, many will come into force after a long period of time and then we will not have time to do anything for environmental protection. Basically, a few major aspects related to the impact of anthropogenic activities on the entire globe, including the continent of Antarctica, are as follows: Green House Effect, Global Warming, Ozone Depletion, Melting of Glaciers, Rise in Sea Level, Submergence of Coastal Nations, Global Climate Change, Floods and Droughts, Effect on Agriculture Productivity, Famine and Pandemics, Economy Imbalance, Ecological Disturbance, etc.Global warming may cause the significant rise in sea level due to tremendous increment in the rate of melting glaciers. If the West Antarctic Ice Sheet melts, this would raise global sea level by about 5m. So, a few stringent international actions are required to reduce greenhouse gas emissions to the level that was 50 years back. Studies of environment and the Antarctic ecosystem are the hot research topics in the world, especially for ozone depletion, global warming glacier melting, and climate change. The Antarctic ecosystem plays an important role to regulate the global climate. All the research work in Antarctica should be done in a sustainable fashion with a minimum disturbance to the Antarctic environment. Atmospheric pollutants in the Antarctic air will be an indication of alarming pollution levels elsewhere, in other parts of the globe. The pollution-free ecosystems of the Earth including Antarctica are the gift of Nature to us. All must have to conserve the pristine ecosystems like our heritage for a better future of Earth and all living beings.

REFERENCES

Akimoto, H. 2003. Global Air Quality and Pollution. *Science*, 302(Dec 5): 1716- 1719.

Associated Press. 2006. Study: Earth 'likely' hottest in 2,000 years, Thursday, June 22, 2006.

BAS. 2000. British Antarctic Survey: Ozone Bulletin, December 2005. (URL: http://www.antarctica.ac.uk/met/jds/ozone/index.html)

BBC. 2005. BBC News. "In Pictures: How the World is changing."

Bharti, Pawan K. 2007. Where is Environmental Science Going in India?, *Current Science*, 92 (4): 414.

Bharti, P. K. and Gajananda, Kh. 2013. Environmental Monitoring and Assessment in Antarctica, In: Environmental Health and Problems (Eds.- Bharti, P.K. and Gajananda, Kh.), Discovery Publishing House, Delhi, pp: 178-186 (ISBN: 978-93-5056-263-5).

Bharti, P. K. and Kumar, P. 2012. Global Climate Change, Lambert Academic Publishing GmbH & Co. KG, Saarbrucken, Germany, pp: 70 (ISBN: 978-3-659-16656-3).

Bharti, P. K. and Gajananda, Kh. 2015. Natural Ecosystem and Climate Change, *Discovery Publishing House*, Delhi, pp: 183 (ISBN: 978-93-5056-749-0).

Caldwell, Martyn M.; Carlos L. Ballaré; Janet F. Bornman; Stephan D. Flint; Lars Olof Björn; Alan H. Teramura; G. Kulandaivelu and Manfred Tevini. 2003. Terrestrial Ecosystems, increased Solar Ultraviolet Radiation, and Interactions with other Climatic change Factors." Published as Part of the UNEP: Environmental Effects of Ozone Depletion and its Interactions with Climate Change: 2002 Assessment. Photochem. Photobiol. Sci., 2, 29–38. DOI: 10.1039/b211159b.

Chauhan, A. and Bharti, P.K. 2016. Climate Change, Disaster Management and Environment, Discovery Publishing House, Delhi, pp: 179 (ISBN: 9789350567845).

Chestnut, L.G., B.D. Ostro, and N.V. Vadakan. 1997. Transferability of Air Pollution Control Health Benefits Estimates from the United States to Developing Countries: Evidence from the Bangkok Study." *American Journal of Agricultural Economics*, 79: 1630-1635.

Cohen, A.J. 2000. Outdoor Air Pollution and Lung Cancer. *Environmental Health Perspectives*, 108: 743–750.

EC. 2002. European Commission Press Release. "Ozone and UV Over Europe: No Signs of Improvement." Annex. Main Conclusions of the Assessment Report on European Research in the Stratosphere. 2002.

Environment Canada, 2005. Clean Air, Climate Change and Stratospheric Ozone Depletion. (URL:http://www.ec.gc.ca/cleanairairpur/Air_Quality,Climate_Change_and_Ozone_ Depletion- WSC6DCEC3F-1_En.htm. as viewed July 6 2005.)

EIA 2006. Turning up the Heat-Linkages between Ozone Layer Depletion and Climate Change: The Urgent Case of HCFCs and HFCs, A Report by the Environmental Investigation Agency, August 2006, pp: 16. Online from http://www.eia-international.org.

Fergusson, Angus. 2001. Ozone Depletion and Climate Change: Understanding the Linkages. Environment Canada. *Meteorological Service of Canada*. 2001.

Guardian Unlimited. 2005. Cold Weather Accelerates Arctic Ozone Erosion. April 26, 2005.

Harris, J.M., Oltmans, S.J., Bodeker, G.E., Stolarski, R., Evans, R.D., and Quincy, D.M. 2003. Long-term Variations in Total Ozone Derived from Dobson and Satellite Data." *Atmospheric Environment*. 37: 3167-3175.

IPCC/TEAP 2002. Special Report."Safeguarding the Ozone Layer and the Global Climate System: Issues Related to Hydrochloro flourocarbons and Perflourocarbons." 2002.

Lovgren, Stefan. 2004. Warming to Cause Catastrophic Rise in Sea Level? *National Geographic News*. April 26, 2004.

McDonnell, W.F. 2000. Relationships of Mortality with the Fine and Coarse Fractions of Long-term Ambient PM10 Concentrations in Nonsmokers. *Journal of Exposure Analysis and Environmental Epidemiology*, 10: 427–436.

Montreal Protocol: The Ozone Hole. (URL:http://www.theozonehole.com/)

NASA, 2000. Science News: Record Setting Ozone Hole, September 2000. (URL:http://science. nasa.gov/headlines/y2000/ast08sep_1.htm)

NASA, 2002. Earth Observatory News. "NASA Scientists Observe "Thinning" of Arctic Ozone Layer during 1999-2000 SOLVE Mission." September 27, 2002.

NASA, 2006a. Global Warming Website. World Book.

(URL: http://www.nasa.gov/worldbook/global_warming_worldbook.html. on July 6 2006).

NASA, 2006b. Jet Propulsion Lab News Release. "Greenland Ice Loss Doubles in Past Decade, Raising Sea Level Faster." February 16, 2006.

Nature, 2005. Arctic Trends Scrutinized. Volume 435. May 5, 2005.

NCAR, 2006. National Center for Atmospheric Research Press Release. "Global Warming Surpassed Natural Cycles in Fueling 2005 Hurricane Season, NCAR Scientists Conclude." June 22, 2006

NERC, 2006. British Antarctic Ozone Survey. *National Environment Research Council*: 2006. (URL:http://www.antarctica.ac.uk/met/jds/ozone/index.html.)

Pope, C. A. 2002. Lung Cancer, Cardiopulmonary Mortality, and Long-term Exposure to fine Particulate Air Pollution. *Journal of the American Medical Association*, 287: 1132–1141

Rai, L.C. & Mallick, N. 1998. Algal Responses to Enhanced Ultraviolet-B Radiation, *PINSA* B, 64(2): 126.

Sheila K. West, Janice D. Longstreth, Beatriz E. Munoz, Hugh M. Pitcher and Donald D. Duncan. 2005. Model of Risk of Cortical Cataract in the US Population with Exposure to Increased Ultraviolet Radiation due to Stratospheric Ozone Depletion. American Journal of Epidemiology. 9 (3): 235-243.

Struck, Doug, 2006. Climate Change Drives Disease to New Territory". Washington Post. May 5, 2006

Thomas Chris, 2004. Feeling the Heat: Climate Change and Biodiversity Loss, Nature. January 2004.

U.S. EPA, 2006. Global Warming Website. Climate: Our Changing Atmosphere. As viewed July 6 2006.

UNEP, 2002. United Nations Environment Programme. "Twenty Questions and Answers about the Ozone Layer." Scientific Assessment of Ozone Depletion, pp: 15

UNEP/GRID, 2001. Arendal Polar Programme Press Release. "Significant Changes Likely in The Arctic From Climate Change." Nairobi/Arendal 22 February, 2001

Venkataraman, C. 2005. Residential Biofuels in South Asia: Carbonaceous Aerosol Emissions and Climate Impacts. Science, 307 (March 4), 1454-1456.

WHO, 2002. Health Effects of UV Radiation. World Health Organization, (URL:http://www.who.int/uv/health/en/)

WHO, 2003. Health Aspects of Air Pollution with Particulate Matter, Ozone and Nitrogen Dioxide, Report on a WHO Working Group, Bonn, Germany, 13–15 January 2003

WMO, 2005. World Meteorological Organization Statement on the Status of the Global Climate in 2005.

Climate Change and Agro-Edaphic System **Pages 20–49**
Edited by: Dr. Alka Chauhan & Dr. Pawan Kumar 'Bharti'
ISBN: 978-93-86841-98-8
Edition: 2019
Published by: Discovery Publishing House Pvt. Ltd., New Delhi (India)

2

Climate Change Scenario in India and Evidences in the Indian Himalayan Region

[1]Bhavika Sharma, Shalini Singh Maurya and Jesmita Brahmacharimayum

ABSTRACT

Climate change is affecting every ecosystem in a number of ways. The timing of water flows and volume going downstream is also affected due to increase in temperatures and melting of snow and glaciers in the upper mountain reaches. As a result, availability of irrigation water decreases. This could lead to increased incidences of pest and disease outbreaks. Ultimately, it affects yield and productivity of agricultural and horticultural crops. The climate change impacts observed in different sectors by souring temperatures include melting of glaciers, decreased production in many agricultural crops, changes in phenology of plants and trees (later or early flowering), increased occurrence of extreme events (floods, cloud bursts, cyclones etc.) and increased desertification etc.. The Paris Agreement aims to bring together all the nations to work for a common cause to undertake efforts to battle climate change and devise strategies to adapt to the effects of climate change and provide support to developing countries to do so. In order to keep check on the rising temperature levels, various adaptation and mitigation strategies have been implemented globally. Clean Development Mechanism (CDM), under Kyoto Protocol, is one such measure which helps in abatement of pollution by offsetting Green House Gas (GHG) emissions by developing countries. China and India lead in the number of CDM projects and these projects do provide a viable solution of offsetting GHGs. The primary aim of the Paris Agreement is to strengthen the global response to the perils of climate change by enhancing the implementation of the Convention in such a manner that the global average temperature remains well below 2°C above pre-industrial levels. It further aims to increase climate resilience by introducing adaptation and mitigation strategies and lower the emissions of GHGs in a way that

[1] ICAR- Indian Institute of Soil and Water Conservation (IISWC), 218, Kaulagarh Road, Near SBI Bank, ONGC, Dehradun, Uttarakhand 248195, India.

the food production is not affected. Its objective is to achieve sustainable development and simultaneously eradicating poverty. Development of sustainable and eco-friendly transportation system can help to offset GHGs and can also provide a solution to the traditional polluting petroleum based fuels. Offsetting GHGs in agricultural fields by making use of paddy husk and agricultural residue for electricity generation can be a viable option. Biomass energy utilization has a great scope in India and since agricultures has maximum contribution of the GDP of India; this form of energy can be utilized to its full potential. It could reduce the amount of waste generated along with production of energy and generation of jobs on a small scale. This could further contribute to eradication of poverty, sustainable development through sustainable agricultural practices and offsetting GHG emissions. The Sustainable Development Goals (SDGs), which are an collection of 17 global goals and 169 targets, have been set by the United Nations and cover a wide range of social and economic developmental issues goals, including poverty, hunger, health, education, gender equality, water and sanitation, energy, climate change, urbanization, environment etc. The SDG 13 aims to strengthen resilience and adaptive capacity to all the climate-related hazards (caused by anthropogenic causes) and natural disasters. The Government of India aims to achieve sustainable development, while keeping changing climatic conditions under a control through National Action Plan on Climate Change (NAPCC), which was released on 30th June 2008. It combines a number of the government's existing national plans mainly dealing with the most important natural resources and constitutes a set of eight missions. National Mission for Sustainable Agriculture (NMSA), National Mission on Strategic Knowledge for Climate Change and National Mission for Sustaining the Himalayan Ecosystem (NMSHE) are the ones specially dealing with climate change and NMSHE specifically caters to the Indian Himalayan Region. Furthermore, individual responses towards climate change by implementation of sustainable practices in day-to-day activities can help to prevent the aggravation of this menace.

Keywords: Climate change, Indian Himalayan Region, NAPCC, SDGs, Paris Agreement

INTRODUCTION

Climate Change and Global Warming

IPCC defines climate change as "statistically significant variation in either the mean state of the climate or in its variability, persisting for an extended period (typically decades or longer)", while Article 1 of the United Nations Framework Convention on Climate Change (UNFCCC) defines climate change as "a change of climate which is attributed directly or indirectly to human activity that alters the composition of the global atmosphere and which is in addition to natural climate variability observed over comparable time periods". Climate change is mainly attributable to alteration of the atmospheric composition caused by human activities, while climate variability is chiefly attributable to natural causes and events such as ice ages. Climate variability has been experienced before as the Earth's average temperature has fluctuated even prior to modernization and industrialization as seen in records maintained by NOAA. For at least the last million years, our planet has experienced both long cold periods referred to as "ice ages", as well as warm periods called "interglacials".

While on the other hand, Global warming according to NOAA refers to "the rise in global temperatures mainly due to the increasing concentrations of greenhouse gases in the atmosphere". It is mainly caused due to the increase in heat-trapping gases that are being constantly added to the atmosphere by human induced activities such as, rapidly increasing industries, burning fossil fuels, accelerating number of vehicles plying on oads etc. Figure 2.1 shows the trend of global temperatures over the past 1700 years.

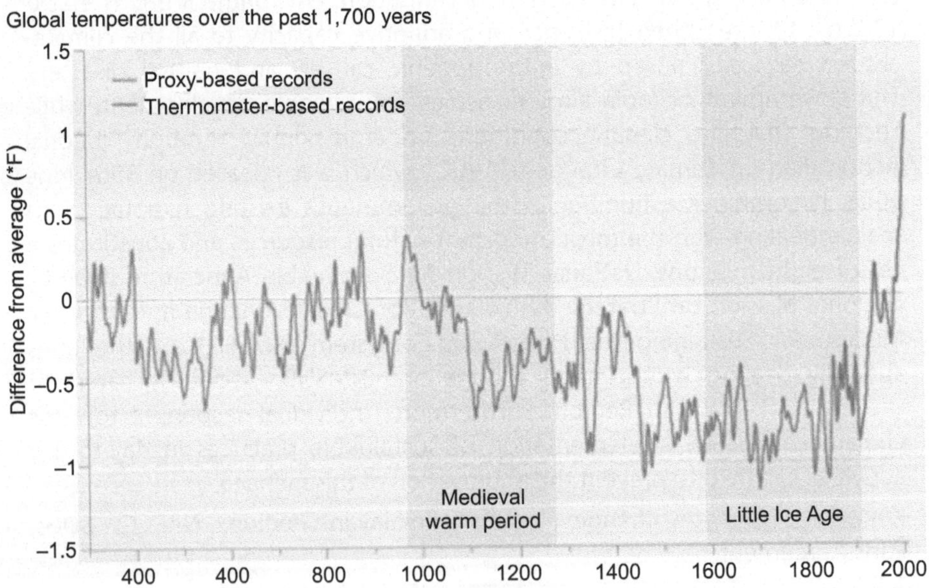

Fig. 2.1: Trend of Global Temperatures over the past 1700 years (Source: NOAA Climate.gov)

Climate Change in the Indian Himalayan Region (IHR)

Himalayas constitute one of the most important mountain systems of the world since they have the largest snow and ice cover outside the polar regions and these are also referred to as the "third pole" (Schild, 2008; Gautam *et. al.*, 2013) and the "water tower of Asia" (Xu *et al.*, 2009; Gautam *et. al.*, 2013). They extend from Indus River in the northwest to the Brahmaputra River in the east

(ICIMOD, 2009) and are responsible for directly or indirectly influencing lives and livelihood of over 300 million people (Schild, 2008; Gautam *et. al.*, 2013) and play a vital role in supporting economy of Asian countries like Nepal and Bhutan, which depend heavily on the Himalayas for services including agriculture, hydropower, water supply and tourism (ICIMOD, 2009).

Himalayas are one of the 34 global biodiversity hotspots (Myers *et al.*, 2000; Chaudhary and Bawa, 2011) and have a total of around 15,000 glaciers, which is the highest concentration in the world. These are known globally for their rich biodiversity and for playing a vital role in regulating the climate of the South Asian region (Saxena *et al.*, 2005; Sharma, 2016). They feed numerous perennial rivers which depend upon the sustainable existence of glaciers and since these are a source of Asia's eight largest rivers (Chaudhary and Bawa, 2011), these have a considerable hydropower potential (GoI, 2010; DST, 2012; Tewari *et al.*, 2017). The Indian Himalayan region (IHR) is home to about 51 million people and most of the people in this region practice hill agriculture.

Himalayas are one of the youngest mountain systems of earth and these have high potential to sustain the human population by providing all the necessary resources required for human civilization. These are capable of sustaining the mankind, provided care is taken in utilizing the resources at a slow pace and a sustainable manner. The rampant construction of buildings and industries in the fragile zone has led to their destruction. Moreover, the overall impacts of climate change are witnessed in the Himalayan region, which is affecting the livelihood of people residing in this region.

DISCUSSION

Climate Change Impacts in IHR

Climate Change Impacts on Extreme Events

Increase in occurrence of extreme events with change in climate is one of the major concerns throughout the world, especially in India. Climate risks and Extreme events given by World Meteorological Organization are shown in Figure 2. In recent years, a number of extreme events have occurred which caused huge losses of life and property. Natural hazards can cause tremendous increase in economic losses (Nicholls *et al.*, 1996). Climate extremes can be categorized into two types: (a) The ones which are based on simple climate statistics occurring every year including extremes like a very low or very high daily temperature, or heavy daily or monthly rainfall amount (b) The ones which are more complex event-driven extremes which do not necessarily occur every year ata given location, including drought, floods, or hurricanes (Nicholls *et al.*, 1996).

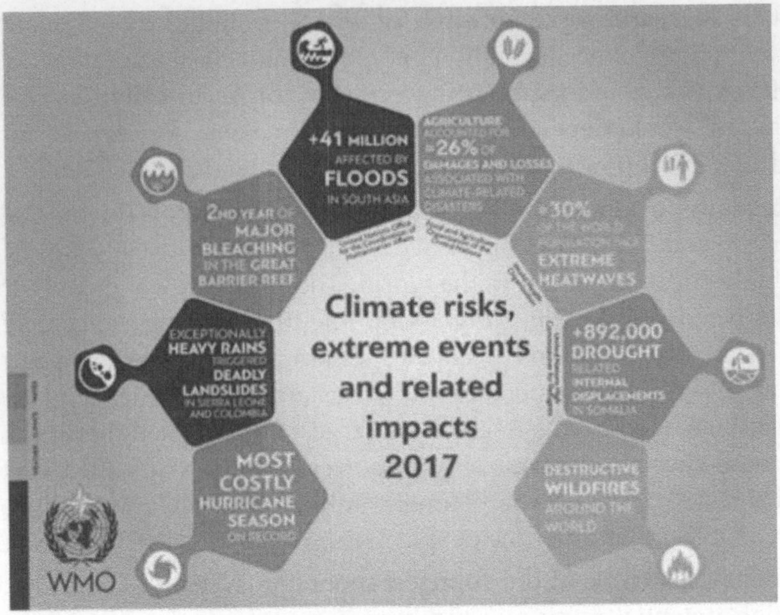

Fig. 2.2. Climate Risks and Extreme Events (Source: World Meteorological Organization)

- **Cyclones**

Some of disastrous tropical storms of the 20th century include the Bombay cyclone (1948), Porbandar cyclone (1976), Kandla cyclone (1998) and Odisha Super Cyclone (October 1999). The Bangladesh cyclone of 1970 and super cyclone of 1999 are the most well documented storms. The Tropical Cyclone of 1970 in the Bay of Bengal killed about 2 lakh people, while super cyclone of 1999, which occurred in Odisha, showed decrease in number of deaths (De *et al.*, 2005). The frequency of tropical cyclones in the North Indian Ocean has significantly increased (20% per hundred years), especially during the months of November and May (which account for maximum number of intense cyclones) (Singh *et al.*, 2000). Though climate change impacts on regional basins could be noticed, the intensity and frequency of tropical cyclone; however, does not seem to be associated with global warming globally. The loss of life has seen a decrease owing to better weather forecasts and warnings, their dissemination and disaster management strategies which have been established by the National Weather Services globally along with World Meteorological Organization (WMO). Regional Meteorological Centres (RMCs) established by WMO play an important role while dealing with Tropical Cyclones; however, damage and destruction do not seem to decrease (De & Joshi, 1999).

- **Sea level rise**

The impact of climate change on sea level rise was revealed by availability of tide gauge. However, for India, longer tide gauge data are few in number.

The spatial pattern of the mean sea level (MSL) variability during 1950-2000 was observed with the use of tide gauge data collected on a global scale (Leuliette, *et al.*, 2004). For assessing the local MSL variability, both tide gauge and satellite data sets can be employed (Chowdhury and Beherab, 2015). By observing the data available through past tide gauging, the estimation of MSL rise for various ports in India has been available. A mean sea level rise of about 2mm/year has been observed in the North Indian Ocean, while Bay of Bengal has experienced a seal level rise of 4 mm/year, leading to non uniformity in sea level variation in the ocean basins. The six tidal gauging stations of India (present in coastal regions) are located in Chennai (Tamil Nadu), Vishakhapatnam (Andhra Pradesh), Bhubaneswar (Odisha), Sagar (Madhya Pradesh), Diamond Harbour (West Bengal) and Haldia (West Bengal). A positive sea level rise has been observed in Chennai, while for Vishakhapatnam with a constant rate of 0.73 mm/year observed from 73 years of data, about 64 mm sea level rise (SLR) has been noticed from 1937 to 2010. For Bhubaneswar, SLR has been observed to be 0.43 mm/year, while for Diamond Harbour, SLR has noticed to be about 4.7 mm per year (Pramanik *et al.*, 2015). A sea level rise of 0.78, 1.14 and 0.75 mm/year has been observed for the stations located in Mumbai, Kochi and Vishakhapatnam respectively, whereas Chennai showed a decrease in sea level (-0.65 mm/year). The estimates do not significantly differ from the earlier study except for Chennai which is explained by examining the monthly mean sea level curve. (Unnikrishnan *et al.*, 2006). The sea level rise estimates for the stations in the Arabian Sea like Mumbai and Kochi and in the Bay of Bengal (Vishakhapatnam) were between 1.06 -1.75mm/yr, with an average rise of 1.29mm/yr, which were in accordance with the global estimates of Inter Governmental Panel on Climate Change (IPCC) (Chowdhury and Beherab, 2015). If the current trend of rise in sea level continues for the next 100 years, out of a total of 3604 Km^2, around 2100 Km^2 of wetland area will be lost in West Bengal and out of a total of 25083 Km^2 area, the maximum loss of coastal wetland projected for Gujarat is approximately 8453 Km^2 (Dwivedi and Sharma, 2005). The list of top 10 countries at risk from sea level rise has been given in Table 2.1.

Table 2.1: Top 10 Countries–Population at Risk from Sea Level Rise, 2008 and 2050 (Source: Wheeler, 2011)

S.No.	Country	Rank		Vulnerable Population (Million)	
		2008	2050	2008	2050
1.	India	1	1	20.6	37.2
2.	Bangladesh	3	2	13.2	27.0
3.	China	2	3	16.2	22.3
4.	Indonesia	4	4	13.0	20.9

5.	Philippines	6	5	6.5	13.6
6.	Nigeria	9	6	4.3	9.7
7.	Vietnam	7	7	5.7	9.5
8.	Japan	5	8	9.8	9.1
9.	United States	10	9	3.8	8.3
10.	Egypt, Arab Rep.	17	10	2.1	6.3

- **Floods and Droughts**

These have been associated with either abundance or scarcity of monsoon rain. Drought conditions prevailed over some parts of India during 1992, 2000 and 2001; while in 2002, almost 29% of the country's area was affected by drought and it was considered as the first all India droughts since 1987. Rainfall in the month of July reached a historical low of 51% below normal in 2002 and the situation was prevented from getting worse due to august rainfall (WMO, 2003). Droughts account for nearly 22% of significant damages caused by all the natural disasters; however, the number of deaths caused by them is relatively less (3%) (De and Joshi, 1998)

With an 10% increased melting of glaciers, rivers in the IHR have shown 3-4 % surplus water in the western Himalaya, while the Eastern Himalayas have witnesses a rise by 30 % increase. Many glacier lakes dammed by moraines have been formed on a glacier terminus in the eastern and central Himalayan region. Owing to its instability, a moraine dam is easily destroyed by any disturbance and lead to an abrupt release of lake water. This could further become a cause of heavy and sudden floods leading to serious damages, along the river channel downstream, affecting communities residing alongside rivers. This phenomenon is called a glacier lake outburst floods (GLOF) (Hasnain 2008). The occurrence of exceptionally heavy rainfall events and associated flash floods in many areas provide us an impetus to study long-term changes in extreme rainfall over India. The occurrence of recent floods in Uttarakhand, in which around 1,10,000 persons were evacuated from flood-hit areas and more than 5000 persons were feared to be dead (Figure 2.3), occurred as a result of downpour of heavy rainfall and consequent floods. (https://www.indiatoday.in/education-today/gk-current-affairs/story/worst-and-deadliest-floods-261643-2015-09-07). The construction of buildings along the river bank added to th damage by increasing vulnerability of communities living close to the fragile zone.

Events of extreme rainfall and flash floods are increasing significantly in India, except some parts of Central India. Though the frequency of heavy rainfall events is decreasing in most of central and north India, the frequency shows an increasing trend in the peninsular, east and North-east India

Fig. 2.3: Devastating Flood of Uttarakhand, 2013
(Source: India Today, 7th September, 2015)

(Guhathakurta *et al.*, 2011). Some of the worst floods which have affected India, since independence, are shown in table 2.2.

Table 2.2: Worst floods of India, Since Independence

S.No.	Affected area	Year	Casualties (No. of deaths)	Economic loss (crore)
1.	Bihar	1987	1,399	6800
2.	Gujarat	2005	123	8000
3.	Maharashtra	2005	1,094	550
4.	Assam	2012	120	3200
5.	Uttarakhand	2013	5,000	12000
6.	Jammu & Kashmir Floods	2014	300	5000

(**Source:** India Today; The Hindu, 2016 and Sharma, 2017)

- **Fog**

There is high moisture availability in the atmosphere, immediately after a western disturbances passes through an area. Both regional and synoptic scale conditions are responsible for fog formation. It affects all forms of transportation, especially the aviation sector, indirectly impacting the economy and also leading to inconvenience to the commuters and may even cause several deaths (De *et al.*, 2005). In general, an increase in temperature affects fog formation negatively. In a research conducted by Klemm and Lin (2016), it was observed that a few tens of a degree rise in temperature can affect the visual range strongly. The IPCC Report (2013) states that there has been an increase of the temperature by a few tenths of a degree over vast areas of the terrestrial surface. Therefore, it was suggested that climate change leads to a decrease of fog.

Assuming equilibrium conditions, two main factors are responsible for reduction in fog, *viz.*, a reduction of the aerosol particle concentration and an increase of the air temperature (Klemm and Lin, 2016). However, an increase in the amount of aerosols liberated into the atmosphere leads to an increase in fog formation. According to a study conducted by De and Dhandekar (2001), there has been an increasing trend in the number of poor visibility days, particularly in most of the airports in North India which experience inconvenience due to fog in winters almost every day. The main causes of this increasing trend may be attributed to increasing number of automobiles plying on roads which release aerosols into the atmosphere and rapid urbanization and industrialization. In India, another possible reason of increase in such incidences may be attributed to the unchecked rise in incidences of crop residue burning in the agricultural fields of North India, which releases particulate matter into the atmosphere. De et al. (2005) also noticed that the main factors affecting visibility include presence of particulate matter and aerosols in the atmosphere along with increase in relative humidity. The year 2008-09 was one of the warmest as well as foggiest winter seasons in Delhi (https://www.ndtv.com/india-news/facts-about-fog-in-delhi-409401). The longest duration of fog that engulfed the Indira Gandhi International Airport, New Delhi, for 179 hours happened in December 1998, while during January in 2003 and 2010, for around 168 and 172 hours, the Delhi Airport was engulfed by fog. (https://www.news18.com/news/india/fog-breaks-7-yr-record-engulfs-delhi-airport-for-172-hrs-332718.html).

- **Cold waves and Heat waves**

Increase in the number of days with abnormally high or low air temperature often referred to heat waves and cold spells is one of the consequences of climate change and climatologists have predicted more frequent heat waves and an increase in the number of days with exceptionally high temperature and heavy precipitation (Climate change, 2007; Parry *et al.*, 2007; Revich and Shaposhnikov, 2012). There is an increase in the rate of mortality during heat waves, which will become more frequent due to global warming (Revich and Shaposhnikov, 2012).

Advancement of cold and dry winds into the subcontinent from the North and occurrence of extremely low temperatures, commonly referred to as cold waves, mainly affect the regions lying 20pN, but along with large amplitude troughs, even states like Maharashtra and Karnataka have experienced cold waves. The maximum number of cold waves is experienced in the state of Jammu and Kashmir, followed by Rajasthan and Uttar Pradesh. (De *et al.*, 2005). As a result of deterioration in the quality of air in urban areas during recent years, more number of deaths has been reported lately (De and Ray, 2000). The November wave, which affected many parts of Karnataka, Gujarat and Maharashtra in 2012, broke 60-year record, when the temperatures dropped to

6 to 7 degrees below normal. In the same year, the North and East India was gripped by the December wave, when the temperatures plummeted to 6 to 10 degrees below normal. (https://www.geographyandyou.com/science/weather-and-climate/cold-waves/). In January 2013, lowest minimum temperatures was recorded in North India, with Delhi receiving record breaking 34 mm rainfall and 1.9 pC was the lowest temperature recorded for the city, Shimla city received record breaking snow in this month and Lucknow and Agra had sub-zero mercury (–0.2 pC). (https://www.skymetweather.com/content/weather-news-and-analysis/january-2013-was-the-coldest-ever-recorded/)

Heat waves occur during summer season, when there is extreme departure from the normal maximum temperatures. A study conducted by Raghavan (1966) indicated that maximum number of heat waves occurs in the month of June and these mostly occur in East Uttar Pradesh, followed by Punjab, east Madhya Pradesh and Gujarat (Saurashtra and Kutch). A study revealed that a significant increase in persistence, frequency and spatial coverage of heat waves was observed during 1991-2000, as compared to the earlier decades of 1971-80 and 1981-90 (Pai *et al.,* 2004). The reason for such changes was attributed to the increased global warming trends during 1991-2000, which was on record the warmest decade during last 140 years (WMO, 2001). Phalodi (Western Rajasthan) holds the record of having the maximum temperature (51 pC) till 2016 (Wu, 2016). The earlier record showed Alwar (Rajasthan) had the highest temperature in May during 1956 (50.6 pC). (De *et al.,* 2005)

- **Forest fires**

Forested landscapes are affected by forest fires which cause huge losses to the economy of a nation as well as seriously impact the biodiversity. Factors like high temperatures during summers, availability of inflammable material such as dry pine needles, steep terrain and high wind velocity are mainly responsible for forest fires (Rothermel, 1983; Roy, 2003). A mountainous terrain leads to rapid spread of forest fires, which is mainly caused by loss of moisture and prevailing high temperature in the upper reaches owing to the upward flowing hot air. Isolated coniferous trees located at higher altitudes catch fire readily due to less moisture availability and high flammability (Bahuguna and Singh, 2002). While some of the forest fire incidences occur accidently, most are caused by human activities such as to scare away wild animals, to burn waste, to hide illegal timber extraction activities, to improve grass growth, to collect honey etc. and even political agitations and community conflicts are responsible for causing these fires (Bahuguna and Singh, 2002; Bhandari *et al.,* 2012).

Forest fires in India are caused advertently for a number of reasons which differ from region to region; for instance, in the North Eastern Himalayan Region, shifting cultivation is the major cause, while in Western Himalayan Region, promoting fresh fodder growth is the main reason and in Central

India, the main purpose is collection of non timber forest products. The purpose of intentional forest burning differs from region to region in the Indian subcontinent. In North Eastern Himalayas, forests are burnt for shifting cultivation. In western Himalayas, forests are burnt to promote fresh fodder growth whereas central Indian forests are burnt to facilitate the collection of non-timber forest products (Spanos *et al.*, 2010). Repeated burning in forests is a major cause of ground flora destruction which leads to changes in plant community structure and reduction in soil nutrient status by causing a decrease in vegetative growth rate (Certini, 2005) and increased soil erosion (Inbar *et al.*, 1998). Moreover, forest fires cause GHG emissions, mainly carbon dioxide, carbon monoxide, methane, hydrocarbons, nitric oxide and nitrous oxide, which are mainly responsible for global warming (Koppmann *et al.*, 2005). Thus, forest fires impact not just the land cover, but also cause destruction of forest ecosystems and biodiversity of an area.

Sendai framework for disaster risk reduction calls for a focused approach within and across the sectors at regional, national and global levels to deal with this hazard. The actions under this framework include understanding the risk, strengthening the management of disaster risk, increasing the resilience by investing in disaster risk reduction, enhancing disaster preparedness for effective response better recovery plans, rehabilitation and reconstruction (UNISDR, 2015). In accordance with the National Fire Prevention and Control guidelines 1999, Indian states they have been encouraged to adopt joint forest management program with community participation to control forest fire.

According to Global Forest Resource Assessment, about 55% of the Indian forest cover, i.e. 3.73 million ha out of 67.5 million ha, experiences fire each year, resulting in an economic loss of more than 4.4 Billion rupees along with other ecological effects (Murthy, 2006). Careful investigation of the spectral signatures received from Remote sensing data along with data collected from ground level assessment; provide a means of evaluation of the damage cause due to forest fires (Gupta et. al. 2018). Continuous monitoring and mapping provide information about the fire prone forests (Chand et al. 2006).

According to latest report on forest fires, 65 fire alerts and at least 57 small and big incidents of fires were reported from forests across Uttarakhand between 19th May, 2018 to 21st May, 2018 in both Garhwal and Kumaon divisions and according to the chief conservator of forest, the economic loss due to fires was estimated to be 3.5 lakhs and 69.71 hectares was gutted by the fires. (https://timesofindia.indiatimes.com/india/70-ha-of-forests-lost-in-ukhand-fires-in-2-ays/articleshow/64264947.cms)

Effective measures to help communities, especially the most vulnerable populations to prepare for and respond to extreme heat events support the evacuation plans and decrease the huge losses to the economy and even lead to a decrease in the number of casualties.

Climate Change Impacts on Agriculture and Food Security

Increasing concentrations of GHGs has been a matter of concern and may directly or indirectly effect agriculture. With the possibility of global climate change, a great emphasis is laid on the world food security and its impacts at a regional level. Climate change is affecting the agriculture sector in many ways, which can vary from region to region. The glaciers and snow cover are melting in major mountain ranges due to increase in temperature. This will affect the timing of water flows and volume going downstream, ultimately reducing the availability of irrigation water. Even slight warming may lead to a reduction in yields in low-latitude regions. This could even lead to changes in the location and incidence of pest and disease outbreaks. Greater frequency and intensity of extreme weather events, such as the El Niño-Southern Oscillation, will increasingly affect climate patterns and food production (FAO, 2016).

The effects of past climate trends on crop production have been observed in several regions of the world (Porter *et al.,* 2014) and negative impacts are more evident than the positive ones. The accurate impacts of climate change on crop yields in future are very difficult to predict and would mainly depend on physical parameters such as temperature, precipitation patterns and CO_2 fertilization along with changes in agro ecosystems (e.g. through reduction in number of pollinators and increased incidence of pest and diseases); and the adaptive responses of human systems (FAO, 2016).

Under normal conditions, weather influences a number of factors including crop growth development, water use and yield during the growing season and even with minor fluctuations from the normal weather, the food production is seriously impaired. Extreme weather conditions, such as floods, droughts, cyclones and hailstorm along with heat and coldwaves, etc., pose direct hazards to crops. Even slight variations in weather during the critical phases of crop development can substantially impact crop yields (Mall *et al.,* 2006). Till the pre industrial period (1850), the concentration of carbon dioxide (CO_2) was in the steady state at 280 ppm and it is rising since then at the rate of 1.5 to 1.8 ppm per year (Mall *et al.,* 2006). Currently its concentration has crossed 400 ppm and the concentration of CO_2 is likely to be doubled by the end of 21st century globally (Keeling *et al.,* 1995). In an experiment conducted by Uprety et al. in 2003 in New Delhi, an increase in rice grain yield was observed due to increase in CO_2 concentration. This was a result of an increased net photosynthetic rate and greater accumulation of sugar which significantly accelerated the development of leaves and tillers and ultimately grain yield.

There are two major crop growing season in India from climate point of view. The summer or '*kharif*' crop growing season (June–September) coincides with southwest monsoon, including crops such as rice, maize, sugarcane, bajra cotton, jute, groundnut, soybean etc. These crops can be harvested throughout the autumn (October–November) or winter (December–February) months and account for more than 50% of the food-grain production and 65% of the oilseeds production of India. The variability in the interannual monsoon rainfall causes large-scale droughts and floods, ultimately affecting the Indian economy (Gadgil *et al.*, 1999a; Mall *et al.*, 2006) and food grain production in India (Parthasarathy and Pant, 1985; Parthasarathy *et al.*, 1992; Selvaraju, 2003; Kumar *et al.*, 2004, Mall *et al.*, 2006). Studies conducted by the Indian Agricultural Research Institute (IARI) point out that with every rise of 1 degree C temperature, there is a possibility of loss of 4-5 million tons in wheat production throughout the growing period (Chaturvedi *et al.*, 2014). The winter or *'rabi'* crop-growing season commences after the summer monsoon, and expands till early summer. The irrigation water required for these crops is provided by rainfall occurring in the post monsoon season and it also provides stored soil moisture (October–November). The major *'rabi'* crops include wheat, barley, mustard, potato, onion and gram etc. The summer monsoon plays a key role for both *kharif* and *rabi* crop production in India (Mall *et al.*, 2006).

There have been reports of declining productivity for many of the cash crops, especially apples, which has been attributed to a failure of pollination services. Pollinators provide pollination services that are crucial for the productivity of agricultural and natural ecosystems. Over three quarters of the world's crops and over 80% of all flowering plants depend on bees as animal pollinators. Globally, the annual contribution of pollinators to agricultural crops has been estimated at about USD 200 billion (ICIMOD, 2012). However, pollinators are currently under threat with declines in pollinator populations and diversity occurring worldwide. This presents a serious threat to agricultural production affecting the livelihoods of farmers, national agricultural economies, and food security. During a brain storming session on Climate variability/change impacts on mountain ecosystem organized by the Department of Environmental Science, YSP University of Horticulture & Forestry, Nauni, Solan (Himachal Pradesh) held on May 7, 2018, the importance of pollinators and their decline in the recent times due to climate change and variability and various anthropogenic activities was highlighted. Both the direct and indirect impacts of climate change on pollinators were explained. As a result of climate change, a shift has been observed in the distribution pattern of bees and loss of ecotypes has also been noticed, which is causing reduced global food availability. A pronounced increase in the incidences of insect diseases due to climate change has also been noticed. The main reasons of this include loss of pollinator habitats and modern agricultural practices, which are dominated by the excessive and indiscriminate use of pesticides and other agrochemicals (Proceedings, 2018). Therefore, there is a need of more robust and improved management strategies with strict implementation of quarantine measures in order to prevent reduction in pollinators' number which can further affect global food supplies (Proceedings, 2018).

An increase in solar radiation as well as erratic rainfall patterns are also impacting agriculture by changing the geographical distribution of areas (an upwards altitudinal shift in cropping has been reported) suited to different cash crops like apple, rajma, potato and carrot (Thandani *et al.*, 2015). Apple is highly sensitive to adversities of climate (Byrne and Bacon, 1992; Partap and Partap, 2002 and Rana *et al.*, 2008). A model demonstrating climatically suitable areas for growing apples suggests that the areas suitable for growing apples has shifted from south to north, from coast to midland, from planes to mountains and from urban centre to suburban areas with the increase in temperature (Seo,2003). An increase of night time temperature may lead to decrease in production of some crops such as rice (Dimri and Dash, 2012). This could also lead to reduction in the winter killing of pests which in turn decrease crop yields. The rising humidity, moisture and milder winters in lower regions (500-1500m a.s.l.) may provide favourable condition to pests and insect diseases. Rust and blight disease are increasing in cereals and potato, while legumes like *Phaseolus* spp. are being infected through the soil borne insects such as *Coleoptera* spp. (locally known as *Uksa/Kurmula*). These insects damage the crops in early stage of seed germination (Maikhuri *et al.*, 2008). In Uttarakhand Hailstorm events are also shifting from March to as late as May in high altitudinal areas and these increase damage to various fruit crops at the flowering and early fruit stages (Thandani *et al.*, 2015). According to an estimate, around 50-60 per cent of the apple crops in parts of the State were destroyed in the year 2011 due to hailstorms (The Hindu, 2011).

The Climate Change, Agriculture and Food Security (CCAFS) have proposed a climate-smart agriculture (CSA) solution that will transform the agricultural systems to support food security under the new realities of climate change. Climate Resilient Agriculture (CRA) deals with the incorporation of adaptation, mitigation and other practices in agriculture which increases the capacity of the system to respond to various climate related disturbances by damage resistance and a quick recovery(Mishra *et al.*, 2016). CSA entails three co-achieving pillars as shown in Figure 2.4.

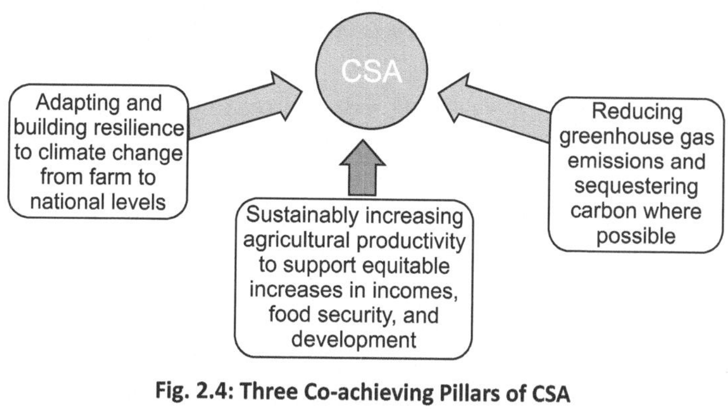

Fig. 2.4: Three Co-achieving Pillars of CSA
(Source: ccafs.cgiar.org)

Keeping in view the food and agriculture security in our country, the Government of India expressed a commitment to make crop insurance more accessible to farmers; for instance, the Maharashtra state government has already adopted a new approach to protect several thousand farmers from the weather uncertainties for key crops. In this approach, payoffs to affected farmers can be determined by calculating the thresholds beyond which crop growth begins to suffer. This scientific technique was developed by CIMMYT scientists, (International Maize and Wheat Improvement Centre), one of the CGIAR centres. The Agriculture Insurance Company of India applied the region- and crop-specific triggers to provide rainfall risk coverage to the crops of almost 1 million resource-poor farmers. Similar social security programmes and policies should be introduced to provide the farmers timely insurance against local supply changes. Introduction of drought resistant varieties and other interventions such as increasing resistance of plants to pests, heat etc. should be worked upon. Lastly, the most important role is played by capacity building, which deals with training the farmers on climate resilient agricultural technologies, motivating them to go for soil testing etc. Recently, extensive use of the crop simulation models to study the climate change impacts on agricultural production and food security has helped to formulate appropriate crop management decisions and strategies to strengthen the climate resilience in agriculture and it is anticipated that in the coming decades, the use of simulation models by policy and decision makers will increase (Mall *et al.*, 2006).

Climate change Impacts on Glaciers and Water Sources

Climatic variations are causing shrinking of significant number of mountain glaciers; for instance, an unusual retreat of the largest glaciers in the Parbati river basin, Kullu district, Himachal Pradesh; namely Parbati glacier has been reported (Kulkarni *et al.*, 2005). A study conducted by Kulkarni *et al.*, 2005 showed that the Parbati glacier had retreated 578 m between 1990 and 2001, with an average of almost 52 m annually and it was suggested that if it continues to retreat at the current rate, it will profoundly affect the availability of water in the basin.

Monitoring such changes is vital, since retreating glaciers might affect the distribution and supply of water in not only the IHR, but will also affect the plain areas which are fed by the rivers originating in the Himalayas. Snowmelt (combined from within and outside the glacier areas) is responsible for approximately 50% of the annual runoff, while glacier melt accounts for about one-third and rain for the remaining part (Engelhardt *et al.*, 2017). All the climate models available currently foresee a near-surface warming trend owing to the increasing emissions of greenhouse gases into the atmosphere. This increase in surface temperatures might have severe impacts on the hydrological cycle, especially in regions where water supply is mainly influenced by melting snow or ice. (Barnett *et al.*, 2005). According to an article published in The Hindu, it has been reported that Himalayas have lost 13 percent in the last forty years. According to this report, Karakoram is the only stable range, while others are retreating at a fast rate, depending upon a number of factors such as location, size, orientation etc., and the rate ranges from a few metres to almost 61 m/year (Gandhi, 2016). The report also mentions that glaciers are retreating faster in Western Himalaya than in Sikkim and the rate of glacial loss in the Himalayas has witnessed an increase over the decades from around 9 Gt/year in 1975-85 to 20 Gt/year in 2000-2010.

As more than one-sixth of the Earth's population is directly or indirectly, dependent upon glaciers for water supply, severe consequences for some of the regions have been predicted with high confidence levels as a result of changes in the hydrological cycle (Barnett *et al.*, 2005). A number of cases of hydrological changes have already happened in many regions of the world, where the perennial rivers have dried up and simultaneously, in other areas where increased incidences of floods have been noticed. Mountain glaciers are shrinking due to climatic variations. Geological Survey of India observed an average retreat of 4.22 to 6.8 m per year for the glaciers of Satluj River basin including the Gara, Gor Garang, Shaune Garang and Nagpo Tokpa (Vohra, 1981). Dobhal et al (1999) observed the shifting of snout of Dokriani Bamak glacier in the Garhwal Himalaya by 586m during 1962 to 1997 with an average of 16.5m per year. This study was however, contradicted by Matny (2000), who observed that the same glacier retreated 20m in 1998 instead of 16.5m over the thirty-five years.

The Saichen glacier and Pindari, Gangotri and the Milam glaciers in the Kumaon region have retreated at a rate of 31.5 m and 23.5 m, 18m and 9.1m per year respectively (Bajracharya *et al.*, 2006). The glaciers lying in Chenab River Basin, including Bara Shigri, Chhota Shigri, Miyar, Hamtah, Nagpo Tokpo, Triloknath and Sonapani retreated at the rate of 6.81 to 29.78 m per year, with the highest and lowest retreat in the Bara Shigri Glacier and Chhota Shigri Glacier respectively (Bajracharya *et al.*, 2006). Banett et al. (2013) investigated changes in glaciers covering an area of ◎200 km2 in the Tista basin, Sikkim, Eastern IHR, between 1990 and 2010 and observed loss of an area of 3.3 ± 0.8% between 1990 and 2010. The climatic data collected from the Gangtok meteorological station (1812 m a.s.l.) for a period of 24 years (1987–2011), showed a 1.0°C rise in the summer minimum temperature and a 2.0°C rise in the winter minimum temperature; thus, indicating hotter summers and warmer winters. The research suggested that glacier retreat was caused mainly attributed to temperature increase and glaciers covered by debris can retreat at a faster rate than debris-free glaciers. Engelhardt et al. (2017) did modeling of glacier mass balance and runoff for Chhota Shigri Glacier lying in the Chenab basin of Western Himalayan region for a span of 60 years (1955-2014) and noticed that the mean annual mass balances of Chhota Shigri were on slightly negative side for the whole evaluation period (1955–2014). Mean annual runoff showed an increasing trend and the annual mean air temperature also increased during the evaluation period; however, the annual mean precipitation did not experience large changes. It was also observed that the monthly runoff increases are greatest in July, due to both increased snow and glacier melt.

A study was conducted from 1976 to 2014 by Pandey et al. (2018) on Pindari glacier which lies in the upper Himalayas of Kumaon region and is the source of Pindar River, a major tributary of Alaknanda River. According to the study, the snout of this glacier has retreated over last four decades (Figure 5), which was carried out using visual interpretation of remote sensing data. Global positioning system coordinates were used to determine the latest snout position in 2014 and the location of snout was marked using a series of periodic Landsat images and manually digitised data. It was reported that the cumulative glacial retreat was 1569.01 metres over the four decades, with an average glacier retreat rate during the study period was 51.23 metres per annum. The glacial loss in the IHR was linked to climate change. This adds to the official confirmation of loss of glaciers in the IHR, which might affect water storage in the area.

It is very likely that some mountain ranges may lose most, if not all, of their glaciers if the current rate of glaciers' retreat owing to global warming continues (Vaughan, 2013). There is a need to extend the model approach to the major glaciers in IHR, since it would help to shed more light for estimation of run-off regime or the coming decades and future developments of glaciers (Engelhardt *et al.*, 2017).

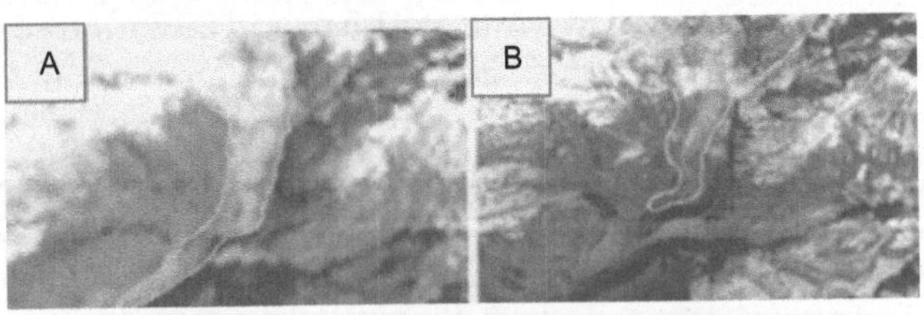

1976 2014

Fig. 2.5: The Position of Pindari Glacier in 1976 and 2014 (Source: Pandey *et al.*, 2018)

ADAPTATION AND MITIGATION STRATEGIES

Role of Paris Agreement

Background

In 1995, during COP 1 (Conference of the Parties), a decision was made by **United Nations Framework Convention on Climate Change** (UNFCCC) parties to accelerate climate efforts by introduction of negotiations towards an initial sub-agreement which was supposed to establish binding targets to reduce emissions of developed countries; however, no new commitments were set for developing countries. UNFCCC is the primary international and intergovernmental forum for negotiating the global response to climate change. The U.S. Senate argued that the agreement should also include greenhouse gas limits for developing countries and thus, the resulting Kyoto Protocol was adopted during COP 3 in 1997. The agreement included a number of "flexible" mechanisms enabling developed countries to use different forms of emissions to achieve their targets economically. It entered into force in 2005 when other countries ratified the agreement. The emission targets extended till 2012 initially. The targets of Kyoto Protocol cover only a small fraction of global emissions; however, one of the elements of the protocol that may sustain is Clean Development Mechanism (CDM), which supports emission reductions of developing countries in the form of tradable emission offsets. On December 12, 2015, world leaders united for the **COP 21** in Paris, and the parties adopted the landmark **Paris Agreement**. The agreement establishes common binding procedural commitments for all countries; however, it allows each nation to decide its nonbinding "**Nationally Determined Contribution**" (NDC). An enhanced transparency framework for tracking each country's actions and to strengthen their NDCs every five years has also been established. The agreement finally entered into force in late 2016.

Role in Climate Change Mitigation

The Paris Agreement brings together all the nations to work for a common cause to undertake efforts to battle climate change and devise strategies to adapt to the effects of climate change and provide support to developing countries to do so. The main objective of Paris Agreement is to strengthen the response of all nations to the threat of climate change by keeping a check on rise in the global temperature in this century below 2 pC above the pre-industrial levels and to ensure efforts are made to limit the temperature rise even further to 1.5 pC. It aims to strengthen the ability of nations to deal with the climate change impacts. (https://www.c2es.org/content/history-of-un-climate-talks/) Under the Protocol, the developed nations accepted binding commitments of emissions reduction targets and decided to decrease their emission levels of mainly four GHGs (Carbon dioxide, Methane, Nitrous Oxide and Sulfur Hexafluoride) by 5.2% of their 1990 levels. (http://www.arthapedia.in/index.php?title=Clean_Development_Mechanism_(CDM))

The Agreement requires all Parties to propose their best strategies and plan of action through nationally determined contributions (NDCs) and suggests that all Parties report about their emissions and other implementation efforts on regular basis. Parties will assess their collective efforts on the progress towards the achievement of targets set under in the Paris Agreement and inform about the groundwork of NDCs in the year 2018.

Status of Ratification

The Paris Agreement became operational thirty days after the date when at least 55 Parties to the Convention which were mainly responsible for at least an estimated 55 % of the total GHG emissions ratified it. It finally came into force on **4th November 2016.** (https://unfccc.int/process-and-meetings/the-paris-agreement/the-paris-agreement/) Accessed on 14.05.2018

India's Stand on CDM Projects

Clean Development Mechanism (CDM) involves funding of GHG abatement projects in developing countries by developed countries (or firms of developed countries). This supports developing countries (where the abatement costs are much lower) by reducing their GHG emissions; while in turn, the developed countries gain by receiving credits in the form of 'certified emission reductions' or CERs which can be used to offset their emission reduction obligations (Toman, 2000; Karp and Liu, 2000; Babu, 2003; Gupta, 2003). Refrigerant-gas manufacturer Gujarat Fluoro-Chemicals (GFL), based in Vadodara, Gujarat became India's first CDM project under Kyoto Protocol and third in the world to have an emission-reduction CDM project certified by the CDM executive board.

India currently has maximum CDM projects of solar energy and second largest number of CDM wind projects. (http://www.cdmpipeline.org/cdm-projects-type.htm). As of 28th February, 2015, total number CDM projects registered globally was 7598, with China and India leading since the commencement of this mechanism. India hosts 20 per cent of projects, while China leads with 50 per cent of the registered projects.

CDM in Indian Agricultural Sector

CDM in Agriculture is one of the sectors, which contributes the GDP of India on a much higher scale and by implementing the Clean Development Mechanism (CDM); it can earn carbon credits and generate an additional revenue source. A limited number of CDM projects have been registered in the agricultural sector so far. The areas in which CDM agriculture projects can be initiated are the biomass and nutrient availability projects. The agriculture residue of crops which are simply burnt can be used for biomass projects for electricity generation. There is a great potential for such projects in India, since every year a large amount of such residue is burnt. This not only affects the soil, but also causes air pollution. Such projects can reduce GHGs emissions and the carbon credits earned can further aid in revenue generation. Secondly, the electricity generated can be employed for operating farm machinery. Another CDM project in Agricultural sector which can be undertaken is offset of Nitrogen fertilizers by employing Rhizobium inoculants. For registering such projects under CDM, such experiments and studies should be supported by evidence in the form of soil test reports displaying differences in results before and after the implementation of the project (Pande and Telang, 2011).

Sustainable Development Goals (SDGs)

The Sustainable Development Goals (SDGs) are an assortment of 17 global goals (Figure 2.6) and 169 targets set by the United Nations, covering a broad range of social and economic developmental issues. These include poverty, hunger, health, education, gender equality, water and sanitation, energy, climate change, urbanization, environment etc. (Press Release, 2014). The SDGs are also referred to as "**Transforming our World: the 2030 Agenda for Sustainable Development**" or simply 2030 Agenda. These goals replaced the Millennium Development Goals (MDGs) which ended in 2015. Unlike the MDGs, the SDG goals apply to all nations equally and its framework does not differentiate between "developed" an "developing" nations. (https://en.wikipedia.org/wiki/Sustainable_Development_Goals).

Fig. 2.6: Sustainable Development Goals
(Source: United Nations Development Programme)

SDG 13 aims to strengthen resilience and adaptive capacity to all the climate-related hazards (caused by anthropogenic causes) and natural disasters in all nations (Table 2.3).

- It further aims to integrate climate change measures into national policies, strategies and planning along with improvement of education, knowledge and awareness among stakeholders and enhancing human and institutional capacity on climate change mitigation, adaptation, impact reduction and early warning.
- It's another objective is to oversee effective implementation of the commitment undertaken by developed-country parties to UNFCCC on Climate Change to a goal of jointly mobilizing $100 billion annually

by 2020 to address developing countries' requirements with respect to the meaningful mitigation actions on implementation and complete functionality of the Green Climate Fund (GCF) through its capitalization.

Table 2.3: Targets and Concerned Ministry or Department for Implementing Sustainable Development Goal No. 13

<table>
<tr><th>S.No.</th><th>Intervention</th><th>Target</th><th>Concerned Ministry or Department</th></tr>
<tr><td>1.</td><td>National Action Plan on Climate Change</td><td>Strengthen resilience and adaptive capacity to climate-related hazards and natural disasters in all countries</td><td>Home Affairs</td></tr>
<tr><td>2.</td><td>National Mission for a Green India</td><td>Integrate climate change measures into national policies, strategies and planning</td><td>MoEF&CC</td></tr>
<tr><td>3.</td><td>National Solar Mission</td><td>Improve education, awareness-raising and human and institutional capacity on climate change mitigation, adaptation, impact reduction and early warning</td><td>MoEF&CC, Information & Broadcasting</td></tr>
<tr><td>4.</td><td>National Mission for Enhanced Energy Efficiency</td><td rowspan="2">Implement the commitment undertaken by developed-country parties to the United Nations Framework Convention on Climate Change to a goal of mobilizing jointly $100 billion annually by 2020 from all sources to address the needs of developing countries in the context of meaningful mitigation actions and transparency on implementation and fully operationalize the Green Climate Fund through its capitalization as soon as possible</td><td rowspan="2">MoEF&CC</td></tr>
<tr><td>5.</td><td>National Mission for Sustainable Habitat</td></tr>
<tr><td>6.</td><td>National Water Mission</td><td rowspan="4">Promote mechanisms for raising capacity for effective climate change-related planning and management in least developed countries, including focusing on women, youth and local and marginalized communities</td><td rowspan="4">MoEF&CC</td></tr>
<tr><td>7</td><td>National Mission for Sustaining the Himalayan Ecosystem</td></tr>
<tr><td>8</td><td>National Mission for Sustainable Agriculture</td></tr>
<tr><td>9</td><td>National Mission on Strategic Knowledge for Climate Change.</td></tr>
</table>

(Source: Niti Ayog)

Climate change Adaptation Strategies for the Indian Himalayan Region

National Action Plan on Climate Change (NAPCC)

One of the pioneer projects of the Government of India to achieve sustainable development, while keeping changing climatic conditions under a control is NAPCC which was released on 30th June 2008. It combines a number of the government's existing national plans mainly dealing with the most important natural resources like water, renewable energy, wildlife, agriculture, and others into a set of eight missions. These missions include:

National Missions

These eight missions have been framed for achieving the main objectives of adaptation and mitigation:

1. **National Solar Mission**: This mission has been designed to promote the development and use of solar energy for power generation and recognizing the need to develop and expand the scope of other renewable sources of energy such as wind energy, biomass, geothermal etc. The ultimate objective of this mission is making solar power competitive with traditional fossil-based energy options.
2. **National Mission for Enhanced Energy Efficiency**: The objectives of this mission are to implement initiatives for enhancing energy efficiency through the institutional mechanism of Bureau of Energy efficiency (BEE) in the Central Government and designated agencies of the state.
3. **National Mission on Sustainable Habitat**: This mission aims to promote energy efficiency as a core component of urban planning, *viz.* to make habitats sustainable through improvements in energy efficiency buildings, public transportation systems and management of solid wastes
4. **National Water Mission**: This mission has been designed to ensure integrated water resource management with broad objectives including Conservation, minimization of wastage and equal distribution of water across all states. Since climate change is expected to worsen water scarcity, this mission targets a 20% improvement in water use efficiency through pricing and other measures.
5. **National Mission for Sustaining the Himalayan Ecosystem**: The mission aims to develop management measures to sustain the mountain ecosystem and safeguarding the Himalayan glaciers, since these are a major source of India's water supply and are likely to recede as a result of global warming. In this mission, community based management of these ecosystems will be encouraged through incentives. Its objective is to conserve wildlife, biodiversity, forest cover, and other ecological values in the Indian Himalayan region.

- **Task Force 1: Natural and Geological Wealth**
- **Task Force 2: Water, Ice, Snow including Glaciers**
- **Task Force 3: Forest Resources and Plant Diversity**
- **Task Force 4: Micro Flora, Fauna and Wildlife and Animal Population**
- **Task Force 5: Traditional Knowledge System**
- **Task Force 6: Himalayan Agriculture**

6. **National Mission for a "Green India"**: This mission aims to enhance the ecosystem services and encompasses carbon sinks. Its goals include the afforestation of 6 million hectares of degraded forest lands and expanding forest cover area to 33% of India's territory.
7. **National Mission for Sustainable Agriculture**: The objective of this mission is to develop strategies to make Indian agriculture resilient to climate change through alternate cropping patterns, development of new climate resilient crop varieties, expansion of weather insurance mechanisms and improving productivity of rainfed agriculture and other practices.
8. **National Mission on Strategic Knowledge for Climate Change**: This mission aims to support the establishment of academic units in institutes and universities to gain a better understanding of climate change, socio-economic impacts and challenges. It envisions enlisting of global community in research and technology development through open source platforms and to fund a high quality and focused research. It also encourages the private sector to take initiatives to develop adaptation and mitigation technologies.

Sustainable Approach at an Individual Level

There are both scientific and nature based solutions of dealing with the changing climate. At a larger scale, air pollution and emission of GHGs need to be addressed to and even stringent laws should be both enacted and followed while dealing with such emissions. At community based and individual levels, we can contribute by following a green approach in everyday life; for instance, by phasing out our old vehicles, encouraging use of public transport system, having days strictly meant only for bicycles and car pooling etc. The industries can maintain their exhausts and discharge coming out of outlets at the source itself, since these are major point sources of air pollution. There is definitely an important role to play by all the stakeholders as well as the officials working in Town Planning Department. Construction of green buildings and eco-friendly houses which reduce the urban heat island effect can also help to a great extent. The use of locally available resources and promoting eco tourism also provides a very viable solution to reduce the climate change impacts. Instead of the huge hotels, the eco lodges can cater to both the issues of sustainability and climate change. These are some of the methods which can widely be practiced.

Since not many physical or chemical methods are readily available to reduce air pollutants at a large scale, the biological/ecological approach may also be followed. These include afforestation, reclamation of waste lands, reducing use of plastic materials which usually take a number of years to recycle, reducing carbon and water footprint, etc. Moreover, the destruction of forests and tree felling should be addressed. Another aspect which causes a large scale destruction of forests is forest fires, which can only be dealt efficiently if enough information is provided to the local communities regarding the delicate nature of trees for e.g. Pine Trees catch fire easily and the communities should be made aware that activities such as burning or smoking should be avoided.

A major component of dealing with climate change is Capacity building. The stakeholders should be equipped with knowledge and information about the impacts of climate change. The local communities are the best tool to reduce the impact of climate change. Apart from this, climate resilient techniques and technology can be shared with them. Even the use of renewable sources can be explained to the stakeholders along the principle of 3 R's (Reduce, Reuse and Recycle). Traditional knowledge acquired by the indigenous and local communities about climate change can also help framing of climate change adaptation policies. Community FM radios can also provide an early warning to equip the local communities of an impending danger or any natural calamity, along with weather forecasts.

Climate change is an issue which occurred over a span of a number of years and was a gradual process due to negligence of humans. The deleterious effects of climate change are being felt lately, but we can deal with this if we together make individual efforts and promote a sustainable environment.

"Climate change needs an immediate action and we need to act together to reduce its effects before it completely eliminates the entire mankind."

Conclusion

Humans have placed an immense pressure on the natural ecosystems of the world and the effects are intensifying with each passing day. India is one of the most vulnerable nations to climate change and the communities living below the poverty line are more vulnerable to the current as well as climate change impacts. Since, the IHR is feeling the repercussions of climate scale largely; awareness and technical interventions would serve as the most vital assets to fight climate change. It is very likely that some mountain ranges may lose most, if not all, of their glaciers at the current rate of retreat of glaciers because of global warming. There is a need to extend the model approach to the major glaciers in IHR, as it will shed more light for estimation future developments of glaciers and run-off regime for the coming decades. The most important aspect is individual response and how well equipped are the stakeholders and for this, introduction to social security programmes and policies is required to provide the farmers insurance against local supply changes. Interventions such as increasing resistance of plants to pests, heat, introduction of drought, frost resistant varieties etc. should be worked upon. Novel strategies are required at this stage to cope with the situation of climate change, as it is one of the most important and challenging tasks we are dealing with currently. The adaptation and mitigation strategies need to be strengthened for building climate resilience among stakeholders. Lastly, the most important role is played by capacity building, which deals with training the farmers on climate resilient agricultural technologies, which in turn will be motivating them to go for soil testing and other such measures.

New arenas of research have opened up due to this challenge and ideas which help in offsetting GHGs should be experimented upon and replicated at a large scale, if successful. Although, major improvements in India's response to climate change has been made in terms of adaptation and mitigation strategies, considerable deficit still exists, which needs to be seriously catered to by accelerating the efforts further. Generation of green jobs can further contribute to eradication of poverty, and offset of GHG emissions.

REFERENCES

Babu P.G., Kumar K.S.K, Saha B. 2003 'Clean Development Mechanism: Issues and Options' in M Toman, U Chakravorty and S Gupta (eds) India and Global Climate Change: Perspectives on Economics and Policy from A Developing Country, Resources for the Future Press, Washington DC

Bajracharya S.R., Mool P.K. and Shrestha B.R. 2006 *The Impact of Global Warming on the Glaciers of the Himalaya, International Symposium on Geo-disasters, Infrastructure Management and Protection of World Heritage Sites*, 25-26 Nov 2006, Nepal Engineering College, Ehime College and National Society for Earthquake Technology Nepal, proceedings, pp. 231 – 242.

Bahuguna V. K. and Singh S. 2002. *Fire situation in India*. International Forest Fire News, 26, 23–27.

Bhandari B. S., Mehta J. P. and Semwal R. L. 2012 *Forest fire in Uttarakhand Himalaya: An Overview*. In G.C.S. Negi and P.P. Dhyani (Eds.) Glimpses of Forestry Research in the Indian Himalayan Region, Special Issue on International Year of Forests–2011 (pp. 167–175), Almora: G.B. Pant Institute of Himalayan Environment and Development.

Banett S., Kulkarni A.V. and Bolch T. 2013. The Influence of Debris Cover and Glacial Lakes on the Recession of Glaciers in Sikkim Himalaya, India, *Journal of Glaciology*, 59 (218), 1035-1046.

Barnett T.P., Adams J.C. and Lattenmaeir D.P. 2005 Potential Impacts of a Warming Climate on Water Availability in Snow-dominated Regions. *Nature*, 438(7066), 303-9.

Byrne D.H. and Bacon T.A. 1992. Chilling Estimation: Its Importance and Estimation. *The Texas Horticulturist*, 18(8): 8–9.

Certini G. 2005 Effects of Fire on Properties of Forest Soils: A Review. *Oecologia*, 143(1), 1–10

Chand T. K., Badarinath K.V.S., Prasad, V.K., Murthy M.S.R., Elvidge C.D. and Tuttle B.T. 2006 Monitoring Forest Fires over the Indian Region using Defense Meteorological Satellite Program-Operational Linescan System Nighttime Satellite Data. *Remote Sensing of Environment*, 103(2), 165–178.

Climate change. 2007 *The Physical Science Basis, in Contribution of Working Group I to the Fourth Assessment Report of the IPCC* (Cambridge, NY, 2007), pp. 10.

Chaturvedi R.K., Kattumuri R. and Ravindranath D. 2014 Mainstreaming Adaptation to Climate Change in Indian Policy Planning. *International Journal of Applied Economics and Econometrics*, 22(1), 23-56.

Chaudhary P. and Bawa K.S. 2011 Local Perceptions of Climate Change Validated by Scientific Evidence in the Himalayas. *Biology Letters*. (http://rsbl.royalsocietypublishing.org/ (Retrieved on 2nd May, 2018).

Chowdhury P. and Behera M.R. 2015 A Study on Regional Sea Level Variation along the Indian coast. *Procedia Engineering*, 116, 1078 – 1084.

De U.S. and Dandekar M.M. 2001 Natural Disasters in Urban Areas. *The Deccan Geographer*, 39(2), 1-12.

De U.S. and Joshi K.S. 1998 Natural Disasters and their Impacts on Developing Countries. *WMO Bulletin*, 47(4), 336-343.

De U.S. and Joshi, K.S. 1999 Interannual and Inderdecadal Variability of Tropical Cyclones over the Indian Seas. *The Deccan Geographer*, 37(1), 5-21.

De U.S., Dube R.K. and Rao G.S.P. 2005 Extreme Weather Events over India in the last 100 years. *J. Ind. Geophys Union*, 9(3), 173-187.

De U.S. and Sinha Ray K.C. 2000 Weather and Climate Related Impacts on Health in Mega Cities. *WMO Bulletin*, 44(4), 340-348.

Dimri A.P. and Dash S.K. 2012 Wintertime Climatic Trends in the Western Himalayas. *Climatic Change*, 111(3-4), 775-800.

Dobhal D.P, Gergan J.T. and Thayyen R.J. 1999 *Recession of Dokriani Glacier, Garhwal Himalaya – An overview*. Symposium on Snow, Ice and Glaciers. A Himalayan Perspective. Geol. Survey India, (In: Abst. Vol.), pp. 30-33.

Dwivedi D. N. and Sharma V. K. 2005 *Analysis of Sea Level Rise and Its Impact on Coastal Wetlands of India*. Proceedings of the 14th Biennial Coastal Zone Conference New Orleans, Louisiana July 17 to 21, 2005.

DST. 2012 *Dynamics of Glaciers in the Indian Himalaya: Science Plan. Himalayan Glaciology Technical Report No. 2*, Science and Engineering Research Board (SERB), Department of Science and Technology, New Delhi, pp. 125 .

Engelhardt M., Ramanathan A., Trude E., Kumar P., Landgren O., Mandal A. and Rasmussen R. 2017 Modelling 60 years of Glacier Mass Balance and Runoff for Chhota Shigri Glacier, Western Himalaya, Northern India. *Journal of Glaciology*, 63(240), 618–628.

FAO. 2016 Climate Change and Food Security: Risks and Responses, Food and Agriculture Organization of the United Nations

Gadgil, S., Abrol, Y. P. and Rao P.R.S. 1999a on Growth and Fluctuation of Indian Food grain Production. *Current Science*, 76(4), 548–556.

Gandhi D. 2016. *Himalayas lost 13 per cent of Glaciers in Forty Years*, The Hindu, June 13th, 2016). (http://www.thehindu.com/sci-tech/energy-and-environment/himalayas-lost-13-per-cent-of-glaciers-in-forty-years/article5554156.ece) Retrieved on 24th May 2018.

Gautam M.R., Timilsina G.R. and Acharya K. 2013 *Policy Research Working Paper 6516, Climate Change in the Himalayas, Current State of Knowledge,* The World Bank Development Research Group, Environment and Energy Team June 2013, pp. 64 .

GOI. 2010 *National Mission for Sustaining the Himalayan Eco-system (NMSHE) under National Action Plan on Climate Change (NAPCC).* Draft Report. Department of Science and Technology, Government of India, pp. 51.

Guhathakurta P., Sreejith O.P. and Menon P.A. 2011 Impact of Climate Change on Extreme Rainfall Events and Flood Risk in India. *Journal of Earth System Science,* 120(3), 359-373.

Gupta S. 2003 *India, CDM and Kyoto Protocol. Economic and Political Weekly,* 38(41), 4292-4298.

Gupta S., Roy A., Bhavsar D., Kala R., Singh S. and Kumar A. S. 2016 Forest Fire Burnt Area Assessment in the Biodiversity Rich Regions Using Geospatial Technology: Uttarakhand Forest Fire Event 2016 *Journal of the Indian Society of Remote Sensing.*

Hasnain S.I. 2008 *Impact of Climate Change on Himalayan Glaciers and Glacier lakes,* Proceedings of Taal 2007: The 12th World Lake Conference: 1088-1091.

ICIMOD. 2009 *Climate Change Impacts and Vulnerability in the Eastern Himalayas* (Edt. Sharma E., Chettri N., Tse-ring K., Shrestha A.B, Jing F., Mool P. and Eriksson M.)

ICIMOD, 2012 *Value of Insect Pollinators to Himalayan Agricultural Economies* (Edt. Partap U., Partap T., Sharma H.K., Phartiyal P., Marma A., Tamang N.B., Ken T. and Munawar M.S.)

Inbar, M., Tamir, M. I., and Wittenberg, L. 1998 Runoff and Erosion Processes after a Forest Fire in Mount Carmel, a Mediterranean area. *Geomorphology,* 24(1), 17–33.

Keeling C.D., Whorf T.P., Wahlen M. and Plich J.V.D. 1995 Interannual Extremes in the Rate of Rise of Atmospheric Carbon Dioxide since 1980. *Nature,* 375(6533): 666–670.

Klemm O. and Lin N. 2016 What Causes Observed Fog Trends: Air Quality or Climate Change? *Aerosol and Air Quality Research.* 16, 1131–1142.

Koppmann R., Czapiewski, K.V. and Reid J.S. 2005 A Review of Biomass burning Emissions, Part I: Gaseous Emissions of Carbon Monoxide, Methane, Volatile Organic Compounds, and Nitrogen containing Compounds. *Atmospheric Chemistry and Physics Discussions,* 5(5), 10455–10516.

Kulkarni A.V., Rathore B.P., Mahajan S. and Mathur P. 2005 Alarming retreat of Parbati Glacier, Beas basin, Himachal Pradesh. *Current Science,* 88(11), 1844-1850.

Kumar K.K., Kumar K.R., Ashrit R.G., Deshpande N.R. and Hansen J. W. 2004 Climate Impacts on Indian Agriculture. *International Journal of Climatology.* 24(11), 1375–1393.

Leuliette E.W., Nerem R.S. and Mitchum G.T. 2004 Calibration Of Topex/Poseidon And Jason Altimeter Data To Construct A Continuous Record Of Mean Sea Level Change, *Marine Geodesy,* 27(1-2), 79-94.

Maikhuri R.K., Rawat L.S., Phondani P. and Farooquee N. 2008 *Impact of Climate Change and Coping Strategies in Nanda Devi Biosphere Reserve (NDBR), Central Himalaya, India*- IMBC-Technical Working Group I: Climate Change Impacts on Biodiversity and Mountain Protected Areas www.icimod.org/resource.php?id=65.

Mall R.K., Singh R., Gupta A., Srinivasan G. and Rathore L.S. 2006 Impact of Climate Change on Indian Agriculture: A Review. *Climatic Change,* 78, 445–478

Matny, L. 2000 *Melting of Erth's Ice Cover Reaches New High.* Worldwatch News Brief, 06 March 2000. (Accessed on 5th June, 2018)

Mishra S, Singh B, Panda K et al (2016) Association of SNP Haplotypes of HKT Family Genes with Salt Tolerance in Indian wild Rice Germplasm.

Murthy M.S.R., Badarinath K.V.S., Gharai B., Rajshekhar G. and Roy P.S. 2006 *The Indian Forest Fire Response and Assessment System (INFFRAS)*, International Forest Fire News (IFFN), No. 34 (January – June 2006, 72-77)

Myers N., Mittermeier R. A., Mittermeier C. G., da-Fonseca G. A. B., Kent J. 2000. Biodiversity Hotspots for Conservation Priorities. *Nature* 40, 853–858

National Action Plan on Climate Change, Government of India. 1-52 (http://www.moef.nic.in/downloads/home/Pg01-52.pdf)

Nicholls N. *et al.*, 1995 *The Science of Climate Change [Intergovernmental Panel on Climate Change* (IPCC), Cambridge Univ. Press, Cambridge, 1996)], pp. 133.

Pai D.S., Thapliya, V. and Kokate P.D. 2004 Decadal Variation in the Heat and Cold Waves over India during 1971-2000, *Mausam*, 55(2), 281-292.

Pande P. and Telang S. 2011 *Analysis of CDM Projects in Indian Agriculture Sector* (http://greencleanguide.com/cdm-and-agriculture/) (Retrieved on 11.05.2018)

Pandey A., Sarkar M.S., Kumar M., Singh G. and Rawat J.S. 2018 Retreat of Pindari Glacier and Detection of Snout Position using Remote Sensing Technology. *Remote Sensing Applications: Society and Environment*. 11, 64-69.

Pramanik M.K., Biswas S.S., Mukherjee T., Roy A.K., Pal R. and Mondal B. 2015 Sea Level Rise and Coastal Vulnerability along the Eastern Coast of India through Geo-spatial Technologies. *J. Geophysics Remote Sensing*. 4(2): 1-8.

Parry M.L., Canziani O.F., Palutikof J.P., Linden P.J. and Hanson C.E. 2007 *Climate Change: Impacts, Adaptation, and Vulnerability, in Contribution of Working Group 11 to the Fourth Assessment Report of the IPCC* (Cambridge Univ. Press, 2007), pp. 976.

Partap U. and Partap T. 2002 *Warning Signals from the Apple Valleys of the Hindu Kush-Himalayas. In: Shreshtha ABM, Editor. Productivity Concerns and Pollination Problems*. Kathmandu: Centre for Integrated Mountain Development, pp. 116.

Parthasarathy B. and Pant G. B. 1985 Seasonal Relationship between Indian Summer Monsoon Rainfall and Southern Oscillation. *Journal of Climate*, 5(4), 369–378.

Parthasarathy B., Rupa Kumar K. and Munot A.A. 1992 Forecast of Rainy Season Good grain Production based on Monsoon Rainfall. *Indian J. of Agric. Science*, 62, 1–8.

Porter, J.R., L. Xie, A.J. Challinor, K. Cochrane, S.M. Howden, M.M. Iqbal, D.B. Lobell, and M.I. Travasso, 2014: Food Security and Food Production Systems. In: Climate Change 2014: Impacts, Adaptation, and Vulnerability. Part A: Global and Sectoral Aspects. Contribution of Working Group II to the Fifth Assessment Report of the Intergovernmental Panel on Climate Change [Field, C.B., V.R. Barros, D.J. Dokken, K.J. Mach, M.D. Mastrandrea, T.E. Bilir, M. Chatterjee, K.L. Ebi, Y.O. Estrada, R.C. Genova, B. Girma, E.S. Kissel, A.N. Levy, S. MacCracken, P.R. Mastrandrea, and L.L.White (eds.)]. Cambridge University Press, Cambridge, United Kingdom and New York, NY, USA, pp. 485-533.

"Press release – UN General Assembly's Open Working Group Proposes Sustainable Development Goals" *(PDF). Sustainable Development.un.org. 19 July 2014*. (Retrieved on 12th May, 2018)

Proceedings on the Brain-storming Session on *"Climate Variability/change Impacts on Mountain Ecosystem vis-à-vis Crafting Adaptation and Mitigation Strategies for Sustainable Livelihood in Himachal Pradesh"* Organized by the Department of Environmental Science, YSP University of Horticulture & Forestry, Nauni, Solan (Himachal Pradesh) on May 7, 2018

Raghavan, K. 1966 A Climatological Study of Severe Heat Waves in India. *Indian J. Met. Geophysics*, 17(4), 581-586.

Rana R.S., Bhagat R.M., Kalia V. and Lal H. 2008 *Impact of Climate Change on Shift of Apple Belt in Himachal Pradesh.* In: ISPRS Archives XXXVIII-8/W3Workshop Proceedings; Impact of Climate Change on Agriculture, pp. 131–137.

Revich B.A. and Shaposhnikov. 2012 Climate Change, Heat Waves, and Cold Spells as Risk Factors for increased Mortality in Some Regions of Russia. *Studies on Russian Economic Development*, 23(2), 195–207.

Rothermel, R. C. 1983 *How to Predict the Spread and Intensity of Forest and Range Fires*. In The Bark Beetles, Fuels, and Fire Bibliography, pp. 70.

Roy, P. S. 2003 *Forest Fire and Degradation Assessment using Satellite Remote Sensing and Geographic Information System*. In Satellite Remote Sensing and GIS Applications in Agricultural Meteorology, pp. 361.

Saxena K.G., Maikhuri R.K. and Rao S. 2005 Changes in Agricultural Biodiversity: Implications for Sustainable Livelihood in the Himalaya. *Journal of Mountain Science*, 2(1), 23–31.

Schild A. 2008 ICIMOD's Position on Climate Change and Mountain Systems. *Mountain Research and Development*, 28(3-4), 328-331.

Selvaraju R. 2003 Impact of El Nino- Southern Oscillation on Indian Food Grain Production. *International Journal of Climatology*, 23(2), 187–206.

Sharma B. 2016 Study on the Impact Assessment of Climate Change on the Social and Economic Status of Farmers in Dharampur Block of District Solan of Himachal Pradesh. *International Journal of Global Environmental Issues*, 15(3), 269-279.

Sharma S. N. 2017 Assam Floods, an Annual Tragedy: A Detailed Report. The Economic Times. https://economictimes.indiatimes.com/news/politics-and-nation/assam-floods-an-annual-tragedy-a-detailed-report/articleshow/59611524.cms (Retrieved on 12th June, 2018)

Seo H.H. 2003 Effects of Climatic Changes Influencing Fruit Tree Harvest. Effects of Climatic Changes Influencing the Korean Peninsula. Suwon-si Gyeonggi-do, Republic of Korea: The Rural Development Administration.

Singh O.P., Alikhan T.M. and Rahman M.S. 2000 Changes in the Frequency of Tropical Cyclones over North Indian Ocean. *Meteorol. Atmos. Phys*, 75 (1-2), 11-20.

Spanos I., Ganatsas P. and Tsakaldimi M. 2010 Evaluation of Postfire Restoration in Suburban Forest of Thessaloniki, Northern Greece. *Global Nest Journal*, 12(4), 390–400.

Tewari V.P., Verma R.K. and Gadow K.V. 2017 Climate Change Effects in the Western Himalayan Ecosystems of India: Evidence and Strategies. *Forest Ecosystems*, 4 (13), 1-9.

Thadani R., Singh V., Chauhan D.S., Dwivedi V. and Pandey A. 2015 Climate Change in Uttarakhand Dehradun: Singh V. Bishen Singh Mahendra Pal Singh (pub), pp. 66.

Toman, Michael A (2000): 'Establishing and Operating the Clean Development Mechanism', Climate Issues Brief No 22, Resources for the Future, Washington DC. Accessed at http://www.rff.org/issue_briefs/PDF_files/ ccbrf22_Toman.pdf

Uprety, D. C. 2003 *Rising Atmospheric Carbon Dioxide and Crops: Indian Studies*, Souvenir: 2ndInternational Congress of Plant Physiology, Jan. 8-12, 2003, New Delhi, 87–93.

UNISDR/GE/2015—ICLUX EN5000. (2015). United Nations, Office for Disaster Risk Reduction. Sendai Framework for Disaster Risk Reduction 2015–2030 (1st Ed.).

Unnikrishnan A.S., Kumar K.R., Fernandes S.E., Michael G.S. and Patwardhan S.K. 2006 Sea Level Changes along the Indian Coast: Observations and Projections. *Current Science*, 90 (3), 362-368

WMO 2003 WMO Statement on the States of the Global Cimate in 2002, WMO No. 949, pp. 12 https://library.wmo.int/opac/doc_num.php?explnum_id=3458 (Retrieved on 12th June, 2018)

Vohra, C.P. 1981 *Note on Recent Glaciological Expedition in Himachal Pradesh* Geol. Survey of India Spec. Publ., 6, 26-29

Vaughan D.G. 2013 *Chapter 4-Observations of the Cryosphere, Climate Change*: The Physical Science Basis, Working Group, contribution to the IPCC Fifth Assessment Report, British Antarctic Survey, pp 37.

Wu, Huizong, 2016 Mercury Rising: India Records its Highest Temperature Ever. CNN, 23rd May, 2016 https://edition.cnn.com/2016/05/20/asia/india-record-temperature/index.html (Retrieved on 26 May, 2018)

Xu J., Grumbine R.E., Shrestha A., Eriksson M., Yang X., Wang Y. and Wilkes A. 2009 The Melting Himalayas: Cascading Effects of Climate Change on Water, biodiversity, and Livelihoods. *Conservation Biology*, 23 (3), 520–530

Facts about fog in Delhi, NDTV Correspondent, 22nd January, 2010, (https://www.ndtv.com/india-news/facts-about-fog-in-delhi-409401 (Retrieved on 26th May, 2018)

Geography and You by Staff Reporter, September 22nd 2017, Cold Waves. https://www.geographyandyou.com/science/weather-and-climate/cold-waves/ accessed on 26th May, 2018

Niti Ayog. http://niti.gov.in/content/SDGs.php (Retrieved on 24th May, 2018)

The Hindu. 2011 Uttarakhand to Install Anti-hail Guns to Save Fruit Crops. http://www.thehindubusinessline.com/industry-and-economy/agribiz/ uttarakhand-to-install-antihail-guns-to-save-fruit-crops/article2414610.ece. (Retrieved on 12th May, 2018)

The Hindu. 2016 Over Rs. 5000 crore loss to J&K due to floods: Assocham http://www.thehindu.com/news/national/over-rs-5000-crore-loss-to-jk-economy-due-to-floods-assocham/article6409726.ece (Retrieved on 12th June, 2018

https://www.climate.gov/news-features/climate-qa/whats-difference-between-global-warming-and-climate-change (Retrieved on 2nd May, 2018)

http://www.downtoearth.org.in/news/indias-first-cdm-project-9597 (Retrieved on 2nd May, 2018)

https://www.news18.com/news/india/fog-breaks-7-yr-record-engulfs-delhi-airport-for-172-hrs-332718.html (Retrieved on 26th May, 2018).

https://www.skymetweather.com/content/weather-news-and-analysis/january-2013-was-the-coldest-ever-recorded/ (Retrieved on 26th May, 2018)

https://www.indiatoday.in/education-today/gk-current-affairs/story/worst-and-deadliest-floods-261643-2015-09-07 (Assessed on 26th May, 2018)

https://timesofindia.indiatimes.com/india/70-ha-of-forests-lost-in-ukhand-fires-in-2-days/articleshow/64264947.cms (Retrieved on 11th June, 2018)

Climate Change and Agro-Edaphic System **Pages 50–73**
Edited by: Dr. Alka Chauhan & Dr. Pawan Kumar 'Bharti'
ISBN: 978-93-86841-98-8
Edition: 2019
Published by: Discovery Publishing House Pvt. Ltd., New Delhi (India)

3

Intergovernmental Panel of Climate Change with Special Reference to Health

[1]Prasann Kumar, [2]Shweta Pathak

ABSTRACT

For 28 years, the Intergovernmental Panel on Climate Change (IPCC) has been assessing the potential risks associated with anthropogenic climate change. Although interest in climate change and health is growing, the implications arising from their interaction remain understudied. Generating a greater understanding of the health impacts of climate change could be key step in inciting some of the changes necessary to decelerate global warming.

Keywords: Agriculture, Biotic, Climate, Density, Intergovernmental, Panel

INTRODUCTION

The evidence of climate change is compelling: sea levels are rising, glaciers are retreating, precipitation patterns are changing, and the world is getting warmer. According to the Intergovernmental Panel on Climate Change (IPCC), the current rate of greenhouse gas emissions is likely to cause average temperatures to rise by 0.2 C per decade, reaching by 2050 the threshold of 2 C above pre-industrial levels. Recent evidence suggests even more rapid change, which will greatly, and in some cases irreversibly, affect not just people, but also species and eco- systems (Elizabeth *et al.,* 2010). Climate change indeed is real. Super typhoon Haiyan is the latest natural disaster that has also led credence to the reality of climate change. This sad occurrence hit land and devastated the Philippines. This record-breaking storm is the strongest storm in history to make landfall. It tore apart buildings and left entire provinces without power or communication. The 370-mile-wide storm packed winds 3.5 times as strong as Hurricane Katrina. Winds reached 195 mph and had gusts of up to 235 mph. Walls of water as high as fifteen feet swept over the country washing away towns on many islands and washed ships ashore where homes

1 Department of Agronomy, School of Agriculture, Lovely Professional University, Jalandhar, Punjab, 144411, India

2 Department of Plant Physiology, I.Ag. Sci., BHU., Varanasi, 221005, U.P., India.

once stood. The U.N. says, "Around 920,000 people were displaced by the storm and a total of 11.8 million people have been affected. Of- ficials said the deadly storm left more than 3850 injured and at least 77 people reported missing across the Philippines." (The Argo, 2013). Climate change is a serious risk to poverty reduction and could undo decades of development efforts. While climate change is global, its negative impacts are more severely felt by poor people and poor countries. They are more vulnerable because of their high dependence on natural resources and limited capacity to cope with climate variability and extremes. Restoring and maintaining key ecosystems can help communities in their adaptation efforts and support livelihoods that depend upon the services of these ecosystems. Moving towards low-carbon societies can help reduce greenhouse gas emissions, improving human health and well-being and creating green jobs. Climate change is a fact of life. We need to act urgently if we are to avoid an irreversible build-up of green- house gases (GHGs) and global warming at a potentially huge cost to the economy and society worldwide. Organisation for Economic Co-operation and Development (OECD) analysis suggests that if we act now, we have 10 to 15 years' "breathing space" during which action is possible at a relatively modest cost. But every year of delay reduces this breathing space, while requiring ever more stringent measures to make a difference. Current financial turmoil is not a reason to delay. Indeed, its macroeconomic consequences will be resolved in a relatively short time, after which growth will resume, while the consequences of inaction on global warming will continue to grow more and more costly over time. This study presents an overview of Global Climate Change with a view to help appreciate the concept, its urgency and to give an insight to the ways it affects society and the natural environment and proffering solutions.A long-term and broad overview of the existing scientific literature in the field of climate change and health is currently missing in order to ensure that all priority areas are being adequately addressed.

2. DEFINING WEATHER AND CLIMATE

Weather is the state of the atmosphere at a specific time in a specific place. Temperature, cloudiness, humidity, precipitation, and winds are examples of weather elements. Thunderstorms, tornadoes, and monsoons are also part of the weather of some places during some seasons. Climate is defined as long-term weather patterns that describe a region. For example, the New York metropolitan region's climate is temperate, with rain evenly distributed throughout the year, cold winters, and hot summers.

Climate Variability and Climate Change

Climate variability refers to variations in the prevailing state of the climate on all temporal and spatial scales beyond that of individual weather events. Variability may be due to natural internal processes within the climate system, or to variations in natural or anthropogenic (human-driven) external forcing. Global climate change indicates a change in either the mean state of the climate or in its variability, persisting for several decades or longer. This includes changes in average weather conditions on Earth, such as a change in average global temperature, as well as changes in how frequently regions experience heat waves, droughts, floods, storms, and other extreme weather. It is important to note that changes in individual weather events will potentially contribute substantially to changes in climate variability. Climate change could occur naturally as a result of a change in the sun's energy or Earth's orbital cycle (natural climate forcing), or it could occur as a result of persistent anthropogenic forcing, such as the addition of greenhouse gases, sulfate aerosols, or black carbon to the atmosphere, or through land-use change.

Climate System

Climate is a complex and interactive system. It consists of the atmosphere, land surface, snow and ice, oceans and other water bodies, and living beings. Among these, the first component, atmosphere characterizes climate. Various external factors influence the internal dynamics of the Climate Systems and these include natural phenomena such as volcanic eruptions and solar radiations, as well as human-induced changes in atmospheric composition. The entire climate system gets the power and energy from the Sun. The radiation balance of the Earth may get modified by three fundamental ways:

(1) by changing the incoming solar radiation;

(2) by changing the fraction of solar radiation that is reflected (called "albedo"); and

(3) by altering the long wave radiation from Earth back towards space Climate, in turn, responds directly to such changes, as well as indirectly, through a variety of feedback mechanisms.

Why "Global Warming" is The Wrong Term

Global warming (as well as global cooling) refers specifically to any change in the global average surface temperature. Global warming is often misunderstood to imply that the world will warm uniformly. In fact, an in- crease in average global temperature will also cause the circulation of the atmosphere to change, resulting in some areas of the world warming more, others less. Some areas can even cool. Unfortunately, although it significantly misrepresents what really happens, the term 'global warming' is still often used by media and others to describe climate change. Climate change is more than a warming trend (which is why the term "global warming" is an inaccurate description of the phenomenon).

Brief History of International Agreements on Climate Change

For the first time in June 1988 at the World Conference on the Changing Atmosphere in Toronto, politicians and scientists conclude "humanity is conducting an unintended, uncontrolled, globally pervasive experiment whose ultimate consequences could be second only to a global nuclear war." The conference recommends reducing carbon dioxide emissions 20% by 2005. In the same year IPCC published its First Assessment Report, which highlighted the increasing accumulation of human-made greenhouse gases in the atmosphere. The first Conference of the Parties (1995) in Canada, realized the need of binding commitments by industrialized countries are required to reduce emissions. In December 1997 around 150 countries signed the Kyoto Protocol, which binds 38 industrialized countries (called Annex 1 countries) to reduce greenhouse gas emissions by an average of 5.2% below 1990 levels for the period of 2008-2012. The Kyoto Protocol became international law on 16 February 2005. For any nation, the more urgent priorities like economic development always tends to take over threats like climate change or global environment change and this is why it is so difficult to achieve a coordinated international response to such issues. Recently, United Nations Climate Change Conference in Bali, Indonesia (December, 2007) was attended by representatives from over 180 countries, together with observers from intergovernmental and nongovernmental organizations. Participants agreed on "Bali roadmap", which provide guide- lines to reach a treaty by the end of 2009 to replace the Kyoto Protocol. That year in April during the UN Climate Talks in Bangkok – the first meeting after the Bali conference—an ambitious timetable had been developed to complete the complex negotiations on a new climate deal in time for the UN Climate Conference in Copenhagen in December 2009.

Greenhouse Effect

A natural system known as the "greenhouse effect" regulates temperature on Earth. Just as glass in a greenhouse keeps heat in, our atmosphere traps the sun's heat near earth's surface, primarily through heat-trapping proper- ties of certain "greenhouse gases". Earth is heated by sunlight. Most of the sun's energy passes through the atmosphere, to warm the earth's surface, oceans and atmosphere. However, in order to keep the atmosphere's energy budget in balance, the warmed earth also emits heat energy back to space as infrared radiation. As this energy radiates upward, most is absorbed by clouds and molecules of greenhouse gases in the lower atmosphere. These re-radiate the energy in all directions, some back towards the surface and some upward, where other molecules higher up can absorb the energy again. This process of absorption and re-emission is repeated until, finally, the energy does escape from the atmosphere to space. However, because much of the energy has been re- cycled downward, surface temperatures become much warmer than if the greenhouse gases were absent from the atmosphere. This natural process is known as the greenhouse effect. Without greenhouse gases, Earth's average temperature would be 19 C instead of +14 C, or 33 C colder. Over the past 10,000 years, the amount of greenhouse gases in our atmosphere has been relatively stable. Then a few centuries ago, their concentrations began to increase due to the increasing demand for energy caused by industrialization and rising populations, and due to changing land use and human settlement patterns.

Greenhouse Gases

The greenhouse gases and their sources are as follows: Water vapour is the most common greenhouse gas but others are very important too. Some occur naturally and some come from human activity. Carbon dioxide or CO_2 is the most significant greenhouse gas released by human activities, mostly through the burning of fossil fuels. It is the main contributor to climate change. Methane is produced when vegetation is burned, digested or rotted with no oxygen present. Garbage dumps, rice paddies, and grazing cows and other livestock release lots of methane Nitrous oxide can be found naturally in the environment but human activities are increasing the amounts. Nitrous oxide is released when chemical fertilizers. Nitrous oxide is released when chemical fertilizers and manure are used in agriculture. Halocarbons are a family of chemicals that include CFCs (which also damage the ozone layer), and other human-made chemicals that contain chlorine and fluorine.

Since Greenhouse Gases Make up such A Small Percentage of the Atmosphere, why do Changes in their Concentrations have such A Big Effect On Climate?

Most greenhouse gases are extremely effective at absorbing heat escaping from the earth and keeping it trapped. In other words, it takes only small amounts of these gases to significantly change the properties of the atmosphere. 99% of the dry atmosphere consists of nitrogen and oxygen, which are relatively transparent to sunlight and infrared energy, and have little effect on the flow of sunlight and heat energy through the air. By comparison, the atmospheric greenhouse gases that cause the earth's natural greenhouse effect total less than 1% of the atmosphere. But that tiny amount increases the earth's average surface temperature from 19 C to +14 C—a difference of about 33 C. A little bit of greenhouse gas goes a long way. Because the concentration of greenhouse gases in the atmosphere is so low, human emissions can have a significant effect. For example, human emissions of carbon dioxide (CO2) currently amount to roughly 28 billion tonnes per year. Over the next century human emissions will increase the concentration of carbon dioxide in the atmosphere from about 0.03% today to almost certainly 0.06% (a doubling), and possibly to 0.09% (a tripling).

Causes of Global Climate Change

Earth's climate changes naturally. Changes in the intensity of sunlight reaching the earth cause cycles of warming and cooling that have been a regular feature of the Earth's climatic history. Some of these solar cycles—like the four glacial-interglacial swings during the past 400,000 years—extend over very long time scales and can have large amplitudes of 5 C to 6 C. For the past 10,000 years, the earth has been in the warm interglacial phase of such a cycle. Other solar cycles are much shorter, with the shortest being the 11 year sunspot cycle. Other natural causes of climate change include variations in ocean currents (which can alter the distribution of heat and precipitation) and large eruptions of volcanoes (which can sporadically increase the concentration of atmospheric particles, blocking out more sunlight). Still, for thousands of years, the Earth's atmosphere has changed very little. Temperature and the balance of heat-trapping greenhouse gases have remained just right for humans, animals and plants to survive. But today we're having problems keeping this balance. Because we burn fossil fuels to heat our homes, run our cars, produce electricity, and manufacture all sorts of products, we are adding more greenhouse gases to the atmosphere. By increasing the amount of these gases, we have enhanced the warming capability of the natural greenhouse effect. It's the human-induced enhanced greenhouse effect that causes environmental concern, because it has the potential to warm the planet at a rate that has never been experienced in human history.

Consequences of Global Climate Change

Although the consequences of climate change could be discussed under a number of different categories, the scope of this discussion limits it to both natural and economic consequences.

Natural Consequences

These are already visible, for instance, temperatures are rising, polar caps are melting, sea level is rising, the desertification increases and the winters in Europe become ever wetter. It has been scientifically demonstrated that Mount Kilimanjaro through the years contains less and less snow as a consequence of global heating. It is questionable whether this mountain in Tanzania will be covered with snow at all in 50 years. It is also concluded that the number of natural disasters increases more and more. Tsunamis, floods and extreme drought occur more.

Frequent than in times past. In the period 1950-1960 worldwide 13 natural disasters have been registered, against 72 in the period 1990-1998. Now already the consequences are clearly demonstrable and most likely they will only increase in extent and frequency in the future. The IPCC predicts that climate change will become apparent in the following main ways:

- By around 2100 global temperatures will have risen by between 1.1 C and 6.4 C. The exact increase depends on future emissions of greenhouse gases and other pollutants and on the combined action of physical and chemical processes in the atmosphere.

- Some parts of the world will receive more precipitation, with others becoming drier.
- In the course of the present century sea levels will rise by between 18 and 59 centimetres. This is because warmer water occupies more space than cold water and because of the retreat of glaciers and polar ice sheets. Our understanding of the melting of the Greenland and Antarctic ice sheets is still incomplete. This, together with the fact that there may be large regional variations in sea level rise, means that in some parts of the world the consequences may be even more dramatic than predicted by IPCC.
- The Gulf Stream, which transports relatively warm water from the Caribbean to Europe, is expected to decline in strength, causing temperatures in northwest Europe to rise less markedly than elsewhere. Standard climate models, however, make no allowance for an abrupt change in the Gulf Stream.

Economic Consequences

Changes in global climate will have enormous consequences for living nature as well as the economy. Even a small rise in mean annual temperature can have a major impact on a region's ecology and biological diversity (Pounds &Puschendorf, 2004). Biodiversity is of crucial importance for the stability of ecosystems as well as for human health (Harvard, 2002). The economic impact of drought, floods and other climate change effects will become quite substantial. Some researchers estimate that these costs are set to rise to between 5% and 20% of global income (Stern, 2006). The IPCC has not yet managed to provide a rock-solid cost estimate of the consequences of climate change. It has estimated the cost of limiting further change, though. If such action is taken, global income will grow by only slightly less than if nothing is done: overall economic growth up to the year 2030 would then be 3 percentage points lower (57% instead of 60%, for example). Avoiding extreme climate change is also important if the "Millennium Development Goals" are to be achieved, formulated by the United Nations as follows:

- Eradicate extreme poverty and hunger.
- Achieve universal primary education.
- Promote gender equality and empower women.
- Reduce child mortality.
- Improve maternal health.
- Combat HIV/AIDS, malaria and other diseases.
- Ensure environmental sustainability.
- Develop a global partnership for development.

That climate policy and the Millennium Goals go hand in hand is readily illustrated. In regions where climate change leads to more severe drought, for example, poverty and hunger will be exacerbated rather than eradicated. Climate change will mean that malaria spreads further round the globe rather than being effectively combated. The multiple impacts of climate change on biodiversity will mean less environmental sustainability, not more. The message is clear: if climate change is not halted, the Millennium Goals will simply not be achieved.

Potential Health Impacts of Climate Change

Global climate change would affect human health via pathways of varying complexity, scale and directness and with different timing. Similarly, impacts would vary geographically as a function both of the environment and topography and of the vulnerability of the local population. Impacts would be both positive and negative (although expert scientific reviews anticipate predominantly negative). This is no surprise since climatic change would disrupt or otherwise alter a large range of natural ecological and physical systems that are an integral part of Earth's life support system. Via climate change humans are contributing to a change in the conditions of life on Earth (figure 3.1).

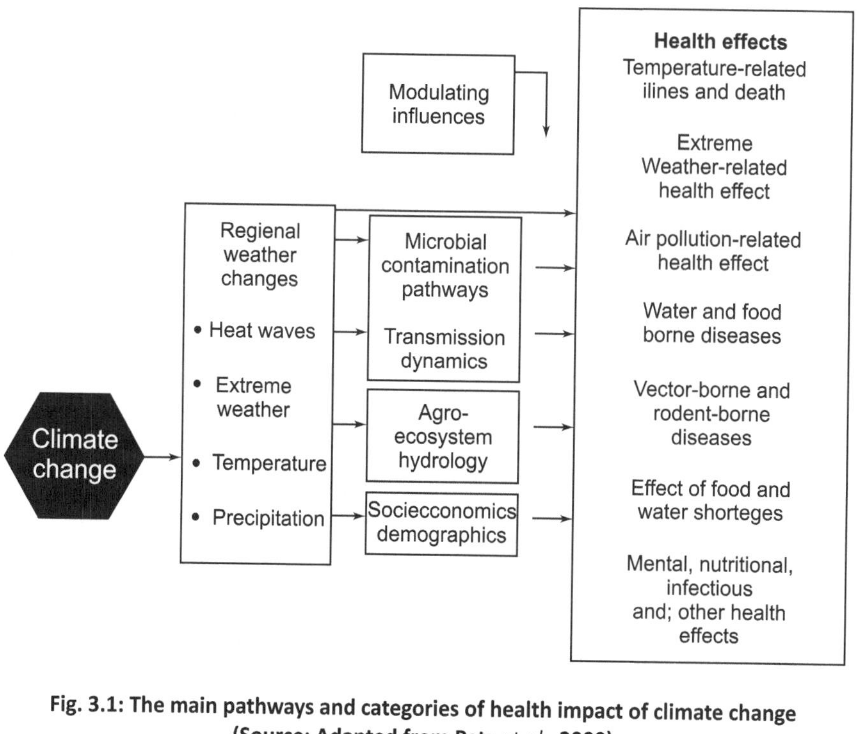

Fig. 3.1: The main pathways and categories of health impact of climate change (Source: Adapted from Patz *et al.*, 2000)

The more direct impacts on health include those due to changes in exposure to weather extremes (heat waves, winter cold); increases in other extreme weather events (floods, cyclones, storm-surges, droughts); and increased production of certain air pollutants and aeroallergens (spores and moulds). Decreases in winter mortality due to milder winters may compensate for increases in summer mortality due to the increased frequency of heatwaves. In countries with a high level of excess winter mortality, such as the United Kingdom, the beneficial impact may outweigh the detrimental (Langford & Bentham, 1995; Rooney et al. 1998). The extent of change in the frequency, intensity and location of extreme weather events due to climate change remains uncertain. Climate change, acting via less direct mechanisms, would affect the transmission of many infectious diseases (especially water, food and vector-borne diseases) and regional food productivity (especially cereal grains). In the longer term and with considerable variation between populations as a function of geography and vulnerability, these indirect impacts are likely to have greater magnitude than the more direct (McMichael & Githeko, 2001; Epstein, 1999). For vector-borne infections, the distribution and abundance of vector organisms and intermediate hosts are affected by various physical (temperature, precipitation, humidity, surface water and wind) and biotic factors (vegetation, host species, predators, competitors, parasites and human interventions). By reflecting the increased retention of heat energy in the lower atmosphere, global warming also affects the atmospheric heat budget so as to increase the cooling of the stratosphere (Shindell *et al.*, 1998) Should this cooling persist, the process of ozone depletion could continue even after chlorine and bromine loading (by human emission of ozone-destroying gases) starts to decline. If so, the potential health consequences of stratospheric ozone depletion (increase in incidence of skin cancer in fair-skinned populations; eye lesions such as cataracts; and, perhaps, suppression of immune activity) would become an issue for climate change.

BACKGROUND

The phenomenon of climate change is a reality that is now universally acknowledged and better understood than it was in 1988 when the Intergovernmental Panel on Climate Change (IPCC) was formed by the World Meteorological Organization (WMO) and the United Nations Environmental Programme (UNEP). There is growing evidence to support the scienti c theories indicating that climate change is adversely affecting human health. However, the impact of climate change on health is quite complex and the same factor may sometimes act as a cause and other times as an effect. The consequences of climate change are likely to lead to an increased demand on health services, which will require adaptation to the growing incidence of climate-related health issues. The need to identify and prevent adverse health impacts is rising to the forefront of climate change policy debates and is becoming a growing priority of the public health community.

METHOD

Scoping review methodology Scoping reviews are a relatively recent method of reviewing evidence-based research, particularly in health and also in other disciplines. There is no single de nition of what a scoping review consists of. A frequently applied de nition is that from Arksey and O'Malley, which states that the aim of a scoping review is to 'map rapidly the key concepts underpinning a research area and the main sources and types of evidence available'. This scoping review framework developed by Arksey and O'Malley in 2005 will be applied for this study. There have been a number of studies since 2005, which enhance the initial framework and have advanced our understanding of this methodology and how to produce a more ef cient and effective study. The key strength of the scoping review method as applied to our study is that it allows for the analysis of a broad research question. Climate change and health is a vast area of research and our intention is to map the breadth of the literature on this topic. The quality of the literature will not be assessed, which is a limitation of scoping reviews. Systematic reviews which have more re ned research questions and narrower study parameters, generally result in fewer, more homogeneous citations which can be more ef ciently assessed forpublications in the eld of medicine and life sciences. Web of Science is a multidisciplinary database, which will capture the non-clinical health aspects of the effects of climate change across a broad range of research areas.

Mitigation Solutions

Between 1970 and 2004 global emissions of greenhouse gases rose by 70%, mainly as a result of rising energy consumption. The CO_2 emissions of electrical power stations, factories, motor vehicles, homes, offices and other sources grew even greater: by 80%. Developed countries are responsible for half the world's CO_2 emissions. While the share of emerging economies like China and Latin America in global CO_2 emissions is rising, it is still far less than that of Europe and the United States taken together (both in absolute terms and per head of the population). If no action is taken, global CO_2 emissions are projected to rise by a further 45% to 110% between 2000 and 2030. In many of the world's regions and countries governments have introduced policies to reduce emissions of CO_2 and other greenhouse gases. This is often referred to as mitigation policy. A case in point is the Kyoto Protocol, under which industrialized countries have committed themselves to a certain cut in emissions; this has not been ratified by Australia or the US, however. The European Union has an additional policy target of reducing its CO_2 emissions by twenty to thirty percent by the year 2020 relative to 1990. One of the key instruments for securing these targets is the European "carbon emissions trading scheme". At the national and local level, too, action is being taken by governments as well as environmental organizations. One example of the latter type of action is Green for sure, a green energy plan presented to the Dutch government in 2007 by the Netherlands' largest environmental and trades unions organizations. Young people themselves can also take action to limit climate change. The first step is for them to realize that many everyday activities—computer gaming, showering, travel, and so on—consume energy and that energy is also required to produce food, clothing, cars, buildings and all kinds of other products. Everyone uses energy and every unit of energy consumed can further exacerbate climate change. It's therefore important to realize that all of us share some of the responsibility for climate change. What we ourselves can do to tackle climate change depends very much on our personal situation. It therefore makes sense to first work out how high your green- house gas emissions are, for example by going to one of the following websites:

- www.carbonfootprint.com
- www.climateneutralgroup.com
- www.carbonneutral.com
- www.CO_2 meter.nl

These sites will then point you to ways of reducing your emissions. There are three golden rules for cutting your personal CO_2 emissions:

(1) Use as little energy as possible.

- Replace old window panes with double-glazing (HR^{++} grade) and improve your home by insulating the floor, cavity-walls, loft and roof.
- Replace your old central heating system with a high-efficiency heater and make sure the system gets regular maintenance.
- Turn your central heating down a degree or two and put it on the night-time setting half an hour earlier.
- Avoid using air-conditioning systems if you can, using a fan, for example; if you do buy an airco, have a good look at the energy label.
- Use power sockets with on-off switches for your adapters, to ensure that energy is not being wasted when equipment is on stand-by.
- Replace old incandescent light bulbs with compact fluorescent ones.
- To save (heated) water, fit a low-energy shower head and take shorter showers; use a solar boiler for your hot water.
- Only use appliances with an A-label or better for energy use.
- Say no to energy-guzzlers like tumble dryers, plasma TVs and water beds.

(2) Try and ensure the energy you do use comes from renewable sources (wind, water, solar).

(3) Compensate for any fossil energy you use by supporting energy efficiency projects or by other means (a variety of schemes are available).

When it comes to reducing emissions of the other main greenhouse gases—methane and nitrous oxide—the single best tip is to eat less meat and more organically grown food.

Adaptation Solutions

Adaptation is processes through which societies make them, selves better able to cope with an uncertain future. Adapting to climate change entails taking the right measures to reduce the negative effects of climate change (or exploit the positive ones) by making the appropriate adjustments and changes (UNFCCC, 2007). The Intergovernmental Panel on Climate Change (IPCC) defines adaptation as 'adjustment in natural or human systems inresponse to actual or expected climatic stimuli or their effects, which moderates harm or exploits beneficial opportunities (IPCC, 2009). The consequences of climate change can be seen all over the world. Sea level rise, flooding, hotter summers and wetter winters are the picture of present and future. The key question is to what extent these changes will persist and how we should adapt to them. Contrary to mitigating measures, adaptive solutions do not contribute to a reduction of the climatological problems. Instead, we reconcile ourselves to the changes and adapt ourselves as best we can to the consequences. This means that much infra structural develop- ment will be needed: raising of dikes, improving of sewer systems, making more space for water and similar measures. We must become conscious of the fact that we will not always be safe anymore (from flooding), but we must adapt ourselves to the changes:

Sea Level Rising/Floods/Water Nuisance

When considering the rising of the sea level and the increased possibility of floods in a country, the Nether-lands for example, there are two courses to a solution. On the one side the Dutch can protect their country even better by raising the dikes and reinforcing the coastal areas. But by doing this, the consequences in case of a failure (the bursting of a dike) will only be worse. In fact, raising dikes will only be like building a high protecting wall around the country, creating a kind of 'bath tub' at the same time. If the protection wall fails the consequences will be greater. Another adaptive solution is learning to live with floods. Instead of concentrating on reinforcing the protecting areas (dunes and dikes) we rather put our efforts in limiting the consequences. This too will reduce the risk. After all, risk is defined as opportunity x consequence. If the opportunity remains the same, but the consequences are less severe, the risk will decrease. And exactly the limiting of the consequences can be started off on local government level. You could think of local policies like "no constructions in lower areas of the country" or on the contrary "specially adapted constructions in lower areas of the country".

Drought and Desertification

The UN-plan that was passed in 1994 underlines a "bottom-up"-approach, with which one wants to find particularly local solutions to prevent desertification together with the local communities. One tries to find the solution in sustainable development, tackling social, economic and ecologic problems at one time. A similar attitude requires quite a co-ordination and close collaboration between regional, national and international bodies, but environmentalists are not convinced that the political will to take measures is strong enough to turn the tide. To resist the advancing desertification, in 1994 the Convention to Combat Desertification (CCD) was established, as a consequence of the Earth summit of 1992. The Convention, which in the meantime has been signed by 191 countries, entered into force in December 1996. To make degraded ecosystems fertile again is a long lasting process and requires an integrated approach of rural development, expansion of irrigation systems and application of new technologies. Still, it is possible. In China the quantity of fertile soil vanishing yearly dropped between 2000 and 2004. In February the Chinese government launched a plan to reclaim 250.000 square kilometres from the desert by 2020 by means of planting trees and grass. Also, the Chinese government wants to invest in dry regions in the efficient use of water and renewable energy sources, such as wind and water. Furthermore it is the opinion of the UN-Environmental organization (UNEP) that where it is difficult to turn the tide, one should make a virtue of necessity. The story of a report that was published 5 June ran as: "As long as deserts become more inhospitable and less suitable for human habitation, we must be imaginative and take advantage of the new situation". UNEP sees an important potential particularly for the exploitation of solar energy, fish-production, research of the medicinal properties of desert plants and the breeding of crops resistant to drought and salinity. Also, new technologies to develop more efficient irrigation systems and to desalinate estuaries could help.

HEAT

Temperature rise caused by climate change can in extreme situations (heat) have a direct negative impact on the human health. Possible health effects in Europe are: problems by heat stress, increase of the spreading of Lyme's disease, effects of bad air quality (summer smog) and an increase of allergies. Population groups at high risk (such as the elderly, children or asthmatic people) may experience stronger effects (a greater sickness bur- den). Policy can play an important role in the limiting of the health effects of climate change. The Netherlands ought to be capable to resist certain health effects of climate change, by means of the maintaining/improving of existing policies or with new policy decisions (fig. 3.2). Little is known about biological or passive adaptation of man to climate change (for example acclimatization, immunization). Possible policy options/adaptation possibilities are amongst others:

- Improving of living conditions, e.g. air conditioning, ventilation.
- Improving of preventive/curative health care, e.g. personnel with special educations, vaccination.
- Monitoring/alarm systems.
- Public information/education. Some adaptation possibilities will be moreeffective and/or cost-effective than others.

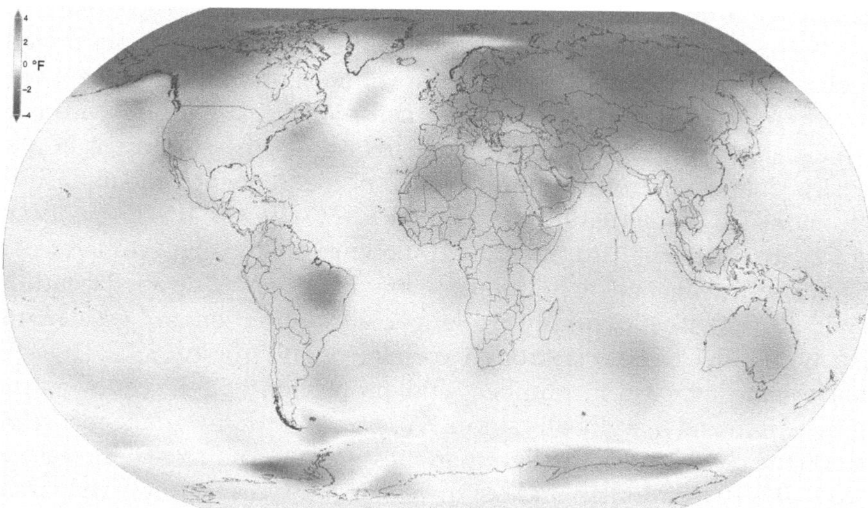

Fig. 3.2: Global temperature baseline
(Source: Based on a review of literature)

CLIMATE EVENTS

Extremes are the infrequent events at the high and low end of the range of values of a particular variable. The probability of occurrence of values in this range is called a probability distribution function (PDF) that for some variables is shaped similarly to a "Normal" or "Gaussian" curve (the familiar bell-shaped curve). People affected by an extreme weather event (e.g., the heavy rainfall in Mumbai in July 2005) wonder whether climate changes due to human influences are responsible. It is difficult to attribute any individual event to a change in the climate. In most regions, instrumental records of variability typically extend only over about 150 years, so there is limited information to characterize how extreme rare climatic events could be. Further, several factors usually need to combine to produce an extreme event, so linking a particular extreme event to a single, specific cause is problematic. In some cases, it may be possible to estimate the anthropogenic contribution to such changes in the probability of occurrence of extremes. As the climate changes and SSTs continue to increase, the conditions that cause tropical storms to form are no longer the same. Higher SSTs are generally accompanied by increased water vapor in the lower troposphere; thus, the moist static energy that fuels convection and thunderstorms is also increased. Hurricanes and typhoons currently form from pre-existing disturbances only where SSTs exceed about 26°C; so, as SSTs have increased, the areas over which such storms can form are potentially expanded. However, many other environmental factors also influence the generation and tracks of disturbances. The 2007 IPCC assessment concluded that there was a risk of increased temperature extremes in India, with more extreme heat episodes in a future climate. This result has been confirmed and expanded in more recent studies. Future increases in temperature extremes are projected to follow increases in mean temperature over most of the world except where surface properties (e.g., snow cover or soil moisture) change. There is still much debate over whether there is likely to be an increase in tropical cyclone intensity. Changes in tropical storm and hurricane frequency and intensity are often masked by large natural variability. ENSO greatly affects the location and activity of tropical storms around the world. Globally, estimates of the potential destructiveness of hurricanes show a substantial upward trend since the mid-1970s, with a trend toward longer storm duration and greater storm intensity, and this activity is strongly correlated with tropical SSTs. One study found a large increase in numbers and proportion of hurricanes reaching categories four and five globally since 1970, even as the total number of cyclones and cyclone days decreased slightly in most basins. The largest increase was in the North Pacific, Indian and Southwest Pacific Oceans. Improved models, ones that prescribed convection constraints based on the relative humidity, were able to simulate the variability and extremes of rainfall quite well over most of India when compared to satellite-derived rainfall but had a tendency to overestimate heavy rainfall events in central India. Several recent studies have addressed possible future changes in heat waves and found that in a future climate, heat waves are expected to be more intense, longer-lasting and more frequent. Based on an eight-member multi-model ensemble, heat waves are simulated to have increased for the latter part of the 20th century and are projected to increase globally and over most regions. Impacts of Climate Change on Natural Ecosystems Observed Changes An analysis of seasonal and annual surface air temperatures for India, using data for 1881–2001 for 25 or more stations, shows a significant annual mean warming of 0.68°C per hundred years. Most of the warming occurs in the post-monsoon and winter seasons. The monsoon temperatures do not show a significant trend in most parts of the country except for a significant negative trend over northwest

India. Maximum daytime temperatures show more of a trend than minimum nighttime temperatures, in contrast to general expectation. Water supply is changing. Almost 67 percent of the glaciers in the Himalayan mountain ranges, the source of major rivers in India, have retreated in the past decade. xliii For India, the IPCCxliv reports increased frequency of hot days and multiple-day heat waves in the past century, with more deaths attributable to heat stress in recent years. Consecutive droughts in 1999 and 2000 led to a sharp decline in water tables in the northwest, and 2000-2002 droughts caused crop failures, leading to mass starvation and impacts on ~11 million people in Orissa. Management decisions about natural hazards can cause conflicts. In 2002, under drought conditions in Andhra Pradesh, the state released dam water for electricity generation but not for irrigation. Poor farmers responded to such policies by smashing the pumps of their richer neighbors. Quarrels over water rights between states can be bitter, too. Tamil Nadu claimed that its neighboring state, Karnataka, violated agreements about sharing water from the Cauvery River. Bangalore is facing acute water scarcity as it attempts to meet the drinking water needs of 7 million people in the city. Public health is affected by currently experienced climate variability and change in the forms of heat and flooding. Between 1980 and 1998, 18 heat waves were reported in India; one in 1988 affected ten states and caused 1,300 deaths. Heat waves in Orissa, in the 1998-2000 period caused an estimated 2,120 deaths, and heat waves in 2003 in Andhra Pradesh caused more than 3,000 deaths.xlvii Flood-related increases in diarrheal disease have also been reported in India.

Economic Growth and Development Since 1990, India as a country has moved aggressively from a centrally planned economy to private ownership of businesses and trade liberalization. It has "developed a diversified industrial base and sophisticated financial sector. Its software subsector—one of the most dynamic in the world—has experienced a sustained and rapid growth. Over the past 25 years, the annual growth rate has been 6 percent, accelerating to a five-year annual average of 8.8 percent, investment at 30 percent of GDP, and booming foreign direct investment. India has made substantial strides in fostering human capital by reducing infant mortality, increasing life expectancy, and improving literacy. The central, democratic government provides stability and some curbs to unbridled free market-ism (or barriers to growth in an alternative characterization), and hordes of entrepreneurs provide the impetus for growth. On the positive side, India's democracy results in equity slightly higher than the global average. The dependency ratio (the percentage of the population dependent on the percentage of the population in the work force) is relatively high, indicating that many people are available for the work force, supporting relatively few people other than themselves. However, the poor condition of people engaged in agriculture and/or born into lower castes reduces the robustness of the overall economy. Climate change, adding to existing problems of the agricultural system, may worsen conditions for the large poor segment of the population enough to severely tax the economic and industrial resources of the central and state governments. Thus, the impacts of climate change are likely to be felt first and foremost in the agricultural sector and associated water availability, with many people affected by lower food productivity (e.g., hunger, malnutrition, and its consequences for education and productive economic life) and burdens on the central and state governments in dealing with smallholders and landless workers who will require assistance. Educational and employment inequalities will exacerbate these conditions. Some (or many) of these workers will migrate to urban areas, placing stress on cities. The need to add to or replace infrastructure affected by climate change (e.g., in the energy and transportation sectors, as well as irrigation systems) will present additional economic costs. Finally, migrants, particularly from Bangladesh, will affect India's economy by providing competition for low cost labor. Food Production and Drinking Water Supply Agriculture and water are inseparable issues, as almost all the water use in India is for irrigation to support high productivity in agriculture. Thus, both the monsoon onset and active/break phase mean a great deal to the agriculture sector. Research indicates that the monsoon active/break phase is related to a tropical phenomenon called the Madden This paper does not represent US Government views. If farmers sow too early and the crop needs water when the monsoon break phase occurs, the whole crop is lost. At the national level, India has abundant water resources for agriculture and drinking, as well as for cooking and sanitation uses. India withdraws 34 percent of its available water annually. However, at state and local levels, there are wide-ranging differences; overexploitation is already problematic and will likely become worse under climate change conditions. Increasing temperatures and increased seasonal variability will likely cause Himalayan glaciers to melt more and more quickly, also leading to increasing danger from floods as glacial lakes burst out of their natural bounds. Changes over decades will include less flow in rivers fed today by snow and ice, with impacts on hydropower, urban water supply, and agriculture. Although there is clear evidence of de-glaciation across the Himalayas, the effect on river flows is likely to be substantially different in different areas. The extent of the changes is very uncertain because, as Sengupta puts it, "River flow data is so scant and recent that it is impossible for scientists to predict how the current rates of glacial retreat will affect river volume."lxx There are major regions, including many of the most highly productive agricultural and industrial regions of India, where water scarcity is already felt in day-to-day life. The retreats of snow and ice cover are important for several local climates, especially those near the Himalayas. The drying effect of an earlier spring snowmelt and, more generally, the earlier reduction in soil moisture is a continuing concern. Already 15 percent of aquifers are in critical condition, a figure that is projected to increase to a "frightening" 60 percent by the year 2030.lxxi Especially in important agricultural areas that have benefited from the Green Revolution, irrigation has led to exploitation of groundwater resources—e.g., 94 percent in Punjab, 84 percent in Haryana, 60 percent in Tamil Nadu, and 51 percent in Rajasthan. Farmers who borrow to dig bore wells for crop irrigation may find that when groundwater tables decline, they cannot repay their loans; some probably will commit suicide. Groundwater depletion has been accelerated by the provision of free or subsidized electricity for agriculture: subsidized rates on irrigation pumps, some state-level free power policies, and supports for agricultural consumers. In many places (northwest India as well as Pakistan) irrigation has resulted in not only overexploitation of water resources, but also increased soil salinity, waterlogging, and siltation of river basins. These problems have been intensified by declining soil fertility, increasing pest damage, and decreasing genetic diversity in crops. Environmental and economic leaders. have called for a second Green Revolution as rates of growth in agricultural production have slowed. This would place more pressure on water resources for irrigation. To partially compensate for increased water demand, the efficiency of irrigation systems can be improved. And in recent years, Water Users Associations (WUAs) have formed to conduct participatory irrigation management; these may promote conservation and water use efficiency. Rainfed agriculture (65 percent of cropped land) will experience climate change impacts, too. Without irrigation, smallholder farmers and landless agricultural workers will likely face household food shortages and loss of livelihoods, requiring government assistance or even international aid, as well as pressures on cities to accommodate migrants from rural areas. 5 "Subseasonal" refers to any timescale shorter than a season. This paper does not represent US Government views. 25 This paper does not represent US Government views. +7 percent, farm-level total net revenue would fall by 9 percent, whereas with a temperature increase of +3.5°C and precipitation change of +15 percent, the fall in farm-level total net revenue would be nearly 25 percent. Aggarwal et al. explored agricultural adaptations to global environmental change in the Indo-Gangetic Plan, concluding that "new information and tools are needed to analyze the trade-offs between the joint socioeconomic and environmental goals, and possible adaptation strategies."Livestock, too, will be affected by climate change. India has the largest livestock population in the world, with animals used as milk producers (especially cattle and buffalo), draft animals, nutrient recycling (manure) and seeding, and as household capital, particularly in landless households. Heat stress lowers production and reproduction, reduces feed and fodder, and increases conditions favorable to disease. For example, outbreaks of foot and mouth disease in cattle are explained 52 percent (in Andhra) and 84 percent (in Maharashtra) by temperature, humidity, and rainfall; mastitis increases in dairy animals during hot and humid weather, which also is associated with increases in flies and cattle ticks. Water availability will be a crucial factor in the continued viability of both crops and livestock, but management is diffuse. Under the Indian constitution, water is the responsibility of the states, not the central government. Thus, water management institutions at the state level have the biggest say in planning and allocation. At the national level, at least five ministries (Water Resources, Environment and Forests, Rural Development, Power, and Urban Development and Poverty Alleviation) are concerned with water, but no organizational mechanism exists to coordinate water management among these ministries. Moreover, efforts to adapt to more variability in water flows by constructing dams and catchments may increase tensions with Bangladesh and Pakistan. While freshwater resources will be affected, the marine environment is and will be changing too. Fisheries stocks may collapse or move in the already-contested waters of the Indian Ocean, potentially affecting livelihoods and food supply for millions of people. The international ocean management regimes will require renegotiation. Human Health Currently, India's public health care system produces relatively poor health outcomes. For India, Healthy Life Expectancy (HALE), which includes adjustment for time spent in poor health, is 53 years for children born in 2003.xc Despite perceived strengths of the national-level public health system (good expertise, written guidelines and standards, and network of research and training institutions), implementation and monitoring of services are weak. Funding for control of communicable diseases has been deemphasized since the 1980s; several infectious diseases, such a tuberculosis and malaria, have reemerged as public health care concerns. In India, unplanned urbanization has contributed to the spread of Plasmodium vivax malaria and dengue. Climate change impacts on health include an expected increase in communicable diseases, such as malaria. Malaria is projected to move to higher latitudes and altitudes in India. An assessment in India projected shifts in the geographical range and duration of the transmission window for Plasmodium falciparum and P vivax malaria. Coping Capabilities in Facing Natural Disasters India is highly vulnerable to natural disasters, and people live on marginal lands or in coastal and delataic cities where they are at greater risk. Floods, regional droughts, cyclones, and earthquakes affect millions of Indians. In the area of disaster mitigation, much has been done to document conditions leading to vulnerability. For example, a Flood Atlas of India and a Vulnerability Atlas of India (1997, revised 2006) have been produced; the latter assesses the vulnerability of housing and infrastructure to earthquakes, cyclones and floods to improve zoning and construction. In India, as in the United States, the primary responsibility for responding to disasters lies at the state level. The Disaster Management Act of 2005 set up the Natural Disaster Management Division in the Ministry of Home Affairs and proclaimed a new emphasis on disaster prevention. The United Nations Development Programxcvii has developed a plan for disaster preparedness and response that attempts to integrate government and other activities. Many Indian states have limited resources and lack their own disaster management plans. Because of these factors, India's disaster response record has been mixed, with delayed response, lack of early warning systems and resources to undertake measures like mass evacuation, inadequate coordination among various government departments, failure to keep essential stores (e.g., sandbags, medicines, and life-saving equipment) on hand, and inadequate coordination with the Army and other service organizations, as well as donors. As an example of disaster response, in 2007 the New York Times reported a United Nations official as saying that about 2,800 people in India, Bangladesh, Nepal, and Pakistan had died in monsoonal floods ("the worst in living memory"), from drowning, waterborne illnesses, snakebites or hunger. For survivors, the land damage meant there would be no near-term agricultural work for millions of landless laborers, leaving them to rely on the sporadic support of aid agencies and government relief organizations. The condition of the 31 million people affected in India was covered internationally but was not featured either in New Delhi newspapers or on national news channels. Infrastructure is affected by climate hazards as well. For instance, 14 percent of the annual repair and maintenance budget of the newly built 760 km Konkan Railway in India is spent repairing damage to track, bridges, and cuttings due to extreme weather events such as rain induced landslides. In spite of preventive targeting of vulnerable stretches of the line, operations must be suspended for an average of seven days each rainy season because of such damage. Systematic disaster preparedness at the community level has helped reduce death tolls; for instance, new warning systems and evacuation procedures in Andhra Pradesh after 1977 reduced deaths from coastal tropical cyclones to 10 percent of the 1977 total by 1997. Climate Change in the Neighborhood The most obvious regional climate change impacts will likely concern water. The Indo-Gangetic Plain stretches from Pakistan's coast across northern India to almost the whole of Bangladesh. The Indus River drains in Pakistan, the Ganges in India, and Bangladesh. Rivers fed by Himalayan snow and ice provide irrigation water for this important agricultural area. India has water agreements with both neighboring countries, and alleged violations of these agreements have caused international disputes. This paper does not represent US Government views. Bangladesh, in particular, depends upon India to allow sufficient fresh water to flow into Bangladesh for every water use and for preventing salt water intrusion. Sea level rise and management decisions have reduced freshwater flows and increased salt-water intrusion in the Indus delta and Bangladesh. This adversely affects the Sundarbans, the largest mangrove forest in the world, which is shared by India and Bangladesh. In addition, flooding has displaced thousands to millions of Bangladeshis, who are subject to outbreaks of xenophobic violence if they resettle in India. Also potentially important are changes in Arabian Sea (e.g., loss of fresh water input due to channeling of Indus river water to agriculture in Pakistan, leading to biogeochemical changes in the Western Arabian Sea); the impacts of aerosols (the "Atmospheric Brown Cloud"), which may diminish winter precipitation in western India and in Pakistan); and changes in the carbon cycle in the Bay of Bengal. Adaptive Capacity The impacts of climate change will be felt differentially, depending upon how well a society can cope with or adapt to climate change, that is, its adaptive capacity. Adaptive capacity is defined by the IPCC as, "The ability of a system to adjust to climate change (including climate variability and extremes) to moderate potential damages, to take advantage of opportunities, or to cope with the consequences."ci Thus, adaptive capacity is distinguished from both climate change impacts and the degree to which those impacts affect the systems that are in place (as discussed in the previous sections). Although the specific determinants (or "drivers") of adaptive capacity are a matter of debate among researchers, there is broad agreement that economic, human, and environmental resources are essential elements. Some components of this adaptive capacity are near term, such as the ability to deliver aid swiftly to those affected by, e.g., flooding or droughts. Other components include a high enough level of education so that people can change livelihoods, a quantity of unmanaged land that can be brought into food production, and institutions that provide knowledge and assistance in times of change. For instance, Yohe and Tolcii identified eight qualitative "determinants of adaptive capacity," many of which are societal in character, although the scientists draw on an economic vocabulary and framing: 1. The range of available technological options for adaptation. 2. The availability of resources and their distribution across the population. 3. The structure of critical institutions, the derivative allocation of decision-making. authority, and the decision criteria that would be employed. 4. The stock of human capital, including education and personal security. 5. The stock of social capital, including the definition of property rights. 6. The system's access to risk-spreading processes. 7. The ability of decisionmakers to manage information, the processes by which these decisionmakers determine which information is credible, and the credibility of the decisionmakers themselves. 8. The public's perceived attribution of the source of stress and the significance of exposure to its local manifestations. Researchers have only recently taken on the challenge of assessing adaptive capacity in a comparative, quantitative framework. A global comparative study of resilience to climate change (including adaptive capacity) was conducted using the Vulnerability-Resilience Indicators. Adaptive capacity, as assessed in this study, consists of seven variables (in three sectors), chosen to represent societal characteristics important to a country's ability to cope with and adapt to climate change: Methodological Description of the Vulnerability-Resilience Indicator Model (VRIM) The VRIM is a hierarchical model with four levels. The vulnerability index (level 1) is derived from two indicators (level 2): sensitivity (how systems could be negatively affected by climate change) and adaptive capacity (the capability of a society to maintain, minimize loss of, or maximize gains in welfare). Sensitivity and adaptive capacity, in turn, are composed of sectors (level 3). For adaptive capacity these sectors are human resources, economic capacity, and environmental capacity. For sensitivity, the sectors are settlement/infrastructure, food security, ecosystems, human health, and water resources. Each of these sectors is composed of one to three proxies (level 4). The proxies under adaptive capacity are as follows: human resource proxies are the dependency ratio and literacy rate; economic capacity proxies are GDP (market) per capita and income equity; and environmental capacity proxies are population density, sulfur dioxide divided by state area, and percent of unmanaged land. Proxies in the sensitivity sectors are water availability, fertilizer use per agricultural land area, percent of managed land, life expectancy, birthrate, protein demand, cereal production per agricultural land area, sanitation access, access to safe drinking water, and population at risk due to sea level rise. Each of the hierarchical level values is comprised of the geometric means of participating values. Proxy values are indexed by determining their location within the range of proxy values over all countries or states. The final calculation of resilience is the geometric mean of the adaptive capacity and sensitivity. • Human and Civic Resources — Dependency ratio: proxy for social and economic resources available for adaptation after meeting basic needs. — Literacy: proxy for human capital generally, especially the ability to adapt by changing employment. • Economic Capacity — GDP (market) per capita: proxy for economic well-being in general, especially access to markets, technology, and other resources useful for adaptation. — Income equity: proxy for the potential of all people in a country or state to participate in the economic benefits available. • Environmental Capacity. Percent of land that is unmanaged: proxy for potential for economic use or increased crop productivity and for ecosystem health (e.g., ability of plants and animals to migrate under climate change). — Sulfur dioxide per unit land area: proxy for air quality and, through sulfur deposition, other stresses on ecosystems. — Population density: proxy for population pressures on ecosystems (e.g., adequate food production for a given population). There is a wide range of adaptive capacity represented by these countries; India ranks low, both in the sample and overall: • Russia ranks 32nd and Libya 34th (in the highest quartile). • Indonesia ranks 45th, Belize 48th, Mexico 59th, and China 75th (in the second quartile). • The Philippines ranks 91st and India 119th (in the third quartile). • Morocco ranks 136th and Haiti 156th (in the lowest quartile). Any country-level analysis must take into account the comparative ranking of the country.

Sample of 11 countries' rankings of adaptive capacity (2005). The contribution of each variable to the overall ranking (slight differences occurring because of the methodology. India ranks low in comparison with Russia and China because of lower human resources (dependency ratio and literacy levels) than China, and both lower human resources and environmental capacity (non-managed land, emissions per total land area, and population density) than Russia. Ranking of Adaptive Capacity in Base Year 0 20 40 60 80 100 Haiti Morocco India Philippines China Mexico Belize Indonesia Libya Russian Federation. Projections are made for two scenarios; rates of growth are based on the IPCC's A1 scenario in its Special Report on Emissions Scenariosciv. Both scenarios feature moderate population growth and a tendency toward convergence in affluence (with market-based solutions, rapid technological progress, and improving human welfare). The scenarios used in this study differ in the rate of economic growth, one modeling high-and-fast economic growth, the other delayed growth. In the high-growth scenario, China overtakes Russia in adaptive capacity, but India retains its relatively low position throughout the entire period in both scenarios. Strengths/Weaknesses in Adaptive Capacity Assessments Even comparative measures of adaptive capacity only allow analysts to ask improved, more focused questions about area or local conditions that contribute to or reduce resilience. It is likely, for instance, that for particular places (e.g., states in India) important variables or domains are not included. For agricultural regions, this might include the extent of irrigation; for urban areas, better measures of education could be important. The measure of unmanaged land does not account for the potential usefulness of that land. However, comparative measures such as these can be an important first step toward determining where to direct resources—for further analysis or additional factors. Aspects of Adaptive Capacity in Base Year 0 200 400 600 Haiti Morocco India Philippines China Mexico Belize Indonesia Libya Russian Federation GDP per capita equity index dependency ratio literacy levels non-managed land (%) emssions/total land population density.

CONCLUSION

Climate change is happening and it is caused largely by human activity. Its impacts are beginning to be felt and will be worsen in the decades ahead unless we take action. The increasing rate of global warming—courtesy of carbon dioxide and other green house gas emissions from human activities—have led to climatic changes and environmental degradation, which in turn have resulted to great challenges in relation to diseases and human health. Many diseases which were previously unknown in certain climatic zones are now finding their way to such areas, due to changes in the weather conditions. Further, many diseases that had been thought extinct are reemerging in areas with altered climatic conditions that favor their comeback. It is therefore important that stakeholders and decision makers at industrial, government and international policy levels come up with stringent and workable means of cutting down on green house gases emission to combat the spread of global warming effects, and the resultant climate change, which has produced devastating impacts especially among poorer nations.Further, there should be increased funding of adaptation and coping programs and projects in affected areas to minimize the impacts on human health and curtail the spread of diseases.

REFERENCES

Harvard, & Chivian, E. (2002). Biodiversity: Its Importance to Human Health Harvard Medical School. IPCC Online, Glossary of Terms Used in the IPCC Third Assessment Report (2001) IPCC_Third_Assessment_Report (Accessed December 2009). http://en.wikipedia.org/wiki/

Langford, I. H., & Bentham, G. (1995).The Potential Effects of Climate Change on Winter Mortality in England and Wales. International Journal of Biometeorology, 38, 141-147.

McCarthy, J. J. (2001). Report of the Intergovernmental Panel on Climate Change. New York, USA: Cambridge University Press.

McMichael, A. J., & Githeko, A. Human Health. In: Climate Change 2001: Impacts, Adaptation, and Vulnerability. Contribution of Working Group II to the Third Assessment.

New Climate Change Fact Sheet, Facts about Climate Change.http://www.the great warming.com/pdf/ClimateChangeFactSheet.pdf

Patz, J. et al. (2000). The Potential Health Impacts of Climate Variability and Change for the United States: Executive Summary of the Report of the Health Sector of the US National Assessment. Environmental Health Perspectives, 108, 367-376.

Pounds, J.A., & R. Puschendorf (2004).Clouded Futures. Nature, 427, 8 January 2004.

RensKortmann (CE Delft), Edgar Peijnenborgh (RPS), Judith Harrewijn, Lindske van Hulst (SME Advies) (2007). Climate Change: Causes, Consequences, and Solutions, Scientific Background to the On-Line Platform Climate Quest.

Rooney, C. et al. (1998). Excess Mortality in England and Wales during the 1995 Heatwave. Journal of Epidemiology and Community Health, 52, 482-486.

Shindell, D. T. et al. (1998). Increased Polar Stratospheric Ozone Losses and Delayed Eventual Recovery Owing to Increasing Greenhouse Gas Concentrations. Nature, 392, 589-592.

Stern, N. (2006). The Economics of Climate Change—The Stern Review. Cambridge: Cambridge University Press SudipMitra, Global Climate Change an Introduction. http://www. climate-leaders.org/wp-content/uploads/global-climatechange-sudipmitra.pdf.

The Argo (2013) Typhoon Haiyan Hits Philippines: Stockton Community Takes Action, The Independent Student Newspaper of the Richard Stockton College of New Jersey. 83.

UNFCCC (UN Framework Convention on Climate Change) (2007). Climate Change: Impacts, Vulnerabilities and Adaptation in Developing Countries (p. 12). Bonn: UNFCCC.

Willetts, E., Guadagno, L., & Ikkala, N. (2010).Addressing Climate Change, Issues and Solutions from around the World (40 p). Editors. Gland, Switzerland: IUCN.

Climate Change and Agro-Edaphic System **Pages 74–102**
Edited by: Dr. Alka Chauhan & Dr. Pawan Kumar 'Bharti'
ISBN: 978-93-86841-98-8
Edition: 2019
Published by: Discovery Publishing House Pvt. Ltd., New Delhi (India)

4

Air Pollution and Climatic Changes

The Global and Regional Perspectives

[1]Akash, Navneet, [2]B.S. Bhandari

ABSTRACT

Human depends on the environment to obtain resource for their survival and development of the civilization. These resources includes food, clean drinking water, timber for construction, fibres for clothing, natural gas and coal for industries. All the human activity affects the environment in different way. The biggest threats to the environment is climate change and pollution. The earth atmosphere is a layer of gases that surrounds the planet and allow us to breathe and live. The atmosphere is made up of Nitrogen, Oxygen and others types of gases. This mixture of gases is known as Air. Air pollution is results from a variety of pollutants like NO2, SO2, CO, CFCs, and Ozone etc. Carbon dioxide, which is a green house gas, warming the earth day by day. As livings things emits carbon dioxide when they breath but carbon dioxide is widely considered to the a pollutants when it is associated with cars, power plants, planes and other human activities involving the burning of gasoline and natural gas. In past 150 years, such activities have pumped so much carbon dioxide into the atmosphere results in climatic changes on earth. Rise in sea level, extinction of animals and plants, extreme weather events, rising ocean temperature are the results of climatic change. This chapter will explore the impacts of climatic changes due to various types of air pollutants and its effects on the survival of earth. Additionally, it will on an out sketch plants as a tools which can reduce the levels of air pollution.

Introduction

Climate is an important factor that influences the quality of air. The emission of various types of pollutants in environment and their dispersion as well as the chemical transformation band deposition can be influenced by meteorological variables such as humidity, temperature, wind (Kinney, 2008). Climate change is expected to worsen the quality of air in densely populated regions of world by changing atmospheric ventilation and dilution, precipitation band other removal processes as well as the atmospheric chemistry (Fiore *et al.*, 20015).

1 Gurukula Kangri University; Haridwar, Uttarakhand, India, 249401
2 H.N.B. Garhwal University; Shrinagar, Uttarakhand, India, 246174

The changes in climate lead to various problems on earth. Every organism gets affected due to the changes in climate. Reduction in the quality of air will directly affect ecosystem in ways that also could affect human health (Haase *et al.,* 2014 and Who, 2013). Different study reveals that climate change has already affected the quality of air. Fang *et al.,* 2013 observed that from 1860 -2000 the global population-weighted fine particle (PM2.5) concentration has been increased by 5% and near-surface ozone concentrations by 2% due to climatic changes. Another study from Silva et al. ,2013 revels that the change from pre-industrial resulted in up to 111,000 and 21,400 additional premature fine particle- and ozone-related deaths due to climate change. As the climate continues to change in future these impacts would be more drastic in future.

Global warming induced by human activity has adverse impact on the environment and its components (Uysal *et al.,* 2003 and Health and Environment Alliance, 2009) . Global greenhouse gas emissions due to the various human activities have been growing with an increase of 70% between 1970 and 2004. The list of greenhouse gases also includes the causative components of air pollution. According to the Intergovernmental Panel on Climate Change 2007 document "most of the observed rise in globally averaged temperatures of earth since the mid-20th century is very likely due to the recorded increase in anthropogenic greenhouse gas concentrations" (Trenberth *et al.,*2007). One of the important green house gas is Carbon dioxide. It is the also due to the anthropogenic greenhouse gas and its emissions increased by 80% between 1970 and 2004 due to various anthropogenic activity (Trenberth *et al.,*2007). The changes in climate resulting from various emission from greenhouse gas affects severely human as well as the other components on the earth. A dramatic increase in the prevalence of the different types of respiratory diseases such as rhino sinusitis and bronchial asthma has been observed in many countries during the last 3 decades in industrialized countries. The key feature of respiratory disease is the development of airway inflammation and bronchial hyper responsiveness in the form of a heightened bronchoconstrictor response not only to allergens to which an individual is sensitized, but also to a range of different stimuli, such as cold air and pollutants. Rising trend in allergic respiratory diseases are the evidence to indicate the higher level of emission from vehicles. The negative effect of air pollution on health has a quantifiable impact, not only in terms of morbidity but also on the mortality of respiratory diseases. The recent increase in morbidity associated with respiratory diseases is the continuous degradation of the quality of air as a result of increasing levels of outdoor air pollutants such as vehicle emissions. The major air pollutants that are toxic, causing serious disease in the human and also effects the flora and fauna which are nitrogen dioxide, sulfur dioxide, and particulate matter. Some other aeroallergens which are derived from pollen grains, lead to bronchial obstruction in predisposed individuals. The pollen allergy is one of the models that study the relationship between respiratory allergic disease and air pollution.

Interactions between Climate and Air Pollution

Climate and air pollution are related to each other in many terms. Changes in climate affect the quality of air directly and indirectly. The major effects of climatic change on the quality of air area degrading the removal process like dispersion, precipitation and amplifying the atmospheric chemistry (Fiore *et al.*,1995), resulting into the severe effects on the organism of earth. Higher concentrations of PM2.5 due to the anthropogenic sources can result from changes in precursor emissions or in meteorology and in the physical as well as the chemical behaviour of various particles into the atmosphere (Liu *et al.*,2010).Besides different anthropogenic emissions, future climate will change the emissions of biogenic volatile organic compounds due to higher temperatures of earth and changed plant metabolism which can alter secondary organic aerosols resulting in changes in secondary particle levels (Carslaw *et al.*,2010). The other thing is wildfires which is associated with climatic changes, could severely reduce air quality in future (Liu *et al.*,2010). The other natural factors are dust particles and storms which also increases in future due to climatic changes (Fuzzi *et al.*,2015). Jacob and Winner (2015), observed that due to climatic change especially due to circulation as well as the decreasing frequency of mid-latitude cyclones, the annual mean particulate matter 2.5(PM) concentrations will change by ± 1 µg/m3 in the united states of America and other European countries. The increasment in global temperature is sometime also due to the Soot (black carbon) which can absorb heat (DeAngelo *et al.*,2013). Sometime at the surface of ozone, the various secondary pollutants formed from the interaction of precursor compounds with the light from sun including UV radiation (Jacob and Winner, 2015). The rate of the formation of these pollutants is temperature depended. So due to the sunny and cloudless days as well as the higher temperatures are more conducive to higher ozone concentrations. Wind play a role in control of ozone levels by dispersing precursor species, thus resulting in the reduction of ozone formation. The formation of ozone near the surface is the results of the chemical reactions which depend on the ozone precursor emission from anthropogenic and natural sources. The precursor are VOCs, CO, CH4. These all react with hydroxyl radical resulting into the formation of ground-level ozone. The rising temperature due to the climatic changes lead to the increasment of natural VOC emission which affect the ozone concentration (Sillman *et al.*,1995). The hydroxyl radical formation is associated with methane gas and another greenhouse gas (Fiore *et al.*,2014). These all interaction into the atmosphere causes different types of diseases and health problems among the organisms. Plants, animals and microbial biomass also get affected due to all these interaction into the environment. Combustible particles can affect cardiopulmonary mortality, hospitalization as well as the respiratory disease like bronchitis, rhinitis, asthma and chronic (WHO, 2013). Recent evidence from different worker revels that the unfair quality of air enhance rheumatic diseases (Sun *et al.*, 2016), diabetes (Thiering *et al.*, 2015), neurodegenerative diseases, cognitive functioning (Clifford *et al.*,2016) and other harmful gases such as the secondary pollutant are related to all circulatory and respiratory mortalities (Who, 2013 and Turner *et al.*,2016) as well as chronic respiratory diseases such as asthma (Who, 2013). Studies showed that higher ozone concentrations causes preterm birth (Olsson and Morgen, 2013), reproductive health (Hansen *et al.*,2010) as well as cognitive decline (Xu *et al.*,2016). Further the primary and secondary pollutants can gear up the climatic change that in turn of public health. The secondary pollutants such as ozone can severely affect the different crop yields which in combination with climate, can affect food security and public health (Patz *et al.*,2014 and McGrath *et al.*,2015). Tai *et al.*, 2014) concluded that climate change could reduce global crop production by > 10% by 2050. It was observed within the latest decade that, there has been a growing interest in the effects of climate change on the levels of future air pollution. It is well known in the world that, the composition of the atmosphere will change due to the various changes in anthropogenic emissions. The climate modelling studies reveals some meteorological parameters will change in the future both due to the natural variability and because of the man-made changes in the composition of the atmosphere. Temperature will continue increase in the future (Houghton, 2001). The increasing temperature will affect the survivals on the blue planet. These climate effects due to air pollution are especially very computer demanding to study, if one wishes to include as many meteorological as well as the chemical processes as possible. Recently a number of sensitivity studies of the effect from specific meteorological parameters on air pollution distribution and anthropogenic emission have been carried out (Zlatev and Brandt, 2005).These all studies reveal that the temperature alone has been altered to suit different temperature scenarios in the world. The sensitivity studies makes it possible to get a general overview in which observed the effect of a specific meteorological parameter on the air pollution in the future. To include all effects of a changing climate and the different level of the emission, much more complicated modelling tools are needed.

Air Pollution: An Overview

In the last few century, the greatest increase in the emissions of air pollutants due to the industrial and economic growth has made poor quality of air. This is a major problem especially in industrialized countries and an emerging problem for the rest of the world in future. The Increased concentrations of many greenhouse gases like CO_2, methane, the earth's atmosphere have already warmed the planet substantially, causing more severe and prolonged heat waves, droughts, and floods, air pollution, temperature variability, forest fires. All of the effects due to climatic changes and pollution cause severe respiratory health risk. (Intergovernmental Panel on Climate Change, 2007 and Solomon *et al.*, 2007). The changes in air quality and climate have a quantifiable impact, not only on the morbidity but also on the mortality for different types of respiratory diseases (Peters *et al.*, 2004 and Dockery *et al.*, 2007). Global earth temperature has markedly risen up over the last five decades due to the greenhouse gas emissions.

Air pollution is the changes in the levels of quality as well as in the purity of the air due to various natural or anthropogenic emissions of biological chemical and biological substances. Different pollutants affecting the air quality include inhalable particles. The inhalable particles are those particles whose aero-dynamic diameter is less than 10 µm (PM10), while fine inhalable particles are less than 2.5 µm (PM2.5) and coarse inhalable particles are 2.5 - 10 µm.(WHO, 2013). The size of these particles surface as well as the chemical composition of the par-ticulate material determine the category of risk that exposure to this agent represents for human health. The fine particles, owing to their smaller size, penetrate deeply into the respiratory system of the living being and severely affect the alveoli. Air pollutants show these effects by causing different types of direct cellular injury or by enhancing the intracellular signalling pathways and transcription factors that are very sensitive to the oxidative stress. (WHO, 2014 and Cecchi *et al.*,2013)

The vehicle exhaust, particle pollution as well as the ground-level ozone are the most important types of harmful pollutants. Ozone is a powerful oxidant which has been associated with persistent structural airway and lung tissue damage as well. In many European country it has been observed that it is contributing to more severe symptoms of asthma as well as in increase in respiratory hospital admissions (Filippidou, 2011). It has been estimated for U.K, in 2020 the annual ozone level >1,500 ppm will associates with deaths of many people due to various respiratory disease. The Positive associations also have been observed between urban air pollution and respiratory symptoms in children. Different study reveals the relations between motor vehicle exhausts and the level of acute or chronic respiratory symptoms in children living near traffic area (Jacob *et al.*, 2009; Gryparis *et al.*, 2004 and-Jerrett *et al.*, 2009) The bad quality of air pollution can negatively influence the development of lungs in children and in adolescents (Gryparis *et al.*, 2004; Epton *et al.*,, 2008 and Gauderman *et al.*, 2007). Different study of different authors have suggested that the Children adversely gets effected due to air pollution. The deficits in lung function was directly correlated with set of pollutants, including acid vapour, nitrogen dioxide, fine particulate matter (PM2.5), as well as the elemental car-bon. The dysfunction in lung during childhood may enhance the risk of respiratory conditions, such as episodic wheezing which happens during a viral infection. However, the larger effect of pollution-related deficits can occur during later in life, since dysfunction in lung is a strong risk factor for complications and death during adulthood. (Li S *et al.,* 2012). The prediction about the effects of climate change due to air pollution and on health-related air pollution is hampered by several limits which are, future emissions which depend on numerous factors like economic development, energy use, population growth, economic development and production. The indoor pollution is another approach and its level of air pollutants other than environmental tobacco smoke which have also been also related to asthma prevalence or symptoms by sparse studies (Hulin *et al.,* 2012; Bentayeb etal., 2013 and Annesi-Maesano *et al.,* 2013). Environmental tobacco smoke is one of the most important categories of risks for respiratory symptoms and diseases in the world. The evidence is also reliable for indoor particulate matter and nitrogen dioxide which have been associated with respiratory diseases like asthma.

Pollutant Categories

The main climatic changes in atmospheric composition is mainly due to the combustion of fossil fuels, excessive use for the generation of energy as well s the transportation. Different types of air pollutants have been reported which differ in their reaction properties, chemical composition, emission as well as the persistence in environment and their ability to be transported in long and short distances as well as their eventual impacts on the survivals. These different pollutants share some similarities which can be grouped to four classes. Some are gaseous pollutants like ozone, $SO_{2,}$ CO, NOx, Volatile Organic Compounds, some are persistent organic pollutants (for e.g. dioxins) and some are heavy metals (for e.g. lead, mercury and particulate Matter(PM)

Table 4.1: List of Some of the Common Environmental Pollutants and their Source

Category	Source of pollutants	Emitted Polluntants
Agriculture	Due to open burning	Carbon monoxide,SPM and VOC
Mining and quarrying	Coal mining	Sulphur dioxide, SPM and NOx,
	Petroleum and natural gas production	Sulphur dioxide
	Non ferrous ore mining	Lead and SPM
	Stone quarrying	SPM
	Beverges and tobacco	VOC, Sulphur dioxide, carbon mono oxide and H_2S
	Textiles and leather industries	VOC and SPM,
	Wood products	VOC, SPM,
	Paper products, printing	SPM,VOC, carbon mono oxide, hydrogen sulphide and Sulphur dioxide

Chemicals manufacturing	Phallic anhydride	carbon mono oxide, SPM and Sulphur dioxide
	Chlor-alkali	chlorine
	Hydrochloric acid	Hydrochloric acid
	Hydrofluoric acid	SiF_4 and Hydrogen fluoride
	Sulphuric acid	SO_3 and Sulphur dioxide
	Nitric acid	Oxides of nitrogen
	Phosphoric acid	F_2 and SPM
	Lead oxide and pigments	Lead and SPM
	Ammonia	Oxides of nitrogen, SPM, Sulphur dioxide , VOC and ammonia
	Sodium carbonate	ammonia and SPM
	Calcium carbide	SPM
	Adipic acid	SPM, VOC, Oxides of nitrogen and carbon mono oxide
	Alkyl lead	Lead
	terephtalic acid, Maleic anhydride	VOC and carbon mono oxide
	Pesticide production, Fertilizers	Ammonia and SPM
	Ammonium nitrate	SPM, Ammonia and nitric acid
	Ammonium sulphate	VOC
	Plastic, Syntheticresins, material, fibres	SPM, CS_2, VOC and H_2S,
	Varnishes, Paints, lacquers	VOC and SPM
	Soap	SPM
	Carbon black and printing ink	SO_2, VOC, NOx, CO, hydrogen sulphide and SPM.
	Trinitrotoluene	Oxides of nitrogen, sulphur dioxide, SPM, SO_3 and nitric acid
Petroleum refineries	Products of petroleum and coal clay products	VOC, F2, SPM, sulphur dioxide and carbon dioxide
	Cement lime and plaster	Sulphur dioxide, SPM and NOx,
Music metal industries	Iron and steel	NOx, SO_2, carbon monoxide VOC and lead
	Non-ferrous industries	sulphur dioxide, F, lead and SPM,
Wholesale and retail trade	Gas, Steam Electricity	Oxides of nitrogen, carbon monoxide,SO_3, lead and sulphur dioxide
Transport	filling operation	VOC
Community services	Municipal incinerators	lead, SPM, sulphur dioxide, Oxides of nitrogen carbon monoxide and VOC

SPM: Suspended particulate matter, VOC: Volatile organic compounds

Source: Economopoulos, 1993

Table 4.2: Particle Penetrability According to Size

Size of particles	Region to which penetration can occur
> 11 μm	Captured in the nostrils but it do not penetrate the lower respiratory tract
7-11 μm	Passage of Nasal
4.7-7 μm	Larynx region
3.3-4.7 μm	primary bronchial region and Trachea
2.1-3.3 μm	Secondary bronchial section
1.1-2.1 μm	Terminal bronchial section
0.65-1.1 μm	Bronchioles section
0.43-0.65 μm	Alveolar section

Source : Wilson *et al.,* 1996 Ghio *et al.,* 1999.

Climate Change and Air Pollution: An Analysis of the Causative Agents of Air Pollution and their Subsequent Effects

Ozone

Ozone is an important greenhouse gas and plays significant role in the radiative budget in the stratosphere through its interactions with both long wave and short wave radiation (Gauss *et al.,* 2003). Ozone is a precursor in oxidizing reactions because it forcefully influences the affect of greenhouse gases as methane and hydrofluorocarbons (Gauss *et al.,* 2006). Ozone also affect indirectly climate due to the limiting sequestration of CO_2 by vegetation (Sitch *et al.,* 2007). The direct radiative affects of ozone provide the positive radiative forcing of the atmospheric gases especially green house gases (Gauss *et al.,* 2003).The ground-level ozone is an important air pollutant that severely affects human and the health of other organism as well as the growth of forests worldwide (Ainsworth *et al.,* 2012). The increasing level of the emission of the precursor of ozone like NOx, CO have affected different lives on earth (Brasseur *et al.,* 2001).

The long-range of trans-Pacific transport of contaminant air masses from Asia is a substantial part of the background ozone in western North America (Vingarzan, 2004). It has been observed that there is significance increasment in the concentration of ozone in the free troposphere during 1984 (0.63-0.34 ppb/ year) in spring season the intercontinental transport across the Pacific is most efficient (Cooper *et al.,* 2010; Law, 2010). The emission from the Asian continent influence, emissions from Canada and Mexico which contribute to background level of ozone concentrations in the eastern region of the United States and in California as well (Wang *et al.,* 2009). In U.S.A, It has also been observed that the highest ozone pollution occurs in the south-western region of United States, especially in California where the fourth highest maximum averages value ranges from 71 to 106 ppb. On the other hand Moderately elevated O3 levels (51 ppb in Montana to 78 ppb in New Jersey) occurs in the U.S.A (Bytnerowicz *et al.*, 2008)

Reactive Nitrogen

Reactive nitrogen generally results from different types human activities in the environment which severely causes harm to human health as well as the ecological problems. The components of nitrogen like NOx results mostly from different combustion processes, while ammonia and N_2O mostly results from agricultural activities. The compounds of nitrogen can affect climate in different ways. The oxide of nitrogen and ammonia contribute to climatic changes indirectly by the altering the production and loss of atmospheric climatic forcers, both aerosols scattering incoming solar radiation and greenhouse gases. These different compounds severely affects climate in different way. The oxide of nitrogen especially N_2O can affect the environment by increasing the ozone formation and also by increasing the removal of CH4 (in cooling effect). So NH3 and NOx can enhance light-scattering aerosols (Pinder *et al.*, 2013). In some areas of U.S.A, the concentration of NOx and nitric acid and atmospheric NOx and nitric acid have decreased as per the report of Chestut, 2005) due to Environmental Protection Agency of the government. Deposition have remained stable, mainly due to a lack of regulatory control of agricultural emission and use of nitrogen as a fertilizer (Davidson *et al.*, 2012). Some of the phytotoxic effects of the reactive nitrogen has been seen by Bytnerowicz *et al.*, 1998. The application of synthetic nitrogen fertilizers as well as the cultivation of N-fixing crops are major parts of the U.S agricultural economy (Smil, 2002 and Houlton *et al.*, 2013). The nitrogen fixation from anthropogenic activity creates essentials industrial products like plastics, nylon and explosive (Domene and Ayers, 2001) but various human problems and environmental issues has developed from the use of unintentional leakage of nitrogen. High rate of mortality, morbidity results from climatic changes and pollution. The contamination of water sources by nitrite, severity of toxic algal blooms as well as the hypoxia in freshwater and coastal marine areas and global climatic change results from the emission of the potent greenhouse and ozone-depleting gas oxides of nitrogen (Davidson *et al.*, 2012).

Sulphur Dioxide and Sulphur Deposition

The level of SO_2 still contributes to acidic deposition and its direct phytotoxic effects are limited to small areas in local geographic areas (Legge *et al.*, 1998; US EPA, 2008). Study revel that wet deposition of sulphur has continuously decreased in recent decades (Greaver *et al.*, 2012; NADP, 2010).

The small scale changes in the concentration of the sulphur dioxide can cause large changes in atmospheric chemistry by several reasons. Sulphur dioxide when oxidized it forms H_2SO_4 which has low vapour pressure for allowing it to adsorb on tiny dry particles and after that to increase the size of those particles by molecular condensation of more acid (Ehhalt,1999). This resulting molecules increases the concentration of aerosol. Sulphur dioxide reacts fastly with OH leaving little OH to oxidize many gases like methane and carbon monoxide. So increasment in the concentrations of methane and carbon monoxide indicate decreasing oxidizing capacity. The sufficient concentration of sulphur dioxide condenses to a liquid below 10°C. The temperature in the troposphere layer decreases with increasing altitude at 6.4°C/km to 55°C at the tropopause and after that increases with altitude in the overlying stratosphere. In most of the cases, troposphere layer and lower stratosphere layer sulphur dioxide is potentially a liquid and this liquid form has good soluble ability and can be oxidized readily by hydrogen per oxide in cloud droplets and also in precipitation (Ehhalt,1999). Study from Ehhalt (1999) revels that 70% of the available sulphur dioxide, oxidized in this way. This type of oxidation process does not lead to nucleation of new particles (Alexander *et al.,* 2005). Laj et al.1990, observed that the depletion of hydrogen peroxide in the ice of Greenland revels that sulphur dioxide reached in Greenland as a gas and after that it was oxidized in precipitation. Another study from Barrie and Hoff (Barrie *et al.,*1984) observed that sulphur dioxide in the arctic region originating from fossil fuel burning in Eurasia.

Effects of Climatic Changes Due to Air Pollution with Special Reference to Plants, Animals and Human Beings

The hazardous pollutants escape to the environment by different types of natural or anthropogenic activities and may severely effects on human, plants as well as the health of the animals. Different types of harmful chemical or pollutants Increases into the atmosphere which differ in their chemical composition, emission, time of disintegration ,reaction properties as well as the ability to diffuse in long distances

Air pollutants like sulphur dioxide, ozone, carbon monoxide, volatile organic compounds (VOCs), particulate matter (PM10 andPM2.5) increasing day by day and resulting in the serious disease in the biotic components. Air pollution affects survivals on earth by many ways. These effects of air pollutants on human health, animals, plants and their mechanism of action are briefly discussed below.

On Humans

The different types of air pollutants severely affects human health in different ways. The composition of air pollutants and their dose as well as the time of exposure resulting into the diverse impacts on human health. The polluted air has bad health effects on human which can range from nausea and difficulty in breathing as well as skin cancer. Air pollutants can include different types of defects like birth defects, reduced activity of the immune system, developmental delays in children, and other diseases. Epidemiological and animal model data revels that primarily affected systems from the pollutants level in air are the cardiovascular and the respiratory system. But the function of several other organs can be also influenced (Cohen *et al.*, 2005; Huang and Ghio, 2006; Kunzli and Tager, 2005; Sharma and Agrawal, 2005). Humans comes direct contact with different level of air pollutants in their surrounding primarily via ingestion and inhalation but the dermal contact represents a minor route of exposure. Air pollution contributes to the contamination of and water and food which makes ingestion in different cases the major route of pollutant intake (Thron, 1996). With the help of respiratory tract and gastrointestinal path, absorption of pollutants may occur in human body, on the other hand a number of toxic substances can be found in the general circulation and some are deposited to different tissues in the body. The elimination occurs only to a certain degree by excretion (Madden and Fowler, 2000).

Different studies from the workers revels that different types of air pollutants affects human in different way in terms of their concentration. Different effects are also observed with the rate of long-term exposure to lower pollutant concentrations. The different symptoms on human such as throat and nose irritation, broncho constriction as well as the dyspnoea, especially in asthmatic individuals which are usually experienced when exposure to increased levels of sulphur dioxide (Balmes *et al.*, 1987), nitrogen oxides (Kagawa, 1985). On the other way, particulate matter which penetrates the alveolar epithelium (Ghio and Huang, 2004), ozone level initiate lung inflammation (Uysal and Schapira, 2003). The patients infected with lung lesions or diseases related to the lungs, pollutant-initiated inflammation will worsen their condition. Some air pollutants like nitrogen oxides increase the susceptibility to respiratory infections (Chauhan *et al.*, 1998) and chronic exposure to ozone and certain heavy metals reduces functional level of lungs (Rastogi *et al.*, 1991; Tager *et al.*, 2005). The high exposure of ozone is also responsible for emphysema, asthma, lung cancer (Kuo *et al.*, 2006; Nawrot *et al.*, 2006). Micro expose of nitrogen dioxide causes Emphysema-like lesions (Wegmann *et al.*, 2005). Another harmful pollutant is dioxins, which induce liver cell damage (Kimbrough *et al.*, 1977), as it indicated by an increase levels of different enzymes in the blood (Mandal, 2005). The Green house gas like carbons monoxide binds to haemoglobin modifying its conformation and reduces its capability to transfer oxygen in blood (Badman and Jaffe, 1996). Oxygen reduction level can severely affect the function of different organs, resulting in the slow reflexes, impaired concentration as well as the confusion. Particulate matter also induces systemic inflammatory changes affecting equally blood coagulation (Riediker *et al.*, 2004). Different level of air pollutants causes changes in blood clotting and induces lung irritation resulting to angina or even to myocardial infarction (Vermylen *et al.*, 2005). Tachycardia, increased level of blood pressure as well as anaemia in human occurs due to an inhibitory effect on haematopoiesis which have been observed as a results of heavy metal pollution like arsenic, mercury, nickel (Huang and Ghio, 2006)).The heavy metals can also induces damages in kidney like tubular dysfunction, excretion of low molecular weight proteins. The can also risk of stone formation or nephrocalcinosis (Damek-Poprawa and Sawicka-Kapusta, 2003; Jarup, 2003; Loghman-Adham, 1997) and renal cancer (Boffetta *et al.*, 1993; Vamvakas *et al.*, 1993).

Table 4.3: Potential Damage Costs of Human being due to Air Pollution at Global Level

Pollutants	Effects	References
Oxides of Nitrogen	Increased incidence of respiratory disease	Birch *et al.*, 2011 and van Grinsven *et al.*, 2013
	Declining visibility—loss of aesthetics	Birch *et al.*, 2011
	Increased effects of airborne disease	Grinsven *et al* 2013
	Increased colon cancer risk	Grinsven *et al* 2013
	cardiovascular and the respiratory system problems	Cohen *et al.*, 2005;
Carbon monoxide	Lung inflammation, systemic inflammatory changes	Riediker *et al.*, 2004.
	Myocardial infraction	Vermylen *et al.*, 2005.
Ozone	Reduces lung function	Rastogi *et al.*, 1991 andTager *et al.*, 2005
	Asthma, emphysema,	Kuo *et al.*, 2006 andNawrot *et al.*, 2006.
Sulphur dioxide	Bronchoconstriction and dyspnoea	Balmes *et al.*, 1987
High level of air pollutants	Affects developing foetus	Schell *et al.*, 2006
	Congenital malformations	Bellinger, 2005

On Animals

In the history of the earth, it has been observed that the composition of the environment has not always been ideal at every moment. The continuing increasing of the global population causes intensive livestock production practices and the counter trade of the large amount in production of meat, eggs as well as the milk resulted in the generation, disposal of large amounts of waste and its accumulation. The aerosolization of different microorganism and their secreted endotoxins, odours, as well as the dust particles are inevitable consequences of the generation and the handling of different types of wastes from the food production chain and from animals. Animals faces different level of the air pollutants from the environment. Although they kept in huge facilities but often diseased due to self-made indoor air pollution. The different effects from may be poor quality of air which they inhale or ingest. In case of air pollution, mostly inhalation triggers the health problems in animals but occasionally deposition of particles from different industrial source exhaust on pasture land which may affect health of animals directly resulting in toxic residue in their eggs, meat, milk or in other products obtained from animals. High level of dioxin in milk of dairy cows and zinc-induced arthritis in growing foals are the few examples of pasture grass pollutants by deposits of smoke from various types nearby industrial activities. Cattle, poultry, Pigs, goats and sheep are kept in indoor areas for a variable part of their life, often for all of their life. These restriction and closed areas affects the health of these animals in different ways. It has been observed that air quality of this area is sometime much better in compare to that of the closed facilities for swine and poultry (Wathes *et al.,* 1998). Dunham (1991), observed that maximal concentrations of gases or pollutants in piggeries are: 2.4 mg dust /m^3; 0.08 mg endotoxin/m^3, 7 ppm ammonia, 105 colony-forming units (CFUs) of total microbes/m^3; as well as 1,540 ppm. carbon dioxide. The different concentrations of bacteria up to 1.1 × 106 CFU/m^3, inhalable dust content of 0.26 mg/m3 and the concentration of ammonia was 27 ppm. These observations have also been reported by Scherer & Unshelm, 1995 in facilities during winter, while at summer lower concentrations but less difference have been found in in- and outdoor temperature in summer and winter.

Many types of pollutants are found in manure which containing enteric bacteria and endotoxin resulting in the negative effects on the health of animals (Pickrell, 1991).

The different concentration of the airborne bacteria and the endotoxin produced by them is related to the level of pen cleanliness. Generation of toxic gasses like ammonia and its higher concentrations in the air are not affected severely to the health of animals, but also by volume of the building, pig flow management and pig density and (Scherer & Unshelm, 1995). Similar factors on the variants levels of ammonia are known to play a role in farrowing units and in poultry houses (Harry, 1978). The pollutants ammonia is considered as one of the most important inhaled toxicant which has negative effect on the health of animals. According to Dodd & Gross (1980) the 1000 ppm level of ammonia for less than 24 hour causes impaired ciliary activity, caused mucosal damage as well as secondary infections in laboratory animals. The respiratory disease in swine is mostly due to the different combination of primary and opportunistic infectious agents, whereby adverse atmosphere and management conditions are the triggers. The primary respiratory infectious agents have capability to cause serious disease on their own, however, often uncomplicated infections have also been observed. If the primary infection becomes complicated serious respiratory disease may occurs in animals by opportunistic bacteria. Some of the pathogens responsible for the various diseases in animals are respiratory syndrome virus, porcine reproductive, and other caused by *Bordetella bronchiseptica, Haemophilus parasuis, Actinobacillus suis, Streptococcus suis, Mycoplasma hyopneumoniae.* It has been reported that, pig or poultry facilities are exposed to the same increased levels of ammonia, carbon monoxide, hydrogen sulphide, as well as the dust particles from feed and manure of the animals (Pickrell, 1991). That is why, workers involved in swine production tend to have greater rates of asthma and types of respiratory infections. The lesions caused due to air pollution in production animals mainly include inflammatory processes.

London was reported to have caused respiratory distress due to severe smog disaster of prize cattle that were housed in the city for a cattle exhibition (Catcott, 1961). The high level of sulphur dioxide is responsible for accompanying emphysema, acute bronchiolitis as well s theand right-sided heart failure.

In another study of Manzo et al. (2010) revels that, dogs with chronic bronchitis and cats with airways inflammatory disease are at dangers level of exacerbating their conditions if exposed to the prolonged urban air pollutants. Both, Indoor and outdoor air pollutants have negatively affects the health of animals.

Table 4.3: Mammals, Birds and Land Invertebrates Affected Due to Air Pollution

Scientific name	Effects due to poor quality of air
Anas rubripes	Observation suggest that increased duckling mortality due to the pollutants level (Haramis,1984)
Lutra lutra	Decline in otter populations due to different level of pollutants which has been suggested for Galloway, Scotland (Fry and Cook, 1984), and also for UK (Mason and Macdonald, 1987)
Lepidoptera	Different studies show a decline in polluted atmosphere Barbour,1986)
Collembola	Decrease in both number and variety in forests experiencing the poor quality of air (Koposzki,1992).
Aphantopus hyperantus	Decline is greatest in areas where high SO_2 levels was found (Heath *et al.,* 1984).
Parnassius Apollo	Decline in polluted areas is due in part to caterpillars ingesting manganese wherethe host plant is growing on acidified soil and also due to the bad air quality(Holm, 1985))

On Plants

Deposition of the ozone in terrestrial ecosystems is mostly controlled by stomata (Ainsworth *et al.,* 2012). These the epidermal cell situated in the plants leaves. There is a strong bonding between stomatal conductance and demage of plants by ozone (Reich and Amundson, 1985). The non-stomatal processes are also essentials and sometimes dominate the total ozone deposition to forests

(Kurpius and Goldstein, 2003). The High level of this green house gas may cause visible injury in foliar parts of plants and affect gas exchange as well as the photosynthesis, resulting in shortened longevity of foliage, reduced plant height and bad health (Grulke *et al.*, 2009). The long-term chronic exposures to ozone can also lower the rate of stomatal conductance and decrease the level of photosynthsis in plants (Reich and Amundson, 1985). The exposure to chronic levels of ozone may limit the ability in closing and opening of the stomata(Grulke *et al.*, 2006), and increasing the water use (Sun *et al.*, 2012 . The long term and short term reduction of stomatal activity caused by the high level of ozone reduce the capability of plants to sequester carbon dioxide and is the basis for the indirect ozone greenhouse effect (Sitch *et al.*, 2007). It has been observed from various study that increased level of the ozone gas since the industrial revolution has decreased the rate of photosynthetic and uptake of carbon dioxide as well as the stomatal conductance of trees by 11% - 13% (Wittig *et al.*, 2007). Study from Felzer *et al.* (2004) revels a 2.6–6.8% reduction rate of the annual net primary productivity in United States in response to the levels of ozone since 1950 with the largest decreases in the late 1980s and early 1990s. The adverse effects of the ozone on loss of carbon sequestration are similar in magnitude to land use change as well as in the offset increases in carbon sequestration due to global warming, N fertilization, CO2. The different levels of nitrogen deposition may have many adverse effects like changes in biodiversity, contamination of water and soils (Greaver *et al.*, 2012; Pardo *et al.*, 2011; US EPA, 2008). The long-and short term reduction of stomatal activity caused by elevated level of ozone, carbon dioxide may also reduce the ability of plants to sequester CO2 which is the basis for the indirect ozone greenhouse effect (Sitch *et al.*, 2007). The Simulation of ozone effects on hardwood of trees in the north-eastern region of United States using 1987–1992 ozone, data showed the declines of annual net primary productivity ranging from 3% to 16% with most pronounced effects at the highest ozone levels as well as on the soils with high water-holding capacity (Ollinger *et al.*, 1997).

Table 4.4: Losses of Phytodiversity due to Different Types of Atmospheric Air Pollutants

Name	Scientific Name	Notes and Source
Lichens	Many foliar species, eg *Usnea, Ramalina.*	Declined due to SO2 pollution.
Bog mosses	*Sphagnum* spp.	Research in the English Pennines reported that many the *Sphagnum* species are damaged by sulphur dioxide and perhaps also by nitrogen dioxide as well as the deposition of nitrogen however *Sphagnum* increases in acidified waters
Woolly fringe moss	*Anuginosum and Racomitrium*	Nitrogen deposition is thought to be at least partly responsible for decline of this moss over most of southern part of Scotland

mosses and liverworts	*Bryum, Hypnum cupressiforme, Grimmia pulvinata*, and *Orthotrichium.*	Susceptible to damage by sulphur dioxide and noitrogen do oxide
Fungi	Many mycorrhizal fungiincluding *Cantharelluscinabrius, Russula* spp, *Lactarius* spp, *Hygrphorus*spp and *Hygrocybe* spp	Mycorrhizal fungi are badly affected by nitrogen deposition in acidified forests and other green house gases.
Blue green algae	*Nostoc, Scytonema* etc	Severely affected due to air high level of air pollutiants
Coniferous trees	*Picea, Larix europeaus* and *abies*	Sensitive to acute damage by ozone and other air other types of pollutants.
Mosses	*Antitrichia curtipendula, Neckera, Orthotrichium,* and *Rhytidiadelphus*	Decline in the many parts of earth due to soil acidification.
Herbaceous species of floweringPlants	Many species, including*Primula veris, Vicia sepium,Trifolium medium, Melica nutans, Hepatica nutans*, etc	Declined due to soil acidification
Broadleaved trees	*Quercus robur, Quercusalba, Acer saccarina, Populus tremulens* and Others	Sensitive to acute damage by green house gases ozone and other airPollutants indirect effects by soil acidification and by increased nitrogen deposition.
Aquatic flowering plants	*echinospora, Littorella, Lobelia dortmanna, uniflora*, and *Isoetes*	Declined due to acidification in freshwaters and streams.

Implications for Air Quality Management

Different types of strategies can be helpful in reducing the levels of the air pollution. For the general regulations of the quality of air effective actions should mainly focus on traffic access control and technological innovation to reduce emission level of low-carbon-motor and energy related emission reduction by improving energy efficiency, or energy switching, ban of coal sales as well as energy conservation. Climate change strategies on the emission of greenhouse reductions also reduced the concentrations of contaminants and provided related health co-benefit.

In energy related strategies, health benefits were obtained mainly from the reduction in the concentrations of sulphur dioxide and the oxide of nitrogen whereas the traffic control strategies was more geographically biased because of the higher health benefit within the immediate catchment of the interventions in a region. Different study of the world has focussed with the strategies aimed to mitigate climatic changes or to reach climate change targets. Green houses gases like carbon dioxide, methane, carbon mono oxide. There is a clear need to develop different models that stimulates the multiple biotic and abiotic factors while designing future ecosystem changes in order to understand the potential risks factors to forest resources. These models could provide science-based outcomes and future scenarios as well as improve the human understanding or thinking of what adaptive or mitigation measures could be recommended to air resource and land managers.

There is ample evidence from models and observations that the twenty first century climate change will worsen the ozone pollution. The emissions of pollutant are expected to respond to climate change. Day by day of the rising of the temperature increase the demand for air conditioning in summer when ozone and particulate matter concentrations are highest. The emission from the evaporation of anthropogenic NMVOCs increases but the effect determined for mobile sources are generally weak in range of 1.3–5% K_1 (Cardelino and Chameides, 1990; Rubin *et al.*, 2006). The level of ozone and its background become an important topic for the management of the air quality. This background also increases significantly in future because of the global rises in methane and oxide of nitrogen like NOx (Fiore *et al.*, 2002). In country like U.S.A, Climate has provide some relief and comfortable in summer. Climate change may provide some relief, at least in summer. Wu *et al.*, 2008b Observed that the U.S. policy-relevant background defined by the U.S. Environmental Protection Agency (EPA) as the surface ozone concentration due to the absence of North - American anthropogenic emissions, will reduces by up to 2 ppb in summer as a result of 2000–2050 climate change. Similar observation was given by Lin *et al.*, 2008b. Further Wu et al. 2008b project that climatic changes will fully offset the impacts of increasing the emission from anthropogenic activities in eastern U.S in summer, as there will still be a 2–5 ppb rises in the PRB in the west. Finally, as the world moves forward to develop energy and transportation policies as well as the other policy directed at mitigating climate change, it will be significant factor into these different policies which co- or dis-benefits for regional air pollution.

The energy policy offers an opportunity to dramatically improve the quality of air through transition to non-polluting sources of energy. In contrast, a switch to biofuels would not necessarily benefit the quality of air and could possibly be detrimental (Jacobson, 2007).

General Regulations for Air Quality Control

These general regulations included the Spain pollution control policies, EU air quality Directives, WHO air quality guidelines, U.S. Environmental Protection Agency guidelines as well as the UK National Air Quality Strategy, Central pollution control board of India, China environment control board. It has been observed that all the study focused on particulate matter, which indicates that particulate matter, particularly PM2.5 (particulate matter) which is the major concerns for public health associated with air pollution level in recent years especially in Europe and other country of this continent. It was reflected in the EU Directive 2008/50/EC regarding the quality of air and clean air for Europe which first set short and long term targets for eradication of PM2.5 (European Commission, 2008). The most of the works aiming in the reduction of the level of air pollution and implemented some targets which was set by the EU. On the other hand, climate change mitigation interventions were based on the proposal of IPCC's Fifth Assessment Report (AR5) to limit global temperature increase to two degree by the end of this century (Schucht *et al.*, 2015). World health organization warned especially the Asian and European countries for their worst strategies to control the levels of air pollutants. However, emission of the greenhouse gas reductions can be achieved simultaneously with air pollutants emission reductions, since both of these are often emitted from the same sources like energy sectors, and transport (Woodcock, et al.2009 and, Aunan *et al.*,1998).

Energy Related Strategies

The need of energy at present time is a global issues. Different types of programme were implemented in Asian and European countries to reduce the emission of air pollution from different types of source of energy. The strategies of energy saving program of Hungary's National Energy Efficiency Improvement as well as the energy conservation programs (Aunan *et al.*, 1998). the ban or reduce the of coal sales in in some country like Dublin, Ireland (Clancy *et al.*, 2002 and the European Commission directives to reduce the sulphur content in liquid fuels for vehicles (Chanel *et al.*, 2014). These programme has reduce the air contaminants so it highlights at global level. These different strategies of different countries of world mainly focused on the eradication of atmospheric pollutants like sulphur dioxide followed by nitrogen oxide black smoke as well as the suspended particles. Complete or partial ban of coal sales obtained the most substantial sulphur dioxide reduction by 33.8% during the study period in Dublin, Ireland (Aunan *et al.*, 1998),. Due to the ban on the unnecessary programme of energy, different co-benefit can be achieved. The carbon emission and particulate matter concentrations decrease accordingly as a by-product by introducing the low carbon emission measures for motor vehicles.

Plants as Phytoremediator of Air Pollutants

Different studies have suggested plants contribute in air pollution reduction (Boonen *et al.*, 2015; Angelo *et al.*, 2013). The different plants species show substantial effect on air pollution control (Escobedo *et al.*, 2011). Number of different studies have identified and quantified various ecosystem services in context of air pollution reduction due to dry deposition function (Nowak, 2000; Nowak *et al.*, 2006). The most important process in removal of pollutants is dry deposition, in which plants removes air pollutant from the troposphere in non-precipitation period (Cavanagh, 2006; Schlesinger, 1979). Dry deposition is mainly depends on nature as well as the property of air pollutant such as gaseous/particles form etc.). Sometime property of surfaces such as size, chemical nature, roughness, and weather variables like wind direction and speed as well as the temperature is also play significant role in removal of pollutants (Roupsard, 2013). Once the air pollutants are accumulated on the surface of plant leaf, they are removed primarily in two different ways. Firstly through stomata (epidermal cell) uptake of gaseous pollutants and leaf interception of particulate matter (Nowak *et al.*, 2006). The first process leads to the diffusion of air pollutant into the inner part of plant leaves. The gases form of pollutants may also be absorbed or react with the surface of plant. Secondly removal may be by re-suspension of intercepted particles from the leaf surfaces through the action of wind. Now it is well known that plant remediate the environmental pollutants by different mechanism. Different plant species like *Penninsetum pedicellatum, Zinnia anguistifolia, Triticum aestivum, Hordeum vulgare, Populus deltoids, Azolla pinnata,* Quercus robur, Fraxinus excelsior, Aesculus hippocastanum, *Zea mays, Astragalus sinicus* removes the environmental pollutants in different way. Below the table is fiven fro various plants species involving removal of atmospheric pollutants.

Table 4.5: Phytoremediation of Atmospheric Pollutants

Plant Species	Pollutants	References
Kolchia	Atrazine, metolachlor and trifluralin	Anderson *et al.*,1994
Penninsetum pedicellatum	Chlorpyrifos and Cypermethrie, Fenvalerate	Dubey and Fulekar., 2011
Fragmites australies (Reed)	Fixed Nitrogen	Haleem *et al.*, 2000
Rye Grass	Chlorpyrifos	Korade and Fulekar., 2009
Zinnia anguistifolia	Mefenoxam	Pai *et al.*, 2001
Alfalfa and alpine blue grass	Hexadecane and PAHs	Nichols *et al.*,1997
Triticum aestivum (Wheat)	2,4-D	Kingley *et al.*, 1994
Hordeum vulgare	2,4-D	Jacobsen, 1997
Sugar beet (cv.Rex)	Polychlorinated biphenyls (PCBS)	Brazil *et al.*, 1995
Rice	Benthiocarb	Sato, 1989
Populus deltoids nigra	1,4-dioxane	Schnoor *et al.*, 1998
Sugarcane	2,4-D	Sandmann and Loose, 1984
Astragalus sinicus	Cd	Sriprang *et al.*,2002
Poplar root extract	1,4-dioxane	Kelley *et al.*, 2001

Zea mays (mays)	3-methylbenzoate	Ronchel *et al.*, 2001
Azolla pinnata (Fern)	Diesel fuel	Cohen *et al.*,2002
Corn		Atrazine

Source: Modified from Kala, 2014

Research and Management needs

The study delve with the empirical evidences provided to support that the different air pollutants have direct implications and addition pressure on the human as well as the ecosystem services. Long-term monitoring of ozone and other green house gases and development of physiologically relevant ozone indices are needed to verify model outputs and understanding of future risk. Different improved techniques are needed to estimate the level of air pollutant exposure. Such techniques would greatly expand our ability to evaluate the future risks caused by various toxic gases and atmospheric deposition of pollutants . Better observation of spatial as well as the temporal distribution of particulate matter and other air pollutants are needed for identification and their sources to develop control strategies. So the study demands more robust studies in the field of air pollution.

Conclusion

This chapter presents the adverse effects of different types of pollutants on human health. As mention above major impairments of different organs can be observed due to the harmful atmospherics pollutants. The observation also focussed that, in view of increased exposure of different pollutants plants are still providing a protective covering to human as well as the animals from different types of air pollutants. Humans burning fossil fuels are currently emitting high level of sulphur dioxide and various gases like carbon mono oxide, oxides of nitrogen every day. Such high level of these gases causing not only global warming but widespread extinction of many species of plants and animals, the different atmospheric pollutants also causing several harmful diseases in human beings. Both carbon and sulphur dioxide emissions must be reduced significantly to reverse global warming, but reducing of sulphur dioxide should be the highest priority in future.

REFERENCES

Ainsworth, E.E., Yendrek, C.R., Sitch, S., Collins, W.J., Emberson, L.D. (2012). The Effects of Tropospheric Ozone on Net Primary Productivity and Implications for Climate Change. *Annu. Rev. Plant Biol.* 63, 637–661.

Alexander, B., Park, R. J., Jacob, D. J., Li, Q. B., Yantosca, R. M., Savarino, J., ... & Thiemens, M. H. (2005). Sulfate Formation in Sea-salt Aerosols: Constraints from Oxygen Isotopes. *Journal of Geophysical Research: Atmospheres, 110*(D10). Thiemens, M.H. & Geophys. M. H. (2005) D10307.D.H. Ehhalt, Phys. Chem. Chem. Phys. 1/24 (1999) 5401.

Angelo, J., Andrade, L., Madeira, L.M., Mendes, A., 2013. An Overview of Photocatalysis Phenomena Applied to NOx Abatement. *J. Environ. Manage.* 129, 522–539.

Anderson, T. A., Kruger, E. L., & Coats, J. R. (1994). Enhanced Degradation of a Mixture of three Herbicides in the Rhizosphere of a Herbicide-Tolerant Plant. *Chemosphere, 28*(8), 1551-1557.

Annesi-Maesano, I., Baiz N., Banerjee, S., Rudnai, P., Rive. (2013). Sin-phonie Group. Indoor Air Quality and Sources in Schools and Re-lated Health Effects. J Toxicol Environ Health B Crit Rev , 16: 491-550.

Aunan, K., Pátzay, G., Aaheim, H. A., & Seip, H. M. (1998). Health and Environmental Benefits from Air Pollution Reductions in Hungary. *Science of the Total Environment, 212*(2-3), 245-268.

Avery, M.A. (2010). Increasings Pringtime Ozone Mixing Ratios in the free Troposphere over Western North America. Nature 463, 344–348.

Badman, D.G., Jaffe, E.R. (1996). Blood and Air Pollution: State of Knowledge and Research Needs. Otolaryngol. Head Neck Surg. 114, 205.

Barbour, D A (1986). Why are There so Few Butterflies in Liverpool? - An answer, *Antenna* 10(2), Royal Entomological Society, London

Balmes, J.R., Fine, J.M., Sheppard, D. (1987). Symptomatic Bronchoconstriction after Short-term Inhalation of Sulfur Dioxide. Am. Rev. Respir. Dis. 136, 1117.

Bentayeb M, Simoni M, Norback D, Baldacci S, Maio S, Viegi G.(2013). Indoor Air Pollution and Respiratory Health in the Elderly. *J Envi-ron Sci Health A Tox Hazard Subst Environ Eng,* 48:1783-9.

Bellinger, D.C. (2005). Teratogen Update: Lead and Pregnancy. Birth Defects Res. A Clin. Mol. Teratol 73, 409.

Barrie, L. A., & Hoff, R. M. (1984). The Oxidation Rate and Residence Time of Sulphur Dioxide in the Arctic Atmosphere. *Atmospheric Environment (1967), 18*(12), 2711-2722.

BirchMB L., Gramig, BM., MoomawWR., DoeringOandReeling, C.J (2011). Why Metrics Matter: Evaluating Policy Choices for Reactive Nitrogen in the Chesapeake Bay Watershed. *Environ. Sci. Technol,* 45 168–74.

Boffetta, P., Merler, E., Vainio, H. (1993). Carcinogenicity of Mercury and Mercury Compounds. Scand. J. Work Environ Health 19, 1.

Boonen, E., Akylas, V., Barmpas, F., Boréave, A., Bottalico, L., Cazaunau, M., Chen, H., Daële, V., De Marco, T., Doussin, J.F., Gaimoz, C., Gallus, M., George, C., Grand, N., Grosselin, B., Guerrini, G.L., Herrmann, H., Ifang, S., Kleffmann, J., Kurtenbach, R., Maille, M., Manganelli, G., Mellouki, A., Miet, K., Mothes, F., Moussiopoulos, N., Poulain, L., Rabe, R., Zapf, P., Beeldens, A. (2015). Construction of a Photocatalytic De-polluting Field Site in the Leopold II tunnel in Brussels. J. Environ. Manage. 155, 136–144.

Brazil, G. M., Kenefick, L., Callanan, M., Haro, A., De Lorenzo, V., Dowling, D. N., & O'gara, F. (1995). Construction of a Rhizosphere Pseudomonad with Potential to Degrade Polychlorinated Biphenyls and Detection of bph Gene Expression in the Rhizosphere. *Applied and Environmental Microbiology, 61*(5), 1946-1952.

Brasseur, G.P., Muller, J.-F., Tie, X., Horowitz, L. (2001). Tropospheric Ozone and Climate: Past, Present and Future. In: Matsuno, T., Kida, H. (Eds.), Present and Future of Modeling Global Environmental Change: Toward Integrated Modeling. TERRAPUB, Tokyo, pp. 63–75.

Bytnerowicz, A., Arbaugh, M., Schilling, S., Fraczek, W., Alexander, D. (2008). Ozone Distribution and Phytotoxic Potential in Mixed Conifer Forests of the San Bernardino Mountains, Southern California. *Environ. Pollut.* 155, 398–408.

Cardelino, C.A., Chameides, W.L. (1990). Natural Hydrocarbons, Urbanization, and Urban Ozone. J. Geophys. Res. 95, 13,971–13,979.

Carslaw, K. S., Boucher, O., Spracklen, D. V., Mann, G. W., Rae, J. G. L., Woodward, S., & Kulmala, M. (2010). A Review of Natural Aerosol Interactions and Feedbacks within the Earth System. *Atmospheric Chemistry and Physics, 10*(4), 1701-1737.

Catcott, E.J. (1961). Effects of Air Pollution on Animals. In: World Health Organization Monograph Series, no.41, WHO, Geneva, pp.221-231.

Cavanagh, J.E. (2006). Potential of Vegetation to Mitigate Road-generated Air Pollution, Retrieved April 21st, 2016 from https://www.niwa.co.nz/sites/niwa. co.nz/files/import/attachments/co1x0405 p05.pdf.

Cecchi, L.D., Amato, G. & Annesi-Maesano, I. (2013). Climate, Urban Air Pollution, and Respiratory Allergy. In: Climate Vulnerability: Understanding and Addressing Threats to Essential Resources, Pielke, R.A (ed). Waltham (MA): Academic Press, 105-13

Chandra, S.V., Garg, N. (1991). A Cross-sectional Study of Pulmonary Function among Workers Exposed to Multimetals in the Glass Bangle Industry, *Am. J. Ind. Med.* 20, 391.

Chauhan, A.J., Krishna, M.T., Frew, A.J., Holgate, S.T. (1998). Exposure to Nitrogen Dioxide (NO2) and Respiratory Disease Risk. *Rev. Environ. Health* 13, 73.

Chanel, O., Henschel, S., Goodman, P. G., Analitis, A., Atkinson, R. W., Le Tertre, A. & Medina, S. (2014). Economic Valuation of the Mortality Benefits of a Regulation on SO2 in 20 European Cities. *The European Journal of Public Health, 24*(4), 631-637.

Chestnut, L., Gand & Mills, D.M. (2005). Afresh look at the Benefits and Costs of the US Acid Rain Program *J. Environ. Manag.* 77 252–66.

Clancy, L., Goodman, P., Sinclair, H., & Dockery, D. W. (2002). Effect of Air-pollution Control on Death Rates in Dublin, Ireland: An Intervention Study. *The lancet, 360*(9341), 1210-1214.

Clifford, A., Lang, L., Chen, R., Anstey, K. J., & Seaton, A. (2016). Exposure to Air Pollution and Cognitive Functioning Across the Life Course–A Systematic Literature Review. *Environmental Research, 147*, 383-398.

Cohen, M. F., Williams, J., & Yamasaki, H. (2002). Biodegradation of Diesel Fuel by an *Azolla*-Derived Bacterial Consortium. *Journal of Environmental Science and Health, Part A, 37*(9), 1593-1606.

Cohen, A.J., Ross Anderson, H., Ostro, B., Pandey, K.D., Krzyzanowski, M., Kunzli, N., Gutschmidt, K., Pope, A., Romieu, I., Samet, J.M., Smith, K., 2005. The Global Burden of Disease due to Outdoor Air Pollution. *J. Toxicol. Environ. Health* A 68, 1301.

Cooper, O. R., Parrish, D. D., Stohl, A., Trainer, M., Nédélec, P., Thouret, V., ... & Leblanc, T. (2010). Increasing Springtime Ozone Mixing Ratios in the Free Troposphere over Western North America. *Nature, 463*(7279), 344.

Davidson, E. A (2009). The Contribution of Manure and Fertilizer Nitrogen to Atmospheric Nitrous Oxide since 1860 *Nat. Geoscience.* 2 659–62

Davidson E .A. (2012). Excess Nitrogen in the US Environment: Trends, Risks, and Solutions. *ESA Issues Ecology* 15 1–16

Damek-Poprawa, M., Sawicka-Kapusta, K. (2003). Damage to the Liver, Kidney, and Testis with Reference to Burden of Heavy Metals in Yellow-necked Mice from Areas Around Steelworks and Zinc Smelters in Poland. Toxicology 186, 1.

DeAngelo, B.J.(2013). Bounding the Role of Black Carbon in the Climate System: A Scientific Assessment. J Geophys Res Atmos. 118(11):5380–552.

Dodd, K.T., Gross, D.R.(1980). Ammonia Inhalation Toxicity in Cats: A Study of Acute and Chronic Respiratory Dysfunction. *Archives of Environmental Health* Vol. 35, pp. 6-14.

Dockery, D.W., Stone, P.H.(2007). Cardiovascular Risks from Fine Particulate Air Pollution. *N Engl J Med*, 356:511-3.

Domene, L.A.F & Ayres, R.U. (2001). Nitrogen's Role in Industrial *Systems J. Ind. Ecology, 5* 77–103.

Donham, K. J. (1991). Association of Environmental Air Contaminants with Disease and Productivity in Swine. *American Journal of Veterinary Research*, Vol. 52, pp. 1723-30.

Dubey, K. K., & Fulekar, M. H. (2011). Effect of Pesticides on the Seed Germination of *Cenchrus Setigerus* and *Pennisetum Pedicellatum* as Monocropping and Co-cropping System: Implications for Rhizospheric Bioremediation. *Romanian Biotechnological Letters, 16*(1) 5908-5918.

Economopoulos, AP. (1993. Assessment of Sources of Air Water and Land Pollution. A Guide to Rapid Source Inventory Techniques and Their Use in Formulating Environmental Control Strategies. Part One: Rapid Inventory Techniques in Environmental Pollution. Part Two: Approaches for Consideration in Formulating Environmental Control Strategies. (Unpublished Document WHO/YEP/93.1.) Geneva: WHO.

Epton, M.J., Dawson, R.D., Brooks, W.M., Kingham, S., Aberkane, T., Cava-nagh, J.A.(2008) The Effect of Ambient Air Pollution on Respiratory Health of School Children: A Panel Study. *Environ Health*, 7:16.

Escobedo, F., Kroeger, T., Wagner, J. (2011). Urban Forests and Pollution Mitigation: Analyzing Ecosystem Services and Disservices. *Environ. Pollut*. 159, 2078–2087.

European Commission (EC). Directive. (2008). 50/EC of the European Parliament and of the Council on Ambient Air Quality and Cleaner Air for Europe. Available online: http://eur-lex.europa.eu/legal-content/

Fang, Y., Naik, V., Horowitz, L. W., & Mauzerall, D. L. (2013). Air Pollution and Associated Human Mortality: The Role of Air Pollutant Emissions, Climate Change and Methane Concentration increases from the Preindustrial period to Present. *Atmospheric Chemistry and Physics, 13*(3), 1377-1394.

Felzer, B., Kicklighter, D., Melillo, J., Wang, C., Zhuang, Q., Prinn, R. (2004). Effects of Ozone on Net Primary Production and Carbon Sequestration in the Conterminous United States using a Biogeochemistry Model. Tellus 56B, 230–248

Fiore, A.M., Jacob, D.J., Field, B.D., Streets, D.G., Fernandes, S.D., Jang, C. (2002). Linking Ozone Pollution and Climate Change: The Case for Controlling Methane. *Geophys. Res. Lett.* 29, 1919.

Fiore, A. M. (2014). Atmospheric Chemistry: No Equatorial Divide for a Cleansing Radical. *Nature, 513*(7517), 176.

Fiore, A. M., Naik, V., & Leibensperger, E. M. (2015). Air Quality and Climate Connections. *Journal of the Air & Waste Management Association, 65*(6), 645-685..

Fry, G. (1984). Australia and the South Pacific. *Diplomacy in the Marketplace: Australia in World Affairs, 90*, 175-77. Filippidou EC, Koukouliata A. Ozone Effects on the Respiratory System. *Prog Health Sci* 2011; 1:144-55.

Fuzzi, S., Baltensperger, U., Carslaw, K., Decesari, S., Denier Van Der Gon, H., Facchini, M. C., ... & Nemitz, E. (2015). Particulate Matter, Air Quality and Climate: Lessons Learned and Future Needs. *Atmospheric Chemistry and Physics, 15*(14), 8217-8299.

Gauderman, W.J., Vora, H., McConnell, R., Berhane, K., Gilliland, F., Thomas, D. (2007). Effect of Exposure to Traffic on Lung Development from 10 to 18 years of Age: A Cohort Study. *Lancet,* 369:571-7.

Gauss, M., Myhre, G., Isaksen, I.S.A., Grewe, V., Pitari, G., Wild, O., Collins, W.J., Dentener, F.J., Ellingsen, K., Gohar, L.K., Hauglustaine, D.A., Iachetti, D. Lamarque, J.-F., Mancini, E., Mickley, L.J., Prather, M.J., Pyle, J.A., Sanderson, M.G. (2003). Radiative Forcing in the 21st Century due to Ozone Changes in the Troposphere and the Lower Stratosphere. *J. Geophys. Res.* 108 (D9), 4292.

Ghio, A.J., Samet J. (1999). Air Pollution and Health: Metals and Air Pollution Particles. Academic Press, p.635-651.

Grulke, N.E., Paoletti, E., Heath, R.L., 2006. Direct Measurements of Foliar Ozone Uptake in Crop and Tree Species. *Environ. Pollut.* 146, 640–647.

Grulke, N.E., Minnich, R.A., Paine, T.D., Seybold, S.J., Chavez, D.J., Fenn, M.E., Riggan, P.J., Dunn, A. (2009). Air Pollution increases Forest Susceptibility to Wildfires: In: A Case Study in the San Bernardino Mountains in southern California.

Greaver, T.L., Sullivan, T.J., Herrick, J.D., Barber, M.C., Baron, J.S., Cosby, B.J., Deerhake, M.E., et al. (2012). Ecological Effects of Nitrogen and Sulfur Air Pollution in the US: What do We Know? *Front. Ecol.* 10 (7), 365–372

Gryparis. A., Forsberg, B., Katsouyanni, K., Analitis, A., Touloumi, G., Schwartz, J. (2004) al. Acute Effects of Ozone on Mortality from the "Air Pollution and Health: A European Approach" Project. *Am J Respir Crit Care Med,* 170:1080-7.

Haase, D., Larondelle, N., Andersson, E., Artmann, M., Borgström, S., Breuste, J., ... & Kabisch, N. (2014). A Quantitative Review of Urban Ecosystem Service Assessments: Concepts, Models, and Implementation. *Ambio, 43*(4), 413-433.

Hansen, C., Luben, T. J., Sacks, J. D., Olshan, A., Jeffay, S., Strader, L., & Perreault, S. D. (2010). The Effect of Ambient Air Pollution on Sperm Quality. *Environmental Health Perspectives, 118*(2), 203..

Haramis, G M (1984). Acid Alteration of Experimental Wetlands: Effects on Diversity Andabundance of Macroinvertebrates and Growth, Behaviours and Survival of Juvenile Black Ducks, Draft Research Summary, US Food and Wildlife Service, Eastern Energy and Land Use Team,Kearneyville, WV

Haleem, D., Von Wintzingerode, F., Moter, A., Moawad, H., & Göbel, U. B. (2000). Phylogenetic Analysis of Rhizosphere-associated β-subclass Proteobacterial Ammonia Oxidizers in a Municipal Wastewater Treatment Plant based on Rhizoremediation Technology. *Letters in Applied Microbiology, 31*(1), 34-38.

Harry, E. G. (1978) 'Air Pollution in Farm Buildings and Methods of Control: A Review'. *Avian Pathology* Vol. 7, pp. 441-454

Heath, J.E, Pollard and Thomas, J.A. (1984); Atlas of Butterflies of Britain and Ireland, Viking Press, London

Health and Environment Alliance. Climate Change.(2009). www.env-health.org/r/93 Date last accessed: 26 May 2009.

Houghton (2001). *Climate Change 2001: The Scientific Basis.* Cambridge University Press.

Huang, Y.C., Ghio, A.J. (2006). Vascular Effects of Ambient Pollutant Particles and Metals. *Curr. Vasc. Pharmacol.* 4, 199.

Hulin M, Simoni M, Viegi G, Annesi-Maesano I. (2012). Respiratory Health and Indoor Air Pollutants based on Quantitative Exposure Assessments. *Eur Respir J,* 40:1033-45.

Intergovernmental Panel on Climate Change (CH). Climate Change (2007). The Physical Science Basis. Geneva: Intergovernmen-tal Panel on Climate Change; 2007 (cited 2007 Jan 01). Available from: http://www.ipcc.ch/pdf/assessment-report/ar4/wg1/ar4_wg1_full_report.pdf.

Jacobsen, C. S. (1997). Plant Protection and Rhizosphere Colonization of Barley by Seed Inoculated Herbicide Degrading Burkholderia (*Pseudomonas*) Cepacia DBO1 (pRO101) in 2, 4-D Contaminated soil. *Plant and Soil, 189*(1), 139-144.

Jacobson, M.Z. (2007). Effects of Ethanol (E85) versus Gasoline Vehicles on Cancer and Mortality in the United States. *Environ. Sci. Technol.* 41, 4150–4157.

Jacob, D.J., Winner, D.A. (2009). Effect of Climate Change on Air Quality. *Atmos Environ* 43:51-63

Jerrett M., Burnett, R.T., Pope, C.A., Thurston, G, & Krewski D. (2009). Long-term Ozone Exposure and Mortality. *N Engl J Med*, 360:1085-95.

Kagawa, J. (1985). Evaluation of Biological Significance of Nitrogen Oxides Exposure. Tokai J. Exp. Clin. Med. 10, 348. Huang, Y.C., Ghio, A.J., 2006. Vascular Effects of Ambient Pollutant Particles and Metals. *Curr. Vasc. Pharmacol.* 4, 199.

Kala. (2014). Rhizoremediation: A Promising Rhizosphere Technology. *IOSR-JESTFT,* 8(8), 23-27.

Kelley, S. L., Aitchison, E. W., Deshpande, M., Schnoor, J. L., & Alvarez, P. J. (2001). Biodegradation of 1, 4-dioxane in Planted and Unplanted Soil: Effect of Bioaugmentation with *Amycolata* sp. CB1190. *Water Research, 35*(16), 3791-3800.

Kimbrough, R.D., Carter, C.D., Liddle, J.A., Cline, R.E.(1977). Epidemiology and Pathology of a Tetrachlorodibenzodioxin Poisoning Episode. Arch. Environ. Health 32, 77

Kingsley, M. T., Fredrickson, J. K., Metting, F. B., & Seidler, R. J. (1994). Environmental Restoration using Plant-microbe Bioaugmentation. *Bioremediation of Chlorinated and Polyaromatic Hydrocarbon Compounds. Lewis Publishers, Boca Raton, Fla,* 287-292.

Kinney, P. L. (2008). Climate Change, Air Quality, and Human Health. *American Journal of Preventive Medicine, 35*(5), 459-467.

Koposzki, H. (1992). Effects of Acid and Nitrogen Deposition on the Mesofauna, Especially the Collembolan. In *Proceedings of Air Pollution and Interactions between Organisms in Forest Ecosystems, 15th IUFRO International Meeting of Specialists on Air Pollution Effects on Forest Ecosystems* (p. 46).

Korade, D. L., & Fulekar, M. H. (2009). Rhizosphere Remediation of Chlorpyrifos in Mycorrhizospheric Soil using Ryegrass. *Journal of Hazardous Materials, 172*(2), 1344-1350.

Kunzli, N., Gutschmidt, K., Pope, A., Romieu, I., Samet, J.M., Smith, K. (2005). The Global Burden of Disease due to Outdoor Air Pollution. *J. Toxicol. Environ. Health,* 68, 1301.

Kuo, C.Y., Wong, R.H., Lin, J.Y., Lai, J.C., Lee, H. (2006). Accumulation of Chromium and Nickel Metals in Lung Tumors from Lung Cancer Patients in Taiwan. *J. Toxicol. Environ. Health* 69, 1337.

Kurpius, M.R., Goldstein, A.H. (2003). Gas-phase Chemistry Dominates O3 loss to a Forest, Implying a Source of Aerosols and Hydroxyl Radicals to the Atmosphere. *Geophys. Res. Lett.* 30 (7), 1371.

Law, K. (2010). More Ozone over North America. Nature 463, 307–308. Vingarzan, R., 2004. A Review of Surface Ozone Background Levels and Trends. Atmos. Environ. 38, 3431–3442.

Laj, H.. Sigurdsson, S.M., Drummey, M.J. Spencer, J.M. Palais, *Nature,* 346 (1990). 45.

Lilleskov, E.A., Liu, L., Lynch, J., Nadelhoffer, K., Perakis, S.S., Robin-Abbott, M.J., Stoddard, J., Weathers, K., Dennis, R.L. (2011). Effects of Nitrogen Deposition and Empirical Nitrogen Critical loads for Ecoregions of the United States. *Ecol. Appl.* 21 (8), 3049–3082.

Lin, J.-T., Patten, K.O., Liang, X.-Z., Wuebbles, D.J. (2008). Effects of Intercontinental Transport on Surface Ozone over the United States at the Present and Future. *Geophys. Res. Lett.* 35, L02805.

Li, S., Williams, G., Jalaludin, B., Baker, P. (2012). Panel Studies of Air Pollution on Children's Lung Function and Respiratory Symptoms: A Literature Review. J Asthma, 49:895-910.

Liu, Y., Stanturf, J., & Goodrick, S. (2010). Trends in Global Wildfire Potential in a Changing Climate. *Forest Ecology and Management, 259*(4), 685-697.

Loghman-Adham, M. (1997). Renal Effects of Environmental and Occupational Lead Exposure. Environ. Health Perspect. 105, 928.Jarup, L., 2003. Hazards of Heavy Metal Contamination. *Br. Med. Bull.* 68, 167.

Madden, E. F., & Fowler, B. A. (2000). Mechanisms of Nephrotoxicity from Metal Combinations: A Review. *Drug and Chemical Toxicology, 23*(1), 1-12.

Mandal, P.K. (2005). Dioxin: A Review of Its Environmental Effects and Its Aryl Hydrocarbon Receptor Biology. J. Comp. Physiol. 175, 221 (B).

Mason, C.F. & MacDonald, S.M. (1987); Acidification and Otter (*Lutra lutra*) Distribution on a British River, *Mammalia* 51(1), 81-87

Manzo, N.D., Slade, R. & Dye, J.A. (2010). Interrelationship of Lung Inflammation and Air Pollutant Exposure on Cellular Oxidative Stress and Epithelial Injury. *Proceedings 27th Symposium of the Veterinary Comparative Respiratory Society*, Plymouth, MA

McGrath, J. M., Betzelberger, A. M., Wang, S., Shook, E., Zhu, X. G., Long, S. P., & Ainsworth, E. A. (2015). An Analysis of Ozone Damage to Historical Maize and Soybean Yields in the United States. *Proceedings of the National Academy of Sciences, 112*(46), 14390-14395.

Nawrot, T., Plusquin, M., Hogervorst, J., Roels, H.A., Celis, H., Thijs, L., Vangronsveld, J., Van Hecke, E., Staessen, J.A. (2006). Environmental Exposure to Cadmium and Risk of Cancer: A Prospective Population-based Study. *Lancet Oncol.* 7, 119.

Neas, L., Williams, R.W., Devlin, R.B. (2004). Particulate Matter Exposure in Cars is Associated with Cardiovascular Effects in Healthy Young Men, *Am. J. Respir. Crit. Care Med.* 169, 934.

Nichols, T. D., Wolf, D. C., Rogers, H. B., Beyrouty, C. A., & Reynolds, C. M. (1997). Rhizosphere Microbial Populations in Contaminated Soils. *Water, Air, and Soil Pollution, 95*(1-4), 165-178.

Nowak, D.J. (2000). Tree Species Selection, Design, and Management to Improve Air Quality. Construction Technology: Annual Meeting Proceedings of the American Society of Landscape Architects.

Nowak, D.J., Crane, D.E., Stevens, J.C. (2006). Air Pollution Removal by Urban Trees and Shrubs in the United States. Urban For. *Urban Greening* 4, 115–123.

Ollinger, S.V., Aber, J.D., Reich, P.B. (1997). Simulating Ozone Effects on Forest Productivity: Interactions Among leaf-, canopy-, and stand-level Processes. *Ecol. Appl.* 7 (4), 1237–1251

Olsson, D., Mogren, I., & Forsberg, B. (2013). Air Pollution Exposure in Early Pregnancy and Adverse Pregnancy Outcomes: A Register-based Cohort Study. *BMJ open, 3*(2), e001955.

Pai, S. G., Riley, M. B., & Camper, N. D. (2001). Microbial Degradation of Mefenoxam in Rhizosphere of Zinnia Angustifolia. *Chemosphere, 44*(4), 577-582.

Pangtey, B.S., Chandra, S.V., Garg, N. (1991). A Cross-sectional Study of Pulmonary Function Among Workers Exposed to Multimetals in the Glass Bangle Industry, *Am. J. Ind. Med.* 20, 391.

Pardo, L.H., Fenn, M.E., Goodale, C.L., Geiser, L.H., Driscoll, C.T., Allen, E.B., Baron, J., Bobbink, R., Bowman, W.D., Clark, C., Emmett, B., Gilliam, F.S., Greaver, T., Hall, S.J.,

Patz, J. A., Frumkin, H., Holloway, T., Vimont, D. J., & Haines, A. (2014). Climate Change: Challenges and Opportunities for Global Health. *Jama, 312*(15), 1565-1580.

Pinder RW, BettezND, BonanGB, Greaver T L, WidierWR, SchlesingerWHand Davidson E A 2013. Impacts of Human Alteration of the Nitrogen Cycle in the US on Radiative Forcing *Biogeochemistry* 114 25–40.

Peters, A., von, S., Heier, M., Trentinaglia, I., Hörmann, A., Wich-mann, H.E, (2004). Exposure to Traffic and the Onset of Myocardial in-farction. *N Engl J Med*, 351:1721-30.

Pickrell, J. (1991). Hazards in Confinement Housing - Gases and Dusts in Confined Animal Houses for Swine, Poultry, Horses and Humans. *Veterinary and Human Toxicology*, Vol. 33: pp. 32-39.

Rastogi, S.K., Gupta, B.N., Husain, T., Chandra, H., Mathur, N., Pangtey, B.S., Schell, L.M., Gallo, M.V., Denham, M., Ravenscroft, J. (2006). Effects of Pollution on Human Growth and Development: An Introduction. *J. Physiol. Anthropol.* 25, 103.

Riebau, A.R., Andersen, C. Wildland Fires and Air Pollution.(1985.). Developments in Environmental Science, Vol. 8. Elsevier, Amsterdam, pp. 365–403. Reich, P.B., Amundson, R.G. (EDs). Ambient Levels of Ozone Reduce net Photosynthesis in Tree and Crop Species. *Science* 230, 566–570.

Riediker, M., Cascio, W.E., Griggs, T.R., Herbst, M.C., Bromberg, P.A., Neas, L., Williams, R.W., Devlin, R.B. (2004). Particulate Matter Exposure in Cars is Associated with Cardiovascular Effects in Healthy Young Men, Am. J. Respir. Crit. Care Med. 169, 934.

Ronchel, M. C., & Ramos, J. L. (2001). Dual System to Reinforce Biological Containment of Recombinant Bacteria Designed for Rhizoremediation. *Applied and Environmental Microbiology, 67*(6), 2649-2656.

Roupsard, P. (2013). Etude Phénoménologique Du dépôt Sec d'aérosols En Milieu Urbain. Ph.D Thesis. University of Rouen.

Rubin, J.I., Kean, A.J., Harley, R.A., Millet, D.B., Goldstein, A.H. (2006). Temperature Dependence of Volatile Organic Compound Evaporative Emissions from Motor Vehicles. J. *Geophys. Res.* 111, D03305.

Sandmann, E. R. I. C., & Loos, M. A. (1984). Enumeration of 2, 4-D-degrading Microorganisms in Soils and Crop plant Rhizospheres using Indicator Media; High Populations Associated with Sugarcane (*Saccharum officinarum). Chemosphere, 13*(9), 1073-1084.

Sato, K. (1989). Interrelationships between Microorganisms and Plants in Soil. Vancura, V. Kunc, F.(Eds.). Elsevier: New York, pp. 335-42.

Schnoor, J. L., Aitchison, E. W., Kelley, S. L., & Alvarez, P. J. J. (1998). Phytoremediation and Bioaugmentation of 1, 4-dioxane. In *Abstr. Adv. Biol. Syst. Rem. Conf* (pp. 87-91).

Schroder, M., Linkert, K.H., Pedersen, S., Takai, H., Johnsen, J.O., Groot Koerkamp, P.W.G., Uenk, G.H., Metz, J.H.M., Hinz, T., Caspary, V. & Linke S.(1998) Emissions of Aerial Pollutants in Livestock Buildings in Northern Europe: Overview of a Multinational Project. *Journal of Agricultural Engineering Research*, Vol. 70, pp. 3-9.

Schlesinger, R.B. (1979). Natural removal mechanisms for chemical pollutants in the environment. *Bioscience* 29, 95–101.

Scherer, M. & Unshelm, J. (1995). Untersuchungen zur Belastung von Mastschweinen sowie der Umgebung von Mastschweinstallen durch Atembaren Feinstaub, Stallspezifische Bakterien und Ammoniak. *Zentralblatt fur Hygiene und Umweltmedizin,* 196, pp. 399-415.

Schucht, S., Colette, A., Rao, S., Holland, M., Schöpp, W., Kolp, P., ... & Brignon, J. M. (2015). Moving towards Ambitious Climate Policies: Monetised Health Benefits from Improved Air Quality could Offset Mitigation Costs in Europe. *Environmental Science & Policy, 50,* 252-269.

Seibert, K., Fuehr, F., Cheng, H. H., (1981). In Theory and Practical Use of Soil-Applied Herbicides Symposium; European Weed Resource Society: Paris, pp. 137-46.

Sharma, R.K., Agrawal, M. (2005). Biological Effects of Heavy Metals: An Overview. *J. Environ. Biol.* 26, 301.

Shine, K.P., Stevenson, D.S., Sudo, K., Szopa, S., Zeng, G. (2006). Radiative Forcing since Preindustrial Times due to Ozone change in the Troposphere and the Lower Stratosphere. *Atmos.*

Chem. Phys. 6, 575–599.

Sitch, S., Cox, P.M., Collins, W.J., Huntingford, C. (2007). Indirect Radiative Forcing of Climatechange through Ozone Effects on the Land-carbon Sink. Nature 448, 791–794.

Sillman, S., & Samson, P. J. (1995). Impact of Temperature on Oxidant Photochemistry in Urban, Polluted Rural and Remote Environments. *Journal of Geophysical Research: Atmospheres, 100*(D6), 11497-11508.

Silva, R. A., West, J. J., Zhang, Y., Anenberg, S. C., Lamarque, J. F., Shindell, D. T., & Horowitz, L. W. (2013). Global Premature Mortality due to Anthropogenic Outdoor Air Pollution and the Contribution of Past Climate Change. *Environmental Research Letters, 8*(3), 034005.

Smil, V. (2002). Nitrogen and Food Production: Proteins for Human Diets. *Ambio* 31 126–31.

Solomon, S., Qin, D., Manning, M., Marquis, M., Averyt, K., Tignor, M.l. (2007). Technical Summary. In: Climate Change. The Physical Science Basis. New York (NY): Cambridge University Press; 2007. 19-940.

Sriprang, R., Hayashi, M., Yamashita, M., Ono, H., Saeki, K., & Murooka, Y. (2002). A Novel Bioremediation System for Heavy Metals using the Symbiosis between Leguminous Plant and Genetically Engineered Rhizobia. *Journal of Biotechnology, 99*(3), 279-293.

Sun, G., McLaughlin, S.B., Porter, J.H., Uddling, J., Mulholland, P.J., Adams, M.B., Pederson, N. (2012). Interactive Influences of Ozone and Climate on Streamflow of Forested Watersheds. Global Chang. Biol. 18, 3395–3409.

Tager, I.B., Balmes, J., Lurmann, F., Ngo, L., Alcorn, S., Kunzli, N. (2005). Chronic Exposure to Ambient Ozone and Lung Function in Young Adults. *Epidemiology* 16, 751.

Tai, A. P., Martin, M. V., & Heald, C. L. (2014). Threat to Future Global Good Security from Climate Change and Ozone Air Pollution. *Nature Climate Change, 4*(9), 817.

Thiering, E., & Heinrich, J. (2015). Epidemiology of Air Pollution and Diabetes. *Trends in Endocrinology & Metabolism, 26*(7), 384-394.

Thron, R.W. (1996). Direct and Indirect Exposure to Air Pollution. Otolaryngol. Head Neck Surg. 114, 281.

Trenberth, K.E., Jones, P.D, Ambenje, P., Bojariu, R., Easterling, Parker, D., Rahimzadeh, F., Renwick, J.A., Rusticucci, M., Soden, B., Zhai, P. (2007). Observations: Surface and

Atmospheric Climate Change. In: Solomon S, Qin D, Manning M, eds. Climate Change 2007: the Physical Science Basis. Contribution of Working Group I to the Fourth Assessment Report of the Intergovernmental Panel on Climate Change. Cambridge, Cambridge University Press, pp. 235-6.

Turner, M.C., Jerrett, M., Pope, C.A., Krewski, D., Gapstur, S.M., Diver,W.R.(2016). Long-term Ozone Exposure and Mortality in a large Prospective Study. *Am J Respir Crit Care Med.* 2016;193(10): 1134–42.

US, E.P.A, (2008). Integrated Science Assessment (ISA) for Oxides of Nitrogen and Sulfur—Environmental Criteria, final report, Washington, DC.

Uysal, N., Schapira, R.M. (2003). Effects of Ozone on Lung Function and Lung Diseases. Curr. Opin. Pulm. Med. 9, 144. Ghio, A.J., Huang, Y.C., 2004. Exposure to Concentrated Ambient Particles (CAPs): A Review. *Inhal. Toxicol.* 16, 53.

Vamvakas, S., Bittner, D., Koster, U. 1(993). Enhanced Expression of the Protooncogenes c-myc and c-fos in Normal and Malignant Renal Growth. *Toxicol. Lett.* 67, 161.

Van Grinsven, H.J.M., Holland, M., Jacobsen, B.H., Klimont, Z., Sutton, M.A.& Willems, W.J. (2013) Costs and Benefits of Nitrogen for Europe and Implications for Mitigation *Environ. Sci. Technol.* 47 3571–9

Vermylen, J., Nemmar, A., Nemery, B., Hoylaerts, M.F. (2005). Ambient Air Pollution and Acute Myocardial Infarction. *J. Thromb. Haemost.* 3, 1955.

Wang, H., Jacob, D.J., Le Sager, P., Streets, D.G., Park, R.J., Gilliland, A.B., Van Donkelaar, A. (2009). Surface Ozone Background in the United States: Canadian and Mexican Influences. *Atmos. Environ.* 43, 1310–1319.

Wathes, C. M., Phillips, V. R., Holden, M. R., Sneath, R. W., Short, J. L., White, R. P. P., & Pedersen, S. (1998). Emissions of Aerial Pollutants in Livestock Buildings in Northern Europe: Overview of a Multinational Project. *Journal of Agricultural Engineering Research, 70*(1), 3-9..,

WHO Regional Office for Europe (DK). (2013). Review of Evidence on Health Aspects of Air Pollution: REVIHAAP Project. Copenhagen: WHO Regional Office for Europe.

WHO Regional Office for Europe (DK). (2014). WHO Expert Meeting: Methods and Tools for Asessing the Health Risks of Air Pollution at Local, National and International Level. Meeting Report. Bonn, Germany, 12-13 May 2014. Copenhagen: WHO Regional Office for Europe.

Wegmann, M., Fehrenbach, A., Heimann, S., Fehrenbach, H., Renz, H., Garn, H., Herz, U., (2005). NO2-induced Airway Inflammation is Associated with Progressive Airflow Limitation and Development of Emphysema-like Lesions in C57bl/6 mice. Exp. Toxicol. Pathol. 56, 341.

Wilson, R., Spengler J. (1996) *Particles in our air*. Harvard University Press, USA.

Wittig, V.E., Ainsworth, E.A., Long, S.P. (2007). To What Extent do Current and Projected increases in Surface Ozone Affects Photosynthesis and Stomatal Conductance in Trees? A Metaanalytic Review of the last 3 decades of Experiments. *Plant Cell Environ.* 30, 1150–1162.

Woodcock, J., Edwards, P., Tonne, C., Armstrong, B.G., Ashiru, O., Banister, D., Beevers, S., Chalabi, Z., Chowdhury, Z., Cohen l.(2009). Public Health Benefits of Strategies to Reduce Greenhouse-gas Emissions: Urban Land Transport. Lancet , 374.

Wu, S., Mickley, L.J., Jacob, D.J., Rind, D., Streets, D.G. (2008). Effects of 2000–2050 Changes in Climate and Emissions on Global Tropospheric Ozone and the Policy-relevant Background Ozone in the United States. J. Geophys. Res. 113, D18312.

Xu, X., Ha, S. U., & Basnet, R. (2016). A Review of Epidemiological Research on Adverse Neurological Effects of Exposure to Ambient Air Pollution. *Frontiers in Public Health,* 4, 157.

Climate Change and Agro-Edaphic System Pages 103–126
Edited by: Dr. Alka Chauhan & Dr. Pawan Kumar 'Bharti'
ISBN: 978-93-86841-98-8
Edition: 2019
Published by: Discovery Publishing House Pvt. Ltd., New Delhi (India)

5

Climate Change and Its Causes

A Moot for Discussion about Some Principle Issues

[1]Prasann Kumar, [2]Shweta Pathak

ABSTRACT

This article discusses the limits of the Anthropogenic Global Warming Theory advocated by the Intergovernmental Panel on Climate Change. A phenomenological theory of climate change based on the physical properties of the data themselves is proposed. At least 60% of the warming of the Earth observed since 1970 appears to be induced by natural cycles which are present in the solar system. A climatic stabilization or cooling until 2030-2040 am forecast by the phenomenological model.

Keywords: Agriculture, Biotic, Climate, Energy, Forage.

INTRODUCTION

Since 1900 the global surface temperature of the Earth has risen by about 0.8 °C (Figure 5.1), and since the 70s by about 0.5°C. This temperature increase occurred during a significant atmospheric concentration increase of some greenhouse gases, especially CO_2 and CH_4, which is known to be mainly due to human emissions. According to the Anthropogenic Global Warming Theory (AGWT) humans have caused more than 90% of global warming since 1900 and virtually 100% of the global warming since 1970 (Appendix A). The AGWT is currently advocated by the Intergovernmental Panel on Climate Change (IPCC), which is the leading body for the assessment of climate change established by the United Nations Environment Programme (UNEP) and the World Meteorological Organization (WMO). Many scientists believe that further emissions of greenhouse gases could endanger humanity. However, not everyone shares the IPCC's views.[1] More than 30,000 scientists in America

[1] The AGWT advocates claim that there exists a scientific consensus that supports the AGWT. However, a scientific consensus does not have any scientific value when it is contradicted by data. It is perfectly legitimate to discuss the topic of manmade global warming and closely scrutinize the IPCC's claims. Given the extreme complexity of the climate system and the overwhelming evidence that climate has always changed, the AGWT advocates' claim that the science is settled is premature in extreme.

[1] Department of Agronomy, School of Agriculture, Lovely Professional University, Jalandhar, Punjab, 144411, India

[2] Department of Plant Physiology, I.Ag. Sci., BHU., Varanasi, 221005, U.P., India

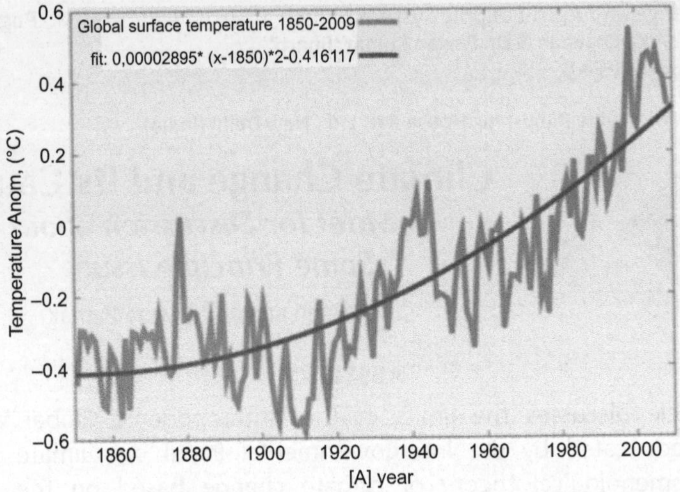

Fig. 5.1: Gobal surface temperature (land and sea) HadCRUT3 (red and its quadratic fit (black) [Climatic Research Unit, http://www.cru.uea.ac.uk/]

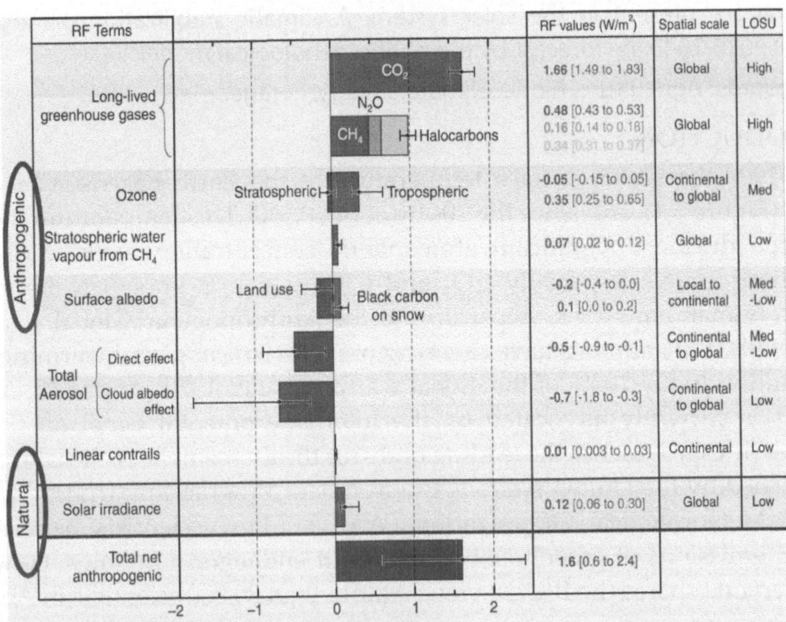

Fig. 5.2: List of radiative forcings held responsible for the global warming since 1750 and used in the models adopted by the IPCC. The figure is adapted from the IPCC Climate Change 2007: Synthesis Report. These forcing are used as inputs of the climate models used by the IPCC to support the AGWT. The table suggests that the total net anthropogenic forcing since 1750 has been 13.3 times larger than the natural forcing. However, labeling on the left of the table, anthropogenic and natural, is misleading because it would imply that the only human activity can change the chemistry of the atmosphere, which is non physical.

(including 9,029 PhDs) have recently signed a petition stating that those claims are extreme, that the climate system is more complex than what is now known, several mechanisms are not yet included in the climate models considered by the IPCC and that this issue should be treated with some caution because incorrect environmental policies could also cause extensive damage [3]. This article briefly summarizes some of the reasons, mostly derived from my own research, why the science behind the IPCC's claim is questionable.[2]

The IPCC's Pro-anthropogenic Warming Bias

First, it should be noted that the IPCC mission states:

> *"The IPCC reviews and assesses the most recent scientific, technical and socioeconomic information produced worldwide relevant to the understanding of humaninduced climate change."*

The above statement implies that the IPCC may provide a colored reading of the scientific literature by stressing those studies that would better justify its own political mission, which evidently focuses on human-induced climate change.[3] Indeed, the existence of an anthropogenic bias appears evident in

[2] On November 19, 2009 a climategate story erupted on the web. This story is seriously undermining the credibility of the AGWT and of its advocates. Thousands of e-mails and other documents were disseminated via the internet through the hacking of a server used by the Climatic Research Unit (CRU) of the University of East Anglia in Norwich, England. These e-mails have been interpreted by some as suggesting serious scientific misconduct and even conspiracy by leading climate scientists and IPCC authors who have strongly advocated AGWT. These emails apparently suggest: 1) manipulation of temperature data; 2) prevention of a proper scientific disclosure of data and methodologies; 3) attempts to discredit scientists critical of the AGWT also by means of internet articles such as those at http://www.realclimate.org (several of these realclimate.org articles are quite shallow and suspiciously inaccurate); 4) attempts to bias Wikipedia articles in favor of the AGWT; 5) and much more seriously, attempts to control which papers appear in the peer reviewed literature and in the climate assessments in such a way to bias the scientific community in favor of the AGWT. Others, however, believe that the contents of those emails have been maliciously misinterpreted by the so-called skeptics. A detailed analysis of these emails can be found in: 1) J. P. Costella (2010), Climategate analysis, SPPI reprint series, (http://scienceandpublicpolicy.org/reprint/climategate analysis.html); 2) S. Mosher and T. W. Fuller (2010), Climategate: The Crutape Letters, CreateSpace publisher; 3) See also United States Senate Report 'Consensus' Exposed: The CRU Controversy, http://epw.senate.gov/public/index.cfm?FuseAction=Files.View&FileStoreid=7db3fbd8-f1b4-4fdf-bd15-12b7df1a0b63.

[3] Further evidence of the IPCC's anthropogenic and political bias was discovered in January 2010: the IPCC's claim that Himalayan glaciers will disappear by 2035 was based on magazine interviews, not on peer-reviewed scientific research which is contrary to the IPCC's own policy. Dr. Lal admitted that this physically impossible event was highlighted in the IPCC report just to put political pressure on world leaders (http://www.dailymail.co.uk/news/article-1245636/Glacier-scientists-says-knew-dataverified.html). Curiously, NASA anticipated the Himalayan glacier melting in 2030 (http://wattsupwiththat.com/2010/01/23/nasaclimate-page-suckered-by-ipcc-deletes-a-moved-up-glacier-melting-date-reference/). Other significant errors and non peer reviewed material in the IPCC have been uncovered such as: Endanger 40 percent of Amazon rainforests; Melt mountain ice in the Alps, Andes, and Africa; Deplete water resources for 4.5 billion people by 2085, neglecting to mention that global warming could also increase water resources for as many as 6 billion people; Slash crop production by 50 percent in North Africa by 2020. http://epw.senate.gov/publcindex.cfm?FuseAction=Files.View&FileStoreid=9cc0e46e-56be-4728-9099-92dbda199bfc.

Figure 5.2 that shows the complete list of the radiative forcings, which, as the IPCC claims, have caused the global climate warming observed since 1750.

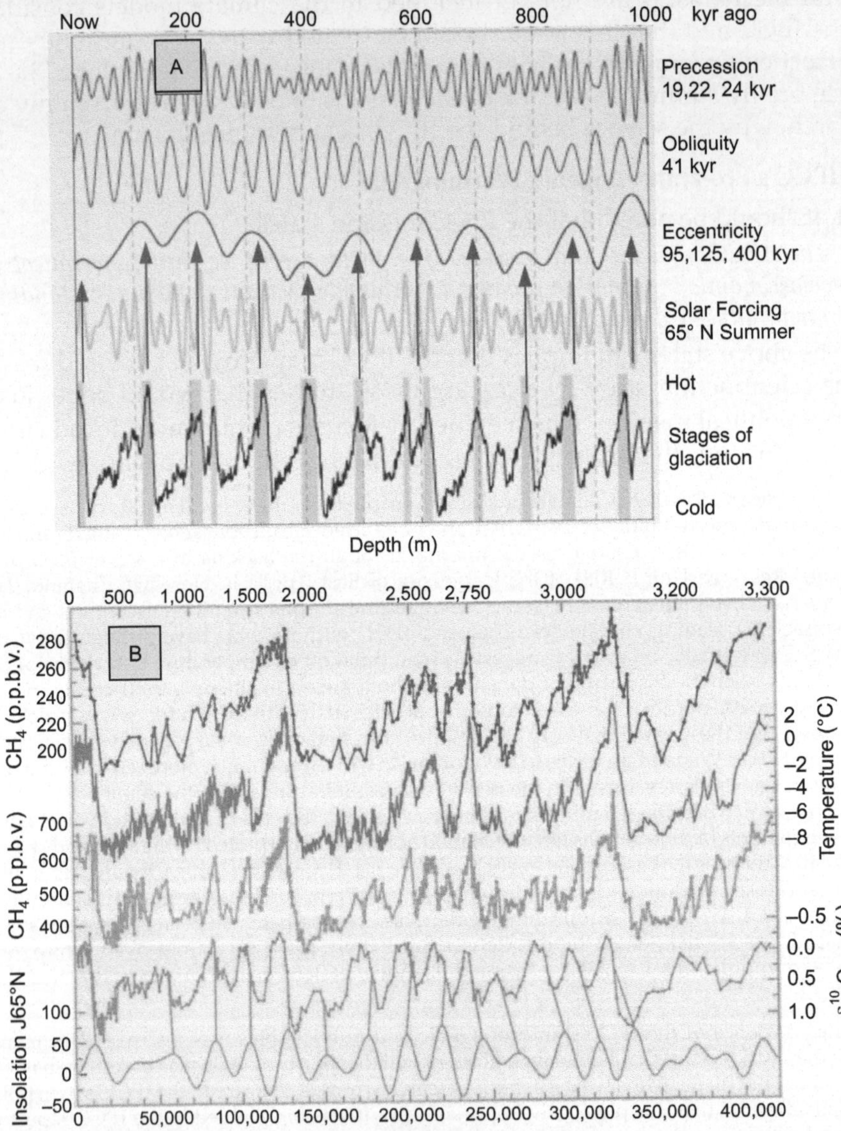

Fig. 5.3: **Cycles of CO_2 and CH_4 that time-lag (with a delay of about 800 years) the temperature cycles observed during the Ice Ages. These glacial cycles were likely induced by the modulation of the solar input into the Earth's system through the Milankovich cycles, which are orbital perturbations of the Earth such as the precession, obliquity and eccentricity. For example, notice the good correspondence between the 100.000 year temperature cycles with the eccentricity, as highlighted in the figure. The figure is adapted from Wikipedia' articles: [A] Milankovitch cycles; [B] Vostok Station.**

This figure divides the climatic forcing into two groups: one group includes only the total solar irradiance and is labeled natural, the other group comprises the rest and is labeled anthropogenic. Thus, the IPCC claims that 100% of the increase of the CO_2 and CH_4 atmospheric concentrations observed since 1750 and the change of all other climate components, except for the total solar irradiance, are anthropogenic. These labels do suggest that without humans the chemical concentrations of the atmosphere and a number of other climatic parameters would remain rigorously unchanged despite a change of the solar energy input! This claim is non physical because as the solar activity increases, the climate warms, and this causes a net increase of atmospheric CO_2 and CH_4 concentration. During warming the ability of the ocean to absorb these gases from the atmosphere decreases because of Henry's law and other mechanisms. A warming would also increase the natural production of atmospheric CO_2 and CH_4 on the land due to the acceleration of the fermentation of organic material, outgassing of (permafrost) soils and other mechanisms. The existence of CO_2 and CH_4 feedback mechanisms are evident in the large CO_2 and CH_4 cycles observed during the ice ages (which were caused by the astronomical cycles of Milankovich) when no human industrial activity existed, see Figure 5.3.

For example, even assuming that the IPCC's forcing estimates in Figure 5.2 are correct, if only 10% of the total increase in greenhouse gases since 1750 has been due to the observed increase of solar activity during the same period, the IPCC, with its labels, has inflated the anthropogenic contribution by 20% and underestimated the solar contribution by 300%. This can be easily extrapolated from the numbers depicted in Figure 5.2. It is evident that if the climatic forcing are labeled as anthropogenic, the presumed consequences, namely climate changes, would also be anthropogenic. This, however, is circular logic.

The Climate Sensitivity Uncertainty to CO_2 Increase

A second fundamental issue concerns how much global warming can be induced by an increase of CO_2 (or CH_4) atmospheric concentration. Indeed, this estimate is extremely uncertain. Also the radiative forcing associated with aerosols is extremely uncertain, as Figure 5.2 shows. The IPCC acknowledges that if the atmospheric concentration of CO_2 doubles the global average temperature could rise between 1.5 and 4.5°C at equilibrium. The variability of climate sensitivity to CO_2 is shown in Figure 5.4, which demonstrates an even wider sensitivity temperature range. If greenhouse gases such as CO_2 are the major causes of global warming, a climate sensitivity to CO_2 increase with a minimum error of 50% (together with the extreme aerosol forcing uncertainty) can only raise strong doubts about the scientific robustness of the IPCC's climate change in interpretation. This error is so large because it is not well known how to model the major climate feedback mechanisms, i.e., water vapor and clouds. Indeed, the AGWT advocates acknowledge that the current models on which the claims of the IPCC are based are significantly incomplete. [4]Rockstrom and 28 other scientists, who strongly promote the AGWT, have confirmed this fact by recently stating: "Most models suggest that a doubling in atmospheric CO_2 concentration will lead to a global temperature rise of about 3°C (with a probable uncertainty range of 2-4.5°C) once the climate has regained equilibrium. But these models do not include long-term reinforcing feedback processes that further warm the climate, If these slow feedbacks are included, doubling CO_2 levels gives an eventual temperature increase of 6°C (with a probable uncertainty range of 4-8°C)."

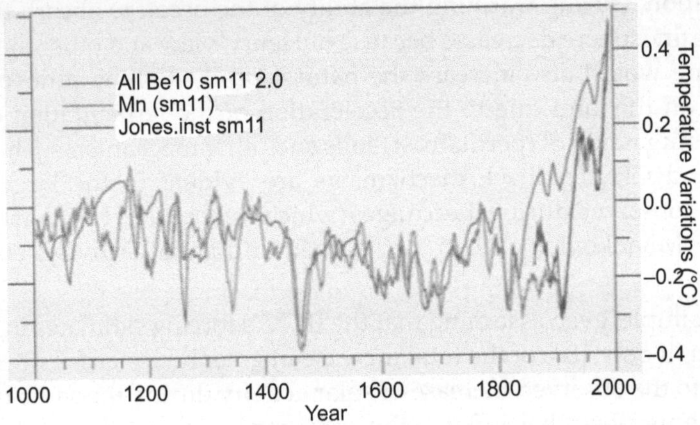

Fig. 5.5: (Red) Mann's Hockey Stick. (Blue) Output response of Crowley's linear upwelling/ diffusion energy balance model using all forcing terms (solar, volcano, CO_2 and aerosol). Instrumental temperature data (black). Note the very good agreement between the model and temperature reconstruction that is claimed by Crowley in his article. Note that from the Medieval Warm Period (1000-1300) to the Little Ice Age (1500-1750) both the model response and Mann's temperature reconstruction show a cooling of about 0.2°C.

The Hockey Stick temperature graph was considered the only global temperature reconstruction available at the time and it required a scientific interpretation. Several scientific groups, for example Crowley, used energy balance models and concluded that the Hockey Stick implied that the climate

[4] Rockstrom et al. have implicitly acknowledged that the IPCC climate models are essentially flawed. This objectively undermines the IPCC's claims because its claims are based on the same climate models that the AGWT advocates acknowledge to be severely incomplete. Evidently, Rockstrom et al.'s claim that future climate models will necessarily confirm and greatly stress the AGWT cannot be considered as a fact. Indeed, it cannot be ruled out that, on the contrary, future climate models will discredit the AGWT by modeling new climate mechanisms that current models lack. 6This larger climate variability was clearly acknowledged by the IPCC in 1990. It was also consistent with the world climate history after AD 1,000 according to ground borehole evidence in a paper published in 1997 (Huang S. H. N. Pollack and P. Y. Shen (1997), Late Quaternary Temperature Changes Seen in Worldide Continental Heat Flow Measurements, Geophysical Research Letters 24, 1947-1950.)

is almost insensitive to solar changes and the anomalous warming observed since 1900 has been almost entirely anthropogenic. In fact, only the (CO_2 and CH_4) GHG forcing function (as deduced from ice core reconstructions) presents a shape that resembles that of a hockey stick. Crowley concluded his article, which shows a good correlation between his climate model and the Hockey Stick, with this statement:

"The very good agreement between models and data in the pre-anthropogenic interval also enhances confidence in the overall ability of climate models to simulate temperature variability on the largest scales." (See Figure 5.5). Crowley's statement reveals the subtle link that exists between the Hockey Stick and the confidence in the sufficient accuracy of the climate models used to claim that the global warming observed since 1900 was almost entirely anthropogenically induced. This interpretation was strongly endorsed by the IPCC in 2001, was popularized by Al Gore in his documentary The Inconvenient Truth, where the Hockey Stick plays a predominant role, and as almost completely implicitly proposed again by the IPCC in 2007. It is important.

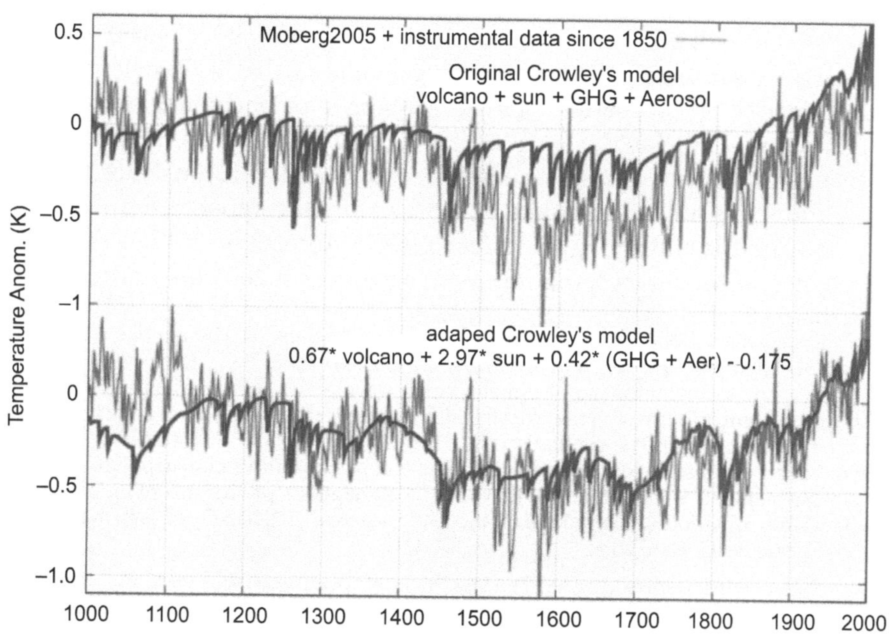

Fig. 5.6: Top: Moberg's temperature (red). Crowley's model (blue) which is also shown in Figure 5. Bottom: In blue Crowley's model once adapted to reproduce the temperature of Moberg et al. (2005) that shows a 0.6°C cooling from MWP and LIA. Note that the solar contribution must be amplified by a factor of while the GHG+aerosol contribution, which is commonly labeled as anthropogenic, must be reduced by a factor of 0.4.

To note that the IPCC's AGWT is based on the interpretation of climate models, such as Hansen's GISS models, developed before 2004/5 which appear to be compatible with the Hockey Stick temperature graph[5]

The Climatic Meaning of Recent Paleoclimatic Temperature Reconstructions

The dates are important because since 2004/2005 the Hockey Stick has been mathematically and physically questioned.[6] An additional open issue is whether the tree rings used by Mann is able to accurately reconstruct the temperature changes, especially over long time scales. Indeed, tree growth does not depend on temperature alone, but on other factors too, such as rain patterns and biological adaptation. These multiple factors may introduce nonlinear relationships and a certain degree of randomness in the data. This may reduce the amplitude of multidecadal and secular oscillations found in the proxy models, in particular when these proxy records are statistically calibrated against the instrumental temperature records, which are only available for the period after 1850, and combined for obtaining a world average. Alternative paleoclimatic reconstructions, which do not use tree rings, have been proposed. These proxy temperature reconstructions suggest a significant pre-industrial climate variability. From the Medieval Warm Period (1000-1300) and the Little Ice Age (1500-1750) these reconstructions show a cooling of at least 0.6°C, three times larger than the Hockey Stick. Figure 6 shows that if Crowley's energy balance model is compared against Moberg's paleoclimatic temperature reconstruction, Crowley's very good agreement between the model and the data vanishes. If the Crowley's model is recalibrated to reconstruct Moberg's temperature, it is easy to calculate that the solar effect must be amplified by a factor of 3 and the anthropogenic effect (GHG + Aerosol) should be multiplied by 0.4. Thus, if Moberg's temperature is accurate, in 2000 the anthropogenic

5 For example, the GISS GCM is compared and found relatively compatible with Mann's Hockey Stick temperature graph in Shindell D.T., G.A. Schmidt, R.L. Miller, and M.E. Mann, (2003), Volcanic and solar forcing of climate change during the preindustrial era. J. Climate 16, 4094-4107. A compatibility with the Hockey Stick temperature graph is also easily visible in the energy balance model (EBM) simulations in Foukal P., C. Frohlich, H. Spruit, T. M. L. Wigley (2006), Variations in solar luminosity and their effect on the Earth's climate, Nature 443, 161-166. In this paper, it is clear that the EBM model simulations predict a cooling between the Medieval Warm Period (1000-1300) and the Little Ice Age (1500-1800) of less than 0.2°C as shown by Mann's Hockey Stick.

6 The problems with Mann's original Hockey Stick temperature graph were first exposed by McIntyre and McKitrick (2005), The M&M Critique of the MBH98 Northern Hemisphere Climate Index: Update and Implications, Energy and Environment 16(1), 69-100. It was shown than Mann's algorithm could produce hockey stick shapes, even with a set of red noise sequences. Note that recently Mann has updated his reconstruction and acknowledged that the preindustrial temperature varied more than previously claimed in his works (Mann M. E., et al. (2008), Proxy-based reconstructions of hemispheric and global surface temperature variations over the past two millennia, Proc Natl Acad Sci USA 105, 13252-13257). However, McIntyre and McKitrick have claimed that also this latest Mann's update presents significant mathematical errors, including some records that would be improperly used.

contribution to global warming was overestimated by 250% because of the Hockey Stick.

Indeed, the Hockey Stick temperature graph does not have any historical credibility because between 1000 and 1400, the Vikings had farms and villages on the coast of Greenland, which would suggest an even milder climate than today, while the following period, from 1400 to 1800, is known as the Little Ice Age. The medieval warm and the following cold period were not only Western and European phenomena, but are also evident in Chinese historical documents. Numerous interdisciplinary studies reporting data from several regions of the world (see the Medieval Warm Period Project[7]) clearly indicate a significant change in pre-industrial climate which seems to be better reproduced by more recent paleoclimatic global temperature reconstructions which do not show a hockey stick shape.[8]

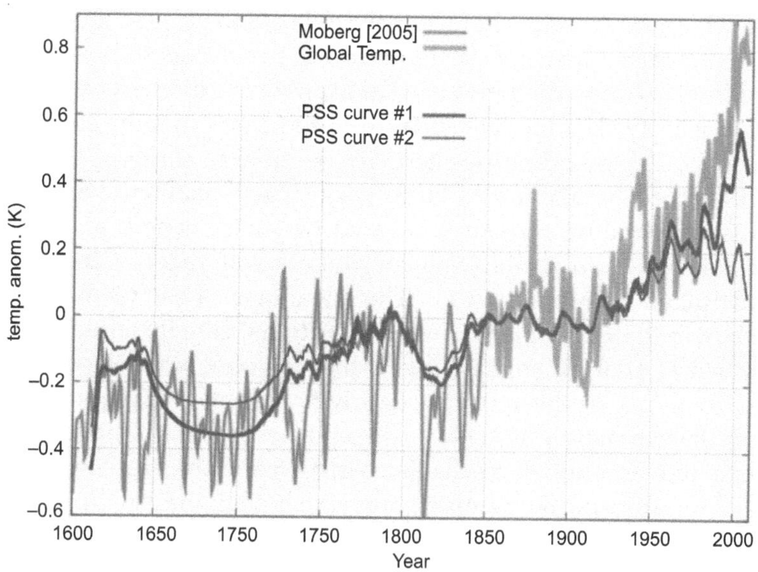

Fig. 5.7: Reconstruction of global surface temperatures over the last 400 years (red and green). In black there is the solar signature on climate as estimated by the empirical model. If since 1980 the TSI satellite composite A in figure 8 (PSS # 1) is used most of the warming observed during the last decades is solar induced. If the TSI satellite composite C in figure 8 (PSS # 2) is using the good correlation between temperature and solar signature abruptly stops in 1980. (Appendix I).

[7] http://www.CO_2science.org/data/mwp/mwpp.php

[8] A nice summary about the findings of nmerous studies published before and after Mann's original work in 1998 and 1999 that Strongly question the validity of the Hockey Stick temperature graph can be found in Heaven and Earth, Global Warming the Missing Science, chapter 2 'History,' by Ian Plimer, Taylor Trade (2009). Apparently, the IPCC's choice in 2001 to strongly highlight Mann's Hockey Stick temperature graph, despite extensive published literature pointing toward a large preindustrial climate variability, can be interpreted as a further evidence of the IPCC's pro-anthropogenic warming bias, as discussed in Section 2.

With the axes upside down by Mann's algorithm because these records are severely compromised by agricultural impact during the last century, e.g., Korttajarvi sediments from Tiljander data. Therefore, these data could not be used for reconstructing the past temperature because they could not be properly calibrated against the instrumental temperature record. (McIntyre S. and R. R. McKitrick (2009) Proxy Inconsistency and Other Problems in Millennial Paleoclimate Reconstructions. Proc Natl Acad Sci USA 106, E10.). See an extended comment by McIntyre here: http://climateaudit.org/2009/10/14/upside-side-down-mann-and-thepeerreviewedliterature/.

The Phenomenological Solar Signature Since 1600

It is possible to use a phenomenological model to interpret climate change. This model can simulate a typical energy balance model to interpret the global surface temperature. However, here the climate sensitivity to solar variations and the thermodynamic characteristic relaxation times are empirically determined in the temperature patterns during the last decades. A secular total solar irradiance reconstruction is used as input of the model as a proxy for the total solar activity. The model can be used to reconstruct the solar signature on climate for the past centuries and it is possible to compare this signature against the paleoclimatic temperature reconstructions. Figure 5.7 shows this result: the temperature signature induced by solar changes as predicted by the phenomenological model well reproduces 400 years of climate change as reconstructed by Moberg et al.. The advantage of the phenomenological approach over that implemented in the traditional climate models, which can be described as analytic engineering, is that the phenomenological approach attempts to measure the climate sensitivity to solar changes through the empirical determination of a kind of response function. This methodology would take into account all mechanisms involved in the process, although the individual microscopic mechanisms are not explicitly modeled.

It is essentially analogous to the method used by an electric engineer to study the electric response properties of an unknown circuit closed inside a box by carefully comparing the patterns of the input and the output signals. The phenomenological approach is essentially a holistic approach[11] that emphasizes the importance of studying a complex macroscopic system by directly analyzing the properties of the whole because of the complex interdependence of its parts rather than analyzing it by separating it into parts. On the contrary, the traditional analytic climate model approach attempts to simulate climate by dividing the climate system into its smallest possible or discernible elements and uses their elemental physical properties alone to interpret the macroscopic system. The limitation of the latter approach is that only those mechanisms and the physical couplings among them that are currently well known can be modeled. All unknown mechanisms and physical couplings remain excluded in an analytic model. Therefore, the analytic modularization may fail to properly model and interpret climate change because it just creates a virtual climate system that may have nothing to do with reality. The risk is scientific reductionism, that is, compensating the current ignorance about the true climatic mechanisms by mistakenly stressing a few of them, such as the anthropogenic GHG and aerosol forcing, in such a way to reproduce some warming trend during a restricted period of time. However, for not mistaking the physics of a complex phenomenon a model should be able to reproduce the data oscillations at multiple time scales. In science, the holistic approach complements the traditional analytical approach. When the two methodologies are appropriately used together, they are considered the most efficient way for studying complex systems. Essentially, the phenomenological approach acknowledges that understanding climate is an inverse-problem that risks to be ill-posed in the analytic approach. For example, the IPCC [1, p. 674] reports that the 11-year solar cycle produces a temperature cycle on the global surface temperature of about 0.1°C that is easy to observe. However, current climate models predict an average solar signature cycle which is three times smaller, approximately 0.035°C (for example, Crowley's model predicts a cycle of about 0.02°C). It is obvious that the current climate models are oversimplified. They are poorly modeling the solar-climate link mechanisms and, therefore, mistaking the real magnitude of the solar effects on climate (Appendix J). The term holistic science is used as a category encompassing a number of scientific research fields. These are multidisciplinary, are concerned with the behavior of complex systems, and recognize feedback within systems as a crucial element for understanding their behavior.

In fact, the IPCC models assume that the sun can influence climate only through total solar irradiance variation, that is used only as a radiative forcing. However, there are additional chemical mechanisms that are stimulated by specific frequencies of the solar radiation (for example, UV alters ozone, which is a greenhouse gas, and light stimulates photosynthesis which influences the biosphere) and there is an additional modulation of clouds, which alters the albedo, that is due to the solar modulation of cosmic ray flux [13,14].[9] All these

[9] A solar induced low cloud cover modulation can greatly affect the climate by greatly enhancing the climatic solar impact because of the potential magnitude of the resulting radiative forcing. This is evident from the fact that cloudy days are significantly cooler than sunny days. In fact, if the clouds were absent the solar radiative forcing warming the Earth's surface would increase by about 30 W/m^2. This value is far larger than the sum of all IPCC anthropogenic forcing in 250 years shown in Figure 5.2. Thus, even a small solar modulation of cloud cover can have a significant impact on climate change. Clouds can also respond quite fast to cosmic ray flux variations and, therefore, they may link some temperature fluctuations to the solar intermittency. Finally, a cosmicray cloud climate link has been suggested to explain the warm and ice periods of the Phanerozoic during the last 600 million years. In fact, the climate oscillations correlate with the cosmic ray flux variations much better than with the CO_2 atmospheric concentration records. In the latter case, most of the cosmic ray flux variation is claimed to be due to the changing galactic environment of the solar system, as

alternative solar-climate link mechanisms are absent in the current climate models because the climate modelers do not know how to model them and the computers are not sufficiently fast to simulate them. The phenomenological model would automatically include all these mechanisms because the climate sensitivity to solar changes is directly, that is phenomenologically, estimated by the magnitude of the temperature patterns that can be recognized as correlated to and, therefore, likely induced by solar changes.

it crosses the spiral arms of the Milky Way (Shaviv, N. J. (2003), The spiral structure of the Milky Way, cosmic rays, and ice age epochs on Earth, New Astronomy 8, 3977; Svensmark H. (2007), Cosmoclimatology: a new theory emerges, Astronomy & Geophysics 48 1, 18-24; Kirkby J. (2009), Cosmic rays and climate, CERN Colloquium, http://indico.cern.ch/getFile.py/access?resId=0&materialId= slides&confId=52576) 13Although it is not possible to verify the accuracy of all satellite measurements, to claim that the TSI proxy models must necessarily be correct is scientifically unsound. TSI proxy models, by definition, are based on the unproven assumptions that a given set of solar related measurements (such as sunspot number records, a few ground based spectral line width records, 14C and 10 Be cosmogenic isotope production and others) can reconstruct TSI. However, TSI proxy models significantly differ from each other and, evidently, this undermines the claim that they are accurate. Thus, although TSI proxy models are useful, they cannot be used to question the accuracy of actual TSI satellite measurements without valid physical reasons. Some of the more popularTSI proxy models were produced by Lean *et al.*, Solanki et al. and Hoyt and Schatten.

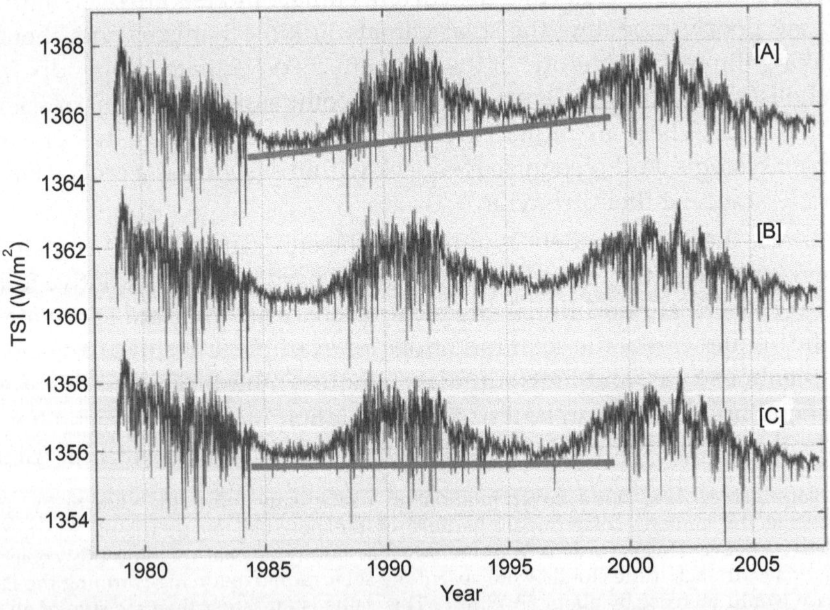

Fig. 5.8: Possible reconstructions of the total solar irradiance using satellite data. The reconstruction 'A' uses the Nimbus7/ERB dataset to fill the ACRIM-gap from 1989.5 to 1991.75; the reconstruction 'C' uses the ERBE/ERBs dataset to adjust the annual trend of the Nimbus7/ERB dataset and uses this altered record to fill the ACRIM-gap from 1989.5 to 1991.75; the reconstruction 'C' is jus the average between the two. The level difference between the minimum in 1986 and 1996 is approximately 0.3 ± 0.4W/m 2 . ACRIM is between 'A' and 'B'; PMOD is similar to 'C'. The red curves indicate the trend between the 1986 and 1996 solar minima.

7. The ACRIM vs. PMOD Satellite Total Solar Irradiance Controversy

Some discrepancy between the temperature reconstruction and the solar signature on climate as seen in Figures 5.6 and 5.7 may also be due to errors in the temperature as well as in the solar proxy records. Figure 5.7 shows two possible empirical solar signatures on climate after 1980. This uncertainty is due to an uncertainty about the behavior of the total solar irradiance. The climate models adopted by the IPCC have used total solar irradiance (TSI) proxy models that claim that total solar irradiance has remained constant since 1980. However, the satellite experimental groups (ACRIM and Nimbus7), which have measured the total solar irradiance since 1978, claim that TSI increased from 1980 to 2000 like the temperature.

However, another group, the PMOD in Switzerland, claimed that the TSI satellite data obtained and published by the above two experimental groups had to be corrected.[10] By doing so, Frohlich obtained a TSI satellite composite that does not show any upward trend from 1980 to 2000. It is important to notice that the experimental groups have always rejected the corrections of their own TSI data proposed by PMOD as arbitrary.[11]

[10]During the ACRIM-gap (1989.5-1992.5) Frohlich altered the Nimbus7 ¨ /ERB results to make them compatible with the ERBE/ERBS results. The Nimbus7 record was shifted downward by 0.86 W/m^2. This shift consisted of: (1) a step function change of about 0.47 W/m 2 which is used to correct a hypothetical sudden change of the sensitivity of the Nimbus7's sensors following a shutdown claimed to have occurred on 09/29/1989; (2) a linear drift of 0.142 Wm 2 / yr from October 1989 through middle 1992 which is supposed to correct a hypothetical gradual sensitivity increase of the same satellite sensors. However, during the ACRIMgap ERBE/ERBS sensors were expected to degrade due to a decrease in their cavity paint absorbency which occurs during the first exposure of these kind of sensors to high solar maximum UV radiation. So, the experimental teams claim that Frohlich's alteration of the published Nimbus7/ERB data, to force them to agree with the lower quality ERBE/ERBS results, is unjustified.

[11]On September 16, 2008, Douglas Hoyt (PI of the Nimbus7/ERB experiment which is fundamental for resolving the ACRIMgap problem, and whose data have been altered to construct the PMOD TSI satellite composite) sent me the following statement that was published in Ref.: "Concerning the supposed increase in Nimbus7 sensitivity at the end of September 1989 and other matters as proposed by Frohlich's PMOD TSI composite: 1. There is no known physical change in the electrically calibrated Nimbus7 radiometer or its electronics that could have caused it to become more sensitive. At least neither Lee Kyle nor I could never imagine how such a thing could happen and no one else has ever come up with a physical theory for the instrument that could cause it to become more sensitive. 2. The Nimbus7 radiometer was calibrated electrically every 12 days. The calibrations before and after the September shutdown gave no indication of any change in the sensitivity of the radiometer. Thus, when Bob Lee of the ERBS team originally claimed thee was a change in Nimbus7 sensitivity, we examined the issue and concluded there was No internal evidence in the Nimbus7 records to warrant the correction that he was proposing. Since the result was a null one, no publication was thought necessary. [3]. Thus, Frohlich's PMOD TSI composite is not consistent with the internal data or physics of ¨ the Nimbus7 cavity radiometer. [4]. The correction of the Nimbus7 TSI values for 1979-1980 proposed by Frohlich is also puzzling. ¨ The raw data was run through the same algorithm for these early years and the subsequent years and there is no justification for Frohlich's adjustment in my opinion."

By preferring the PMOD total solar irradiance satellite composite to the ACRIM one the IPCC message was that the global warming observed since 1980 could not be naturally interpreted and, therefore, it had to be 100% anthropogenic. Figure 5.8 shows three alternative reconstructions of the total solar irradiance using satellite measurements since 1978. The IPCC has

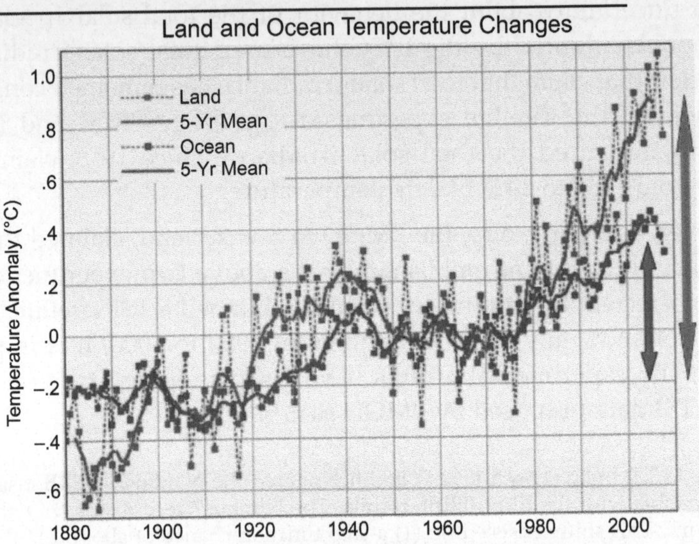

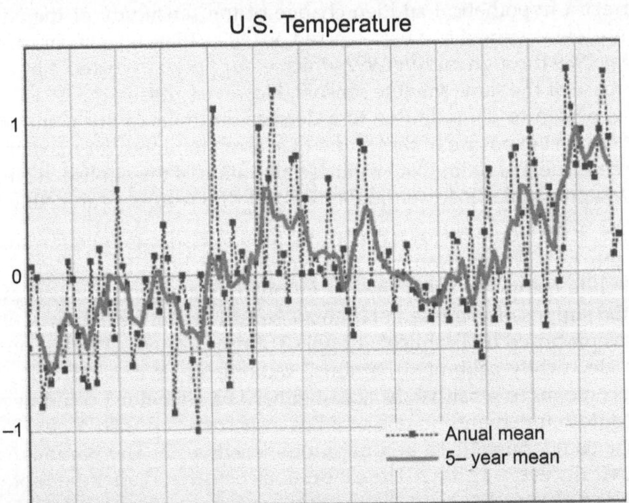

Fig. 5.9: Left: Global surface temperature records of the ocean and the land. Note the significant difference observed between the two records since 1970. The land apparently warmed at a double rate than the ocean. Right: Global surface temperature record relative to the United States of America. Note that this record highlights the existence of a large 60-70 year cycle and shows a smaller upward secular trend. (GISTEMP: http://data.giss.nasa.gov/gistemp/)

adopted a reconstruction, similar to C, which is compatible with PMOD's claim. However, the figure clearly indicates that the latter composite shows the lowest 1986-1996 decadal trend but, as the figure suggests, total solar irradiance could very likely have increased from 1980 to 2000.

Problems with the Global Surface Temperature Record

Once again it is the uncertainty in the data that makes it difficult to correctly interpret climate change. Even the global warming of about 0.8°C since 1900 may be uncertain. In fact, during this period the land warmed by about 1.1°C, while the oceans warmed by about 0.6°C (Figure 5.9). This difference appears to be too significant to be explained only by the different thermal inertia between the ocean and the land regions. It could be partially due to an underestimation of the urban heat island effect by at least 10-20%, to land use changes or perhaps to the fact that several meteorological stations located in cold regions were closed after 1960.[12] The US temperature record present a smaller warming trend since 1880 than the global temperature records. Given the better quality of this record, this finding may suggest that part of the reported global warming may be spurious. If the warming trend has been overestimated (or if it was partially due to land use changes), the effect of CO_2 and CH_4 on climate change has to be reduced for this reason as well.

A large 60 year Cycle in the Temperature Record

A reasonable alternative is to extract any relevant physical information from the temperature fluctuations. It has been observed that several multi-secular climatic and oceanic records present large cycles with periods of about 50-70 years with an average of 60 years Figure 5.10 shows the global temperature record detrended of its quadratic upward trend depicted in Figure 5.1. This sequence has been filtered of its fast fluctuations (by applying a six year moving average smooth algorithm) and it has been plotted against itself with a time-lag of about 60 years. The figure clearly suggests the existence of an almost perfect cyclical correspondence between the periods 1880-1940 and 1940-2000. The peak in 1880 repeats in 1940 and again in 2000. The smaller peak in 1900 repeats in 1960. This 60-odd year oscillation cannot be associated with any known anthropogenic phenomenon.

[12]The other IPCC model scenario runs also fail to reproduce this 60-year cycle. These climate model simulations can be downloaded from the IPCC Data Archive at Lawrence Livermore National Laboratory (http://climexp.knmi.nl/selectfield co2.cgisomeone@somewhere). However, this is not the only shortcoming of the climate models adopted by the IPCC. These models have predicted an increase in the warming trend with altitude in the tropic troposphere due to anthropogenic GHG emissions, but balloon and satellite temperature observations have shown a significant disagreement with the model predictions. (Douglass D. H., J. R. Christy, B. D. Pearson and S. F. Singer (2007), A comparison of tropical temperature trends with model predictions, Intl. J. Climatology, DOI: 10.1002/joc.1651). A list of comparison of model predictions with actual observations and the incompatibility between the two was prepared by Douglas Hoyt: Greenhouse Warmng Scorecard Updated 4/2/2006.

On the contrary, Figure 5.11 shows the global temperature as reproduced by a typical climate model such as the GISS ModelE, one of the major climate models adopted by the ICC 2007. The failure of the model to reproduce the 60 year cycle is evident from the Indeed, all IPCC climate models have the same failing.

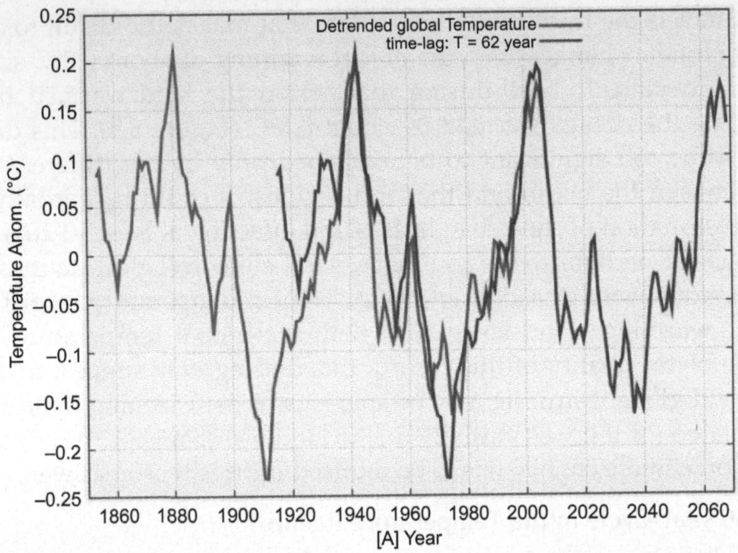

Fig. 5.10: The 60 year cycle modulation of the temperature. (Red) global temperature detrended of its quadratic upward trend which is shown in Figure 1. (Blue) the same record time-lag shifted of about 60 years. Note the perfect symmetry between the periods 1880-1940 and 1940-2000 that excludes the fact that these cycles could have had an anthropogenic origin. Even a smaller peak in 1900 repeats in 1960. This overwhelming clear finding, by alone, contradicts the AGWT and the IPCC's claim that 100% of the warming observed from 1970 to 2000 is anthropogenic.

The existence of a natural 60 year cycle with a total (min-to-max) amplitude of at least 0.3°C, as Figure 10 shows, implies that at least 60% of the 0.5°C warming observed since 1970 is due to this cycle. Considering that longer natural cycle can be present and that solar activity was stronger during the second half of the 20th century than during the its first half, the natural contribution to the warming since 1970 may have been even larger than 60%. Human emissions can have contributed at most the remaining 40%, or less, of the warming observed since 1970 (if no overestimation of the global warming is assumed as Section 8 would suggest), not the 100% as claimed by the IPCC. This 60 year cycle has just entered into its cooling phase and this will likely cause a climate cooling, not a warming, until 2030-40, as Figure 10 would suggest.[13]

[13] There is strong observational evidene that the ocean has been cooling since 2003 (Loehl C. (2009), Cooling of the global ocean since 2003, Energy & Environment 20, No. 1 & 2, 101-104).

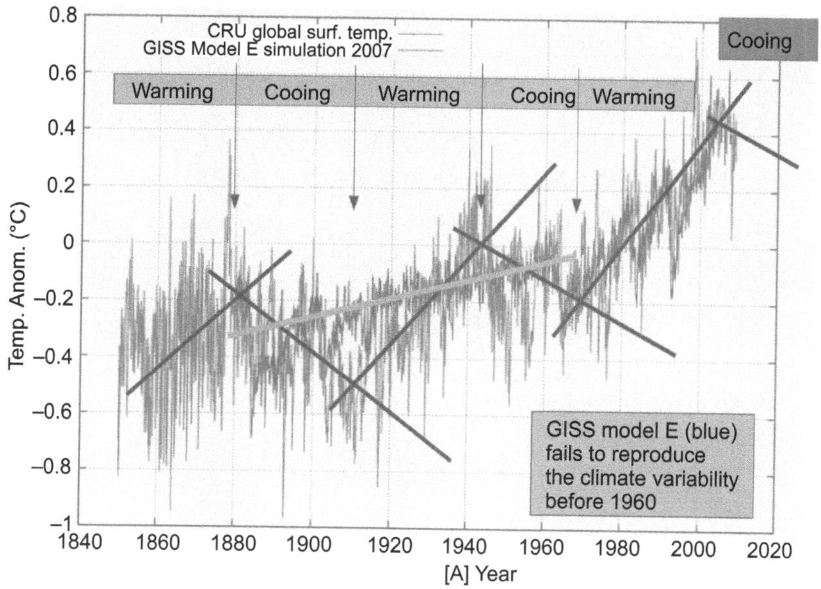

Fig. 5.11: Global temperature (red) against the temperature prediction of the GISS ModelE adopted by the IPCC. The temperature shows a clear cycle of about 60 years, which herein is emphasized by black segments. This 60 year cycle has been explicitly shown in Figure 5.10. This cycle is clearly not reproduced by the climate model simulation. The climate simulation clearly crosses from 1880 to 1970 the black segments instead of reproducing the 60 year modulation of the temperature.

The latter result is quantitatively consistent with the results depicted in Figures 6-8 that suggest a significant change in pre-industrial climate, in contrast to the Hockey Stick, and that solar activity has increased from 1980 to 2000 as Willson of the ACRIM team claims in contrast to PMOD Frohlich's claim. In fact, they are consistent with a reduction of the anthropogenic contribution by 250% as calculated above in Figures 6 and 7. The independent results depicted in Figures 6, 7 and 10 are consistent with each other and would imply that if the CO2 atmosphere concentration doubles, the temperature could rise between 1.0 and 1.5°C, which is significantly less than the IPCC's estimate of 1.5-4.5°C. This result clearly indicates that the possible impacts that anthropogenic GHGs can have on global climate change should be greatly diminished. Consequently, the IPCC's claims about imminent and catastrophic consequences that human emissions are causing and will cause, are unsubstantiated: these claims should be greatly moderated. The existence of a large 60-year natural cycle in the global temperature essentially points toward the conclusion that nature, not human activity, rules the climate.

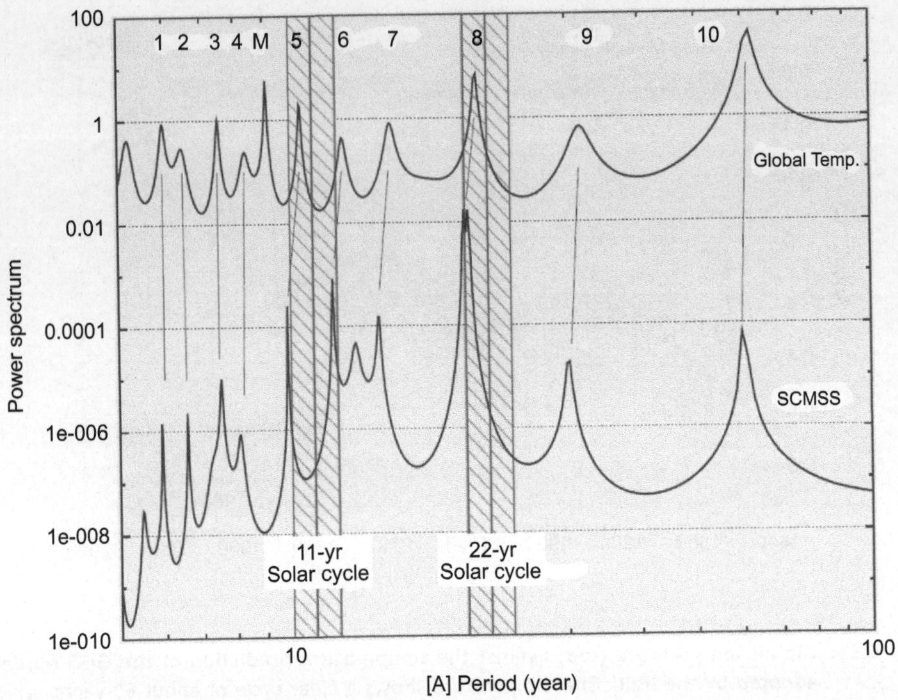

Fig. 5.12: Spectral analysis of the global temperature from 1850 to 2009 (above), and of the speed of the center of mass of the solar system SCMSS (below). Cycles 5 and 8 are also close to the 11 ± 1 and 22 ± 2 year solar cycles. The M cycle in the spectrum of the temperature at about 9 year is absent in the SCMSS record. However, it corresponds to a lunar cycle (Appendix Q-W).

Astronomical Origin of the Climate Oscillations

If the temperature is characterized by natural periodic cycles the only reasonable explanation is that the climate system is modulated by astronomical cycles. Natural cycles known with certainty are the 11 (Schwabe) and 22 (Hale) year solar cycles, the cycles of the planets and luni-solar nodal cycles. Jupiter has an orbital period of 11.87 years while Saturn has an orbital period of 29.4 years. These periods predict three other major cycles which are associated with Jupiter and Saturn: about 10 years, the opposition of two planets; about 20 years, their synodic cycle; and about 60 years, the repetition of the combined orbits of the two planets. The major lunar cycles are about 18.6 and 8.85 years. Figure 5.12 shows a spectral analysis of the global surface temperature and of a record that depends on the orbits of planets (the speed of the sun relative to the center of mass of the solar system). The two records have almost the same cycles. The temperature record contains the cycles of the planets combined with the two solar cycles of 11 and 22 years and a lunar cycle at about 9.1 years.[14] (See also Appendixes Q-V).

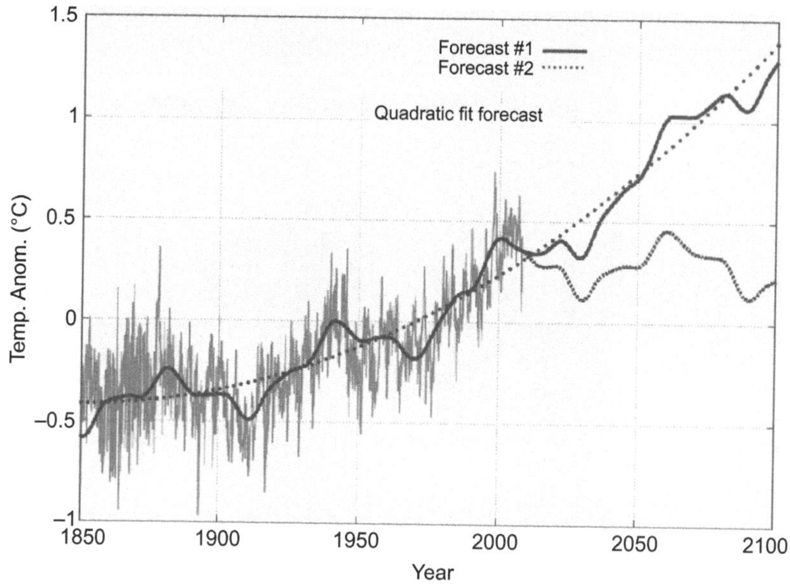

Fig. 5.13: Global temperatures (red) and the reconstruction of temperature using only the 20 and 60 year planetary cycles (in black). The dashed curve indicates simply the quadratic trend of the temperature.

These cycles can be used to reconstruct the fluctuations of the temperature. For example, it is possible to adopt a model using only the major 20 and 60 year cycles plus a quadratic trend of the temperature and the reconstruction of Figure 5.13 is obtained. Other natural cycles associated with the Sun are evident in Figures 6 and 7. The model reconstructs with great accuracy the temperature oscillations since 1850. It suggests that until 2030-2040 the temperature may remain stable if the upward trend in temperature observed from 1850 to 2009 continues in the near future[21] or the global temperature cools if the trend of the secular solar activity decreases, as other independent considerations would suggest.

For example, an imminent relatively long period of low solar activity may be predicted on the basis that the latest solar cycle (cycle #23) lasted from 1996 to 2009, and its length was about 13 years instead of the traditional 11 years. The only known solar cycle of comparable length (after the Maunder Minimum) occurred just at the beginning of the Dalton solar minimum (cycle

[14]The temperature cycle 'M' shown in Figure 12 appears to be exactly at 9.1 ± 0.1 years. This period is exactly between the period of the recession of the line of lunar apsides, about 8.85years, and half of the period of precession of the solar-luni nodes, about 9.3 years.

#4, 1784-1797) that lasted from about 1790 to 1830. The solar Dalton minimum induced a little ice age that lasted 30-40 years as shown in Figure 5.7. Therefore, it is possible that the Sun is entering into a multi-decde period of low activity, which could produce cooling of the climate. (Appendix W).

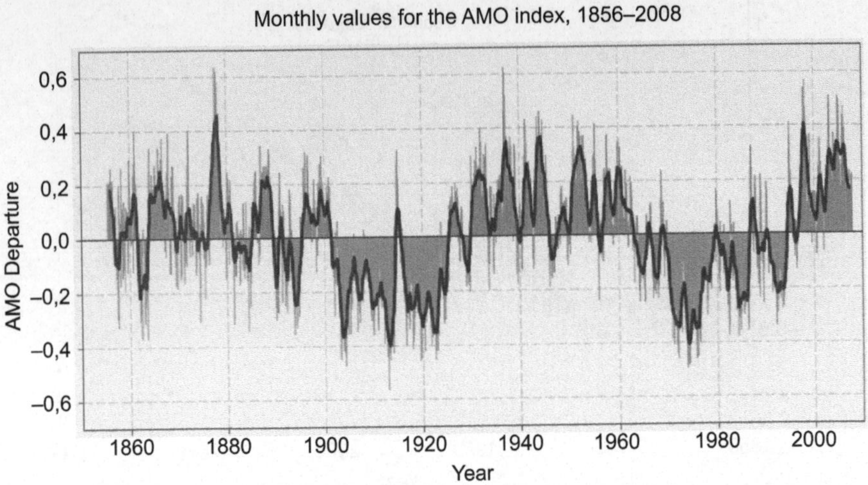

Fig. 5.14: Monthly value of the Atlantic Multidecadal Oscillation (AMO) index. Note the evident 60-year cycle. The figure is adapted from Wikipedia at the voices: Atlantic Multidecadal Oscillation.

The physical mechanisms involved in the process are likely numerous. The gravitational forces of the planets can partially modulate the solar activity. For example, it was noted that the alignment of Venus, Earth and Jupiter presents cycles of approximately 11 years that are in phase with the 11-year solar cycles and multi secular reconstructions of solar activity reveal 60-year cycles associated with the combined orbit of Jupiter and Saturn and other longer cycles. Solar changes could modulate climate change through various physical and chemical processes as explained in Section 6, which are currently not included in the models, as explained in Section 6. There is also the possibility that the Earth's orbital parameters are directly modulated by the gravitational forces of Jupiter, Saturn and the Moon, and the Sun's magnetic force in such a way that the length of day is modulated and/or other planetary parameters are altered. For example, the rotation of the Earth on its axis shows 60-year cycles that anticipate those of the temperature by a few years. Variations in the Earth's rotation and tides caused by the lunar cycles can drive ocean oscillations, which in turn may alter the climate. For example, the Atlantic Multidecadal Oscillation (AMO) and the Pacific Decadal Oscillation (PDO) present clear

60-year cycles and other faster cycles, see Figures 14 and 15. None of these mechanisms are included in the models adopted by the IPCC.[15]

Conclusion

The analysis of several records suggests that the IPCC's claim that humanity is running an imminent danger because of anthropogenic CO_2 emissions[16]

[15] Some of the strongest AGWT advocates are rapidly acknowledging that no significant global warming has been observed since at last 10 years contrary to the IPCC projections. Other factors, besides anthropogenic GHGs, are responsible of climate changes. In February 2010 Phil Jones, the ex director of the CRU center for climate change and the academic at the center of the climategate, has admitted that there has been no global warming since 1995. http://www.dailymail.co.uk/news/article-1250872/Climategate-Uturn-Astonishment-scientist-centre-global-warming-email-row-admits-data-organised.html In 2009 Susan Solomon et al. (Irreversible climate change due to carbon dioxide emissions, PNAS 106 1704-1709) predicted a large, imminent and irreversible warming since 2000 due to anthropogenic emissions. However, in January 2010 Solomon et al. (Contributions of stratospheric water vapor to decadal changes in the rate of global warming, Science 10.1126/science.1182488) acknowledged that stratospheric water vapor, not just anthropogenic CO_2 and CH_4, is an important climate driver of decadal global surface climate change that has largely contribute both to the warming observed from 1980-2000 (30%) and to the slight cooling observed after 2000 (25%). Stratospheric water vapor concentration can also be indirectly driven by UV solar irradiance variations through ozone modulation and its contribution would be included in the phenomenological model herein presented.

[16] The AGWT advocates claim, by using climate model projections, that an increase in anthropogenic CO_2 concentration in the atmosphere will lead to ecological disasters, including wild swings in weather patterns, extended desertification, spread of hotclimate infectious diseases, greater risks of severe damaging weather phenomena such as Katrina-like hurricanes, melting of the glaciers in a few decades that, in turn, will leave hundreds of millions of people without fresh water, cause the extinction of polar bears and raise so much the ocean level that all coasts and their cities will be severely flood beginning, of course, with New York [Al Gore (2006), An Inconvenient Truth, documentary movie]. After that, an increase in anthropogenic CO_2 will reach the tipping point and activate a runaway greenhouse effect that will let the oceans boil away and, ultimately, transform the Earth into a Venus-like state (as James Hansen claimed during his AGU 2008 scientific talk (2008-12-17) "Climate Threat to the Planet"). All this AGWT apocalypticism is extensively rebutted in Climate Change Reconsidered [3] by using scientific research based on actual data. Al Gore's movie has been elegantly rebutted by Christopher Monckton of Brenchley in "35 Inconvenient Truths: The errors in Al Gores movie" SPPI (2007), http://scienceandpublicpolicy.org/monckton/goreerrors.html Regarding the hypothetical tipping point and the runaway greenhouse effect that the Earth would be risking, it should be noted that the atmospheric CO_2 concentration was many times higher than today in almost all earlier geologic periods when no runaway greenhouse effect occurred (Hayden H. C. (2007), A Primer on CO_2 and Climate, Vales Lake Publishing, LLC.). For example, during the Jurassic period (150-200 million years ago) the CO_2 concentration was at least 5 times higher than today (about 2000 ppmv), and during the Cambrian period (500-550 million years ago) it was at least 10-15 times higher than today (4000-6000 ppmv). Interestingly, during the late Ordovician period (490-440 million years ago) the Earth experienced an extremely cold glacial period despite the fact that the CO_2 concentration was at least 10 times higher than today. In fact, most of the greenhouse effect that keeps the Earth warm is regulated by water vapor, not by CO_2. The water vapor concentration, together with the low cloud cover percentage, are not well understood yet but they are likely strongly influenced by the solar changes and cosmic rays. During the last few years there has been a tendency among the AGWT advocates to declare CO_2 to be a pollutant. This is a further serious mystification of the reality. For human health CO_2 is completely innocuous even at a concentration 10 times larger that the 0.039% (390 ppmv) actual atmospheric value. Moreover, CO_2 is as essential to life as oxygen and water.

Carbon dioxide is the major food for plants, which in turn are food for animals, and of course for humans too. Indeed, an increase in atmospheric CO_2 concentration would lead to accelerated plant growth and, therefore, to increased food production. In fact, in man-made greenhouses CO_2 is enriched at 2, 3 or 4 times the natural concentration (about 1000 ppmv) because this causes plants to grow faster and improves plant qality. Thus, an increase of atmospheric CO_2 concentration may also benefit humanity.

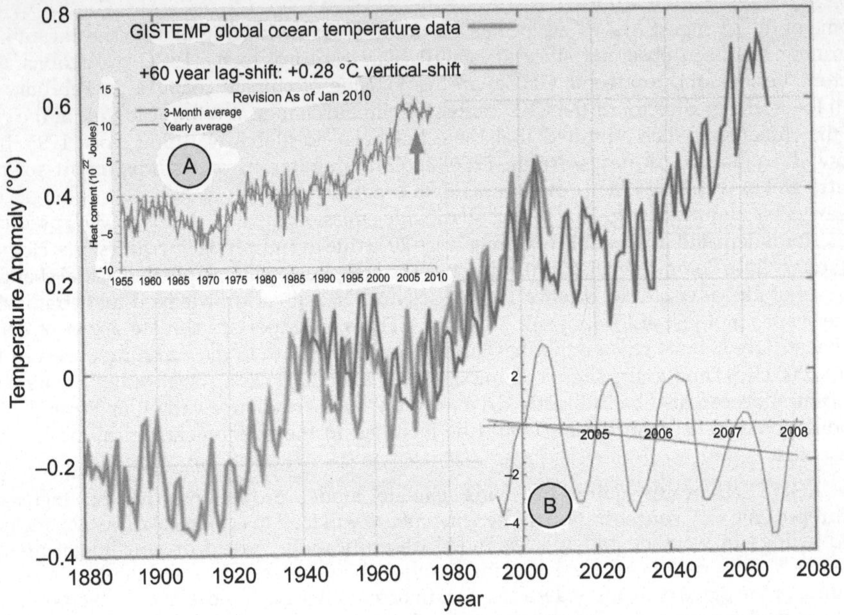

Fig. 5.15: GISTEMP global surface ocean temperature record (shown also in Figure 9) plotted against itself with a 60 year lag shift and a vertical translation. The figure clearly indicates an almost perfect matching between the 1880-1940 and 1940-2000 periods. This further proves the existence of a 60-year natural cycle driving climate change. In particular, note the almost perfect correspondence between the warming trends during the 1910-1940 and 1970-2000 periods. The upward trend during the former period (1910-1940) appears even slightly higher than the upward trend during the latter period (1970-2000) suggesting a warming deceleration. This finding strongly contradicts the IPCC's claim that 100% of the warming observed since 1970 can only be explained with anthropogenic emissions. The figure also suggests a slight ocean cooling until 2030-2040, as does the climateplanetary model of Figure 13, which started in 2002-2003. The upward trend between the first and second half of the last century correlates well with the increased solar activity occurring between the first and second half of the 20th century, as indicated by all solar models (see Ref. and Figure 5.7). If the upward warming trend observed since 1880 continues the ocean will not likely warm more than 0.5°C by 2100. The insert A shows the latest update (Jan/2010) of the Ocean Heat Content (OHC) data from the National Oceanographic Data Center (NODC) (http://www.nodc.noaa.gov/OC5/3M HEAT CONTENT/). This record shows a decrease of the ocean heat content since 2003. This record significantly differs from an earlier version, which showed a slight increase, published in Levitus et al. (2009), Global ocean heat content 1955-2008 in light of recently revealed instrumentation problems, Geophys. Res. Lett. 36, L07608. The insert B depicts ocean heat content as measured by Argo. Argo is a network of over 3000 floats scattered across the globe that measure temperature and salinity of the upper ocean. A cooling trend from 2003 to 2008 is found. Loehl C. (2009), Cooling of the global ocean since 2003, Energy & Environment 20, No. 1&2, 101-104. Both inserts are compatible with a forecast suggesting that ocean temperature will decrease until 2030-2040.

is based on climate models that are too simplistic. In fact, these models fail to reproduce the temperature patterns and the temperature oscillations at multiple time scales. (See also Appendixes H, J, X-Z). These models exclude several mechanisms that are likely to affect climate change related to natural temperature oscillations that have nothing to do with man. Indeed, these oscillations, such as a large 60 year cycle, appear to be synchronized with the oscillations of the solar system. By ignoring these natural mechanisms, the IPCC, also through a questionable choice of data and labels as explained in Section 2, has greatly overestimated the effect of an anthropogenic forcing by a factor between 2 and 3 just to fit the observed global warming in particular from 1970 to 2000, as the climate model depicted in Figure 11 shows. However, a detailed climatic reconstruction suggests that the phenomenological model depicted in Figures 13 and 15 is more satisfactory and is likely to be more accurate in forecasting.

REFERENCES

Boeker E. and R. van Grondelle, Environmental Science, Wiley, 2001.

Crowley T. J., (2000), "Causes of Climate Change Over the Past 1000 Years" Science 289, 270-277.

Frohlich C. and J. Lean (1998), The Sun's Total Irradiance: Cycles, Trends and Related Climate Change Uncertainties since 1978. ¨ Geophys. Res. Lett. 25, 43774380. Frohlich C. (2006), Solar Irradiance Variability Since 1978: Revision of the PMOD Composite ¨ during Solar Cycle 21. Space Sci. Rev. 125, 53-65.

Hansen, J. et al. (2007), Climate Simulations for 1880-2003 with GISS modelE, Clim. Dyn. 29, 661-696.

Hung C-C., (2007), Apparent Relations Between Solar Activity and Solar Tides Caused by the Planets, report NASA/TM2007-214817. http://gltrs.grc.nasa.gov/Citations.aspx?id=330

Huang S. (2004), Merging Information from different Resources for New Insights into Climate Change in the Past and Future, Geophys. Res. Lett. 31, L13205.

IPCC AR4-WG1: Solomon, S., D et al. (eds) in Climate Change 2007: The Physical Science Basis.Contribution of Working Group I to the Fourth Assessment Report of the Intergovernmental Panel on Climate Change, (Cambridge University Press, Cambridge, 2007).

Idso C. and S. F. Singer, (2009), Climate Change Reconsidered: 2009 Report of the Nongovernmental Panel on Climate Change (NIPCC), Chicago, IL: The Heartland Institute. http://www.climatechangereconsidered.org/

Kirkby J. (2007), Cosmic Rays and Climate, Surveys in Geophys. 28, 333-375.

Klyashtorin L.B. and Lyubushin, A.A. (2007). Cyclic Climate Changes and Fish Productivity. Moscow, VNIRO Publishing. & Klyashtorin, L.B., V. Borisov, and A. Lyubushin (2009), Cyclic Changes of Climate and Major Commercial Stocks of the Barents Sea, Mar. Biol. Res. 5, 4-17.

Knutti R., G. C. Hegerl (2008), The Equilibrium Sensitivity of the Earths Temperature to RadiationChanges, Nature Geoscience 1, 735-743.

Loehle C., and Mc Culloch, J.H., (2008), Correction to: A 2000-year Global Temperature Reconstruction based on Non-tree ring proxies. Energy Environ. 19, 93100.

Li Y. Y., K. J. Willis, L. P. Zhou, and H. T. Cui (2006), The Impact of Ancient Civilization on the Northeastern Chinese Landscape: Palaeoecological Evidence from the Western Liaohe River Basin, Inner Mongolia, The Holocene 16, 1109-1121.

Mann, M. E., R. S. Bradley and M. K. Hughes, (1998), Global-scale Temperature Patterns and Climate Forcing over the Past Six Centuries. Nature 392, 779-787. Mann M. E., R. S. Bradley, and M. K. Hughes, (1999), "Northern Hemisphere Temperatures during the Past Millennium: Inferences, Uncertainties, and Limitations," Geophysical Research Letters 26, 759-762.

Moberg A., D. M. Sonechkin, K. Holmgren, N. M. Datsenko and W. Karlen, (2005), "Highly variable Northern Hemisphere′ Temperatures Reconstructed from low- and high-Resolution Proxy Data," Nature 443, 613-617.

Mazzarella, A. (2008), Solar Forcing of Changes in Atmospheric Circulation, Earth's Rotation and Climate, The Open Atmospheric Science Journal 2, 181-184.

McKitrick R. and P. Michaels (2007), Quantifying the Influence of Anthropogenic Surface Processes and Inhomogeneities on Gridded Global Climate Data, J. of Geophysical Research, 112, D24S09.

Ogurtsov, M. G., Y. A. Nagovitsyn, G. E. Kocharov, and H. Jungner (2002), Long-period Cycles of the Suns Activity Recorded in Direct Solar Data and Proxies, Solar Phys. 211, 371-394.

Rockstrom J., ¨ et al. (2009), A Safe Operating Space for Humanity, Nature 461, 472-475.

Scafetta N., (2009), Empirical Analysis of the Solar Contribution to Global Mean Air Surface Temperature Change, J. of Atm. and Sol.-Terr. Phys. 71, 1916-1923.

Scafetta N., Climate Change and Its Causes: A Discussion about Some Key Issues, at the U. S. Environmental Protection Agency, DC USA, February 26, 2009.

Scafetta N., and R. C. Willson (2009), ACRIM-gap and TSI Trend Issue Resolved using a Surface Magnetic Flux TSI Proxy Model, Geophys. Res. Lett. 36, L05701. Willson, R. C., and A. V. Mordvinov (2003), Secular Total Solar Irradiance Trend during Solar Cycles 21-23, Geophys. Res. Lett., 30(5), 1199-2002.

Svensmark H, Bondo T and Svensmark J. (2009), Cosmic Ray Decreases Affect Atmospheric Aerosols and Clouds, Geophys. Res. Lett. 36, L15101.

Climate Change and Agro-Edaphic System **Pages 127–146**
Edited by: Dr. Alka Chauhan & Dr. Pawan Kumar 'Bharti'
ISBN: 978-93-86841-98-8
Edition: 2019
Published by: Discovery Publishing House Pvt. Ltd., New Delhi (India)

6

Soil Microorganisms and Climate change

[1]P. Dhevagi, [2]C. Ponniah

ABSTRACT

Microorganisms present in the soil are important for many ecological processes that support the life. It plays an important role in the ecosystem especially the production and utilisation of green house gases. Since the global climate is changing continuously, it is important to understand the possible feedbacks from soil to the atmosphere. Extra plant growth due to increased CO_2 inflow accelerates soil microorganisms with extra energy. But at least some of that extra carbon also provides fuel to microorganisms whose byproducts, nitrous oxide and methane, end up in the atmosphere. Due to severe impact of climate change, series steps have been taken to reduce the impact by rectifying the source of causes. This article focuses on the action and reaction of soil microbial community to climate change.

Keywords: Soil microorganisms–Factors Influencing-climate change.

Introduction

Early microbiologists recognised that if there were no decomposers in the soil, we would have been buried in organic debris long ago. In recent years, our knowledge about soil microbes has been greatly advanced, which makes us to understand the role of these organisms in the transformation of matter in soil processes and plant growth. Microbes in the soil are important to us in maintaining soil fertility / productivity, cycling of nutrient elements in the biosphere and sources of industrial products such as enzymes, antibiotics, vitamins, hormones, organic acids etc. At the same time certain soil microbes are the causal agents of human and plant diseases.

Pasteur established the fact that the mechanism of decomposition of organic matter by microorganisms depends not only upon the nature of the organisms but also upon the environmental conditions under which the process is taking

[1] Assistant Professor, Department of Environmental Sciences, Tamil Nadu Agricultural University, Coimbatore – 641003

[2] Special Officer (Vigilance and Disciplinary Proceedings) and Professor (ENS), Tamil Nadu Agricultural University, Coimbatore-641003.

place. Soil microorganisms (Flora & Fauna), just like higher plants depends entirely on soil for their nutrition, growth and activity. Microorganisms found in the soil are vital to many of the ecological processes that sustain life such as nutrient cycling, decay of plant matter, consumption and production of trace gases, and transformation of metals (Panikov, 1999). Thus, soil microbial communities play a critical role in ecosystem processes. These processes were governed by environmental variables, such as soil type and texture, temperature, moisture or pH, also management practices such as cropping systems (Cavigelli *et al.*, 2005). All these factors play a great role in determining not only the number and type of organism but also their activities. Variations in any one or more of these factors may lead to changes in the activity of the organisms which ultimately affect the global climate (Kratz and Jane, 2014).

Due to severe impact of climate change, series steps have been taken to reduce the impact by rectifying the source of causes. Since soil microorganisms plays an important role in the ecosystem especially the production and utilisation of green house gases, it is the right time to understand how soil microorganisms are influenced by climatic factors and vice versa.

Types of Soil Microorganisms

Soil is now believed to be a living system, containing a dynamic population of organisms/microorganisms. The soil organisms are broadly classified into two groups viz soil fauna and soil flora. Soil fauna divided into microfauna (Protozoa, Nematodes) and macrofauna (Earthworms, moles, ants & others) and Soil Flora divided into microflora and macroflora. Microflora includes bacteria, fungi, yeast, actinomycetes and algae eg. BGA and macroflora includes roots of higher plants.

Cultivated soil and the soils rich in organic matter contain much more population than fallow land, sandy and eroded soils. Soil microbial communities remain mysterious mainly because of their extraordinary complexity (Sadowsky and Schortemeyer, 1997). Soil microbial communities generally consist of autotrophs, heterotrophs, aerobes and anaerobes. For example, most agricultural soils contain both aerobic and anaerobic locations within the pore structure of the soil particles; thus, other than with a rice paddy, it can be misleading to call a soil aerobic or anaerobic (Granatstein and Bezdicek, 2003). However, this field of study has recently benefited from the combination of molecular techniques to describe microbial communities with more sophisticated phylogenetic techniques for analyzing and comparing communities.

Factors Affecting Soil Microorganisms

Microbial processes can significantly shape the effects that global climate change has on terrestrial ecosystems. Climate change studies often focus on life at the macroscopic scale and due to advanced phylogenetic technique, attention towards microscopic level also increased in recent days. There are many physical factors which affect the activity of the soil biota (Killham, 1993). The major soil factors which influence the microbial population, distribution and their activity in the soil are 1. Soil fertility, 2. Cultural practices 3. Soil moisture, 4.Soil temperature 5. Soil aeration 6. Light 7. Soil pH 8. Organic matter 9. Food and energy supply 10. Nature of soil 11. Microbial associations and 12. Root exudates.

Soil minerals are weathered by bacteria and fungi either as a direct source of energy for the soil biota (chemoautotrophs) or a consequence of the production of acids. The organic matter is consisting of three components, each differing in composition and function. The biologically active fraction is the smallest and turns over every 1-5 years and is the most important for microbes, nutrient cycling, and disease suppression. Microbial biomass carbon generally makes up 1-5% of the soil carbon. The organic matter, serves as a source of food nutrients as well as energy required by the soil organisms. Nutrients (macro and micro) and organic constituents of humus are responsible for absence or presence of certain type of microorganisms and their activity. For example activity and presence of nitrogen fixing bacteria is greatly influenced by the availability of molybdenum and absence of available phosphate restricts the growth of *Azotobacter*.

Pesticide, fungicide and weedicide application have their effect on soil organisms. These chemicals are either degraded by the soil organisms or leaves toxic residues, which are hazardous to microbial activity in the soil. Tillage operations facilitate aeration; moisture and temperature thereby increase the biological activity of organisms. Crop rotation with legume maintains N_2 fixing bacteria and there by improve soil fertility. Liming of acid soils increases the population of bacteria and actinomycetes and lowers the fungal population. Fertilizers and manures applied to the soil supply food and nutrition not only to the crops but also to microorganisms in soil and thereby proliferate the activity of microbes. Cover cropping increased the absolute amount of all microbial groups, but Gram-positive bacteria decreased in proportion under cover crops (Buyer *et al* 2010).

Soil moisture serves as source of nutrients, supplies hydrogen / oxygen and acts as solvent and carrier of other food nutrients to the microorganisms. Microbial activity and population proliferate best in the moisture range of 20 to 60%. Under water logged conditions due to lack of soil aeration (Oxygen) anaerobic microflora become active and the aerobes get suppressed. While in the absence of adequate moisture in soil, some of microbes die out due to tissue dehydration and some of them change their forms into resting spores or cysts to overcome the adverse conditions. Direct sunlight is highly injurious to most of the microorganisms except algae. Therefore upper portion of the surface soil is usually devoid of microorganisms. Ultraviolet light can damage

DNA which induces mutations in the organisms resulting in death of the organism or biochemical changes through metabolic pathways. Photochemical degradation will lead to structural changes making them more or less easy to be degraded.

Microorganisms interact with each other giving rise to antagonistic or symbiotic interactions. The association existing between one organism and another influences the population and activity of soil microbes to a great extent. Root exudates and sloughed off material of root surfaces provide an abundant source of energy and nutrients and thus directly or indirectly influence the quality as well as quantity of microorganisms in the rhizosphere region. Vetch shoots increased the amount and proportion of Gram-negative bacteria, fungi, and arbuscular mycorrhizal fungi in the rhizosphere of tomato plants (Buyer *et al* 2010).

Soil reactions also influence the type of bacteria present in soil. For example nitrifying bacteria *(Nitrosomonas & Nitrobacter)* and diazotrophs like *Azotobacter* are absent or inactive in acid soils, while diazotrophs like *Beijerinckia, Derxia,* and sulphur oxidizing bacteria like *Thiobacillus thiooxidans* are active in acidic soils. pH directly affects the solubility of elements. At acidic pH, aluminium becomes more soluble and hence more available to the organisms with increased toxicity. Essential minerals can become unavailable at extreme pH. For example, phosphorous and managanese become increasingly unavailable at high pH values.

Soil temperature influences the biological, physical and chemical processes, microbial activity and population in soil. Though microorganisms can tolerate extreme temperature (such as – 60° or + 60°C) conditions, most of the soil microorganisms are mesophilic (25 to 40°C) and optimum temperature is 37°C. Seasonal changes in soil temperature affect microbial population and their activity especially in temperate regions. Cellular processes do not work so efficiently and as the temperature increases away from their upper limit there are irreversible changes to the cell properties leading to cell death. Higher soil temperatures under certain treatments increased the proportion of Gram-positive bacteria and the imposed treatments were much more significant than soil temperature, moisture, pH, and texture in controlling microbial biomass and community structure (Buyer *et al* 2010). As global temperatures continue to rise and precipitation patterns change, it becomes more important to understand possible feedbacks to the climate system (Christensen *et* al. 2007, Meehl *et al.* 2007).

A study was conducted by Kirschner *et al* 2002, reveals that a significant enhancement of bacterial growth followed after rainfall, suggests that the high salt concentration had inhibited bacterial activity. The increase in temperatures would lead to increased decomposition by fungi. Since one by-product of decomposition is carbon dioxide, rising temperatures may lead to greater carbon dioxide release from the soil

Aeration (oxygen and sometimes CO_2) in the soil is essential for better growth of microorganisms. Microbes consume oxygen from soil air and gives out carbon dioxide. Activities of soil microbes is often measured in terms of the amount of oxygen absorbed or amount of CO_2 evolved by the organisms in the soil environment. Under high soil moisture level / water logged conditions, gaseous exchange is hindered and the accumulation of CO_4 occurs in soil air which is toxic to microbes.

Increasing concentrations of atmospheric carbon dioxide (CO_2) can affect biotic and abiotic conditions in soil, such as microbial activity and water content (Zak *et al* 2000, Pendall *et al* 2004). In turn, these changes might be expected to alter the production and consumption of the important greenhouse gases nitrous oxide (N_2O) and methane (CH_4) (Pendall *et al* 2004, Smith *et al* 2003). They showed using meta-analysis, that increased CO_2 (ranging from 463 to 780 parts per million by volume) stimulates both N_2O emissions from upland soils and CH_4 emissions from rice paddies and natural wetlands (Table 6.1).

Table 6.1: Microorganisms and Reaction in the Production and Consumption of Atmospheric Trace Gases (Conrad, 1996)

Trace gas	Production in		Consumption in	
	Upland soil	Wetland soil	Upland soil	Wet land soil
H_2	N_2 – Fixing bacterias	Fermenting bacteria	Abiontic soil hydrogenases	Methanogens, sulphate reducers, ferric iron reducers (Knallgas bacteria)
CO	Chemical conversion of organic carbon	Uncharacterised anaerobic bacteria	Ammonium oxidizers	Uncharacterised anaerobic bacteria (carboxytrophs)
CH_4	Unknown	Methanogens	Unknown methanotrophs	Common methanotrophs
OCS	Microbes with thiocyanate hydrolase, unknown reaction	Microbes with thiocyanate hydrolase, unknown reaction	Microbes with anhydrase, unknown reaction	Microbes with carbonic anhydrase, unknown reaction
N_2O	Nitrifiers, denitrifiers, DNRA	Denitrifiers, DNRA	Denitrifiers	Denitrifiers
NO	Nitrifiers, denitrifiers, DNRA, chemical decomposition of nitrite	Denitrifiers, DNRA	Denitrifiers, heterotrophic bacteria, methanotrophs,	Denitrifiers, (heterotrophic bacteria, methanotrophs)

Soil Microbes and Climate Change

Climate change affects not only plants and animals and but also soil microbes. The effect of climate change on soil microorganisms is given in Fig. 6.1. Climate change affects soil carbon through various ways, both directly and indirectly. With reference to the direct effects even 1°C increase can cause increased ecosystem respiration in sub arctic peat land (Dorrepaal *et al* 2009). Direct effects include the influence on soil microbes and green house gas production, because increased temperature stimulates microbial activity and carbon dioxide production. Indirect effect results from increased productivity, which alters soil physic conditions, root exudates, litter and microbial activity. Heterotrophs convert the organic carbon to carbondioxide and autotrophs do the opposite. Work done so far suggest that the transfer of carbon through roots of plants to the soil plays an important role in regulating ecosystem responses to climate change (Bardgett, 2008, 2011, Dorrepaal *et al* 2009 and Schuur *et al,* 2009) Soil is a vast carbon dioxide factory. As these microorganisms consume carbon-based materials found in soil, they release carbon dioxide gas into the atmosphere as a normal part of their metabolism. The fungi, like other soil microbes, utilize carbon in the soil for growth, releasing carbon dioxide as a by-prduct.

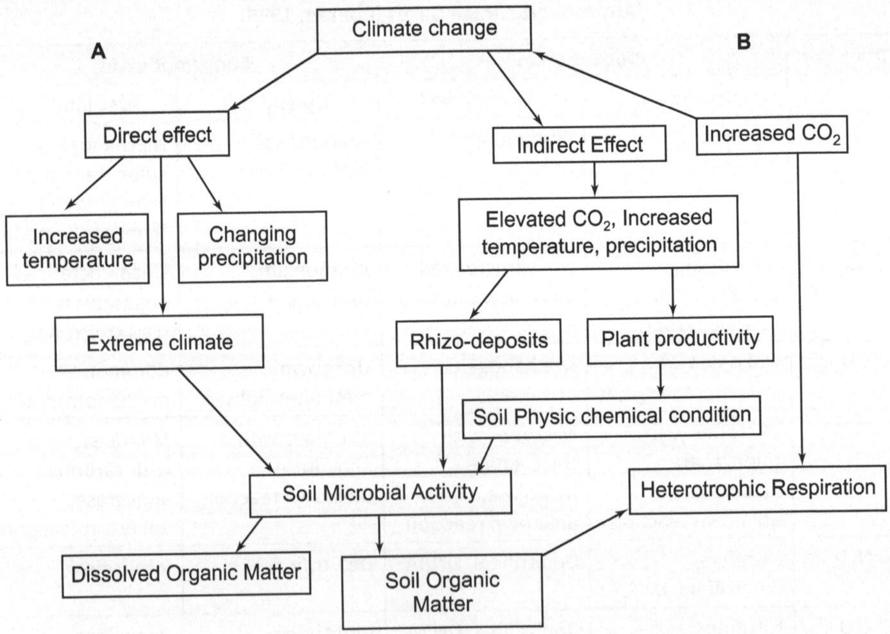

Fig. 6.1: Effect of Climate change on Soil Microorganisms (Bardgett *et al* 2008)

Long periods of drought and heavy rainfall may lead to a change in the nutrient balance in soils. In extreme cases, it may even increase greenhouse gas emissions like carbon dioxide (CO_2), methane (CH_4), nitrous oxide (N_2O), and nitric oxide (NO), but the exact responses may not be known.

Rising temperatures are also having an effect on snowpack and glaciers and that could be detrimental to the communities of microorganisms living below them. As global temperatures rise and glaciers retreat, these microorganisms lose their habitat and may become extinct. The microbial activity under the snowpack is high in coniferous forests especially high in the late winter as the snowpack provides ideal temperatures and moisture for the growth of snow mold. To the average suburban dweller, snow mold may just be another disease that damages the lawn, but in the coniferous forest ecosystem, these mats serve an important function. Snow mold are extremely rapidly growing at very low temperatures – below freezing and contribute about 10-30% of the total year-round carbon dioxide production at these sites. As global temperatures rises the late winter period of subfreezing temperatures will shorten, and snow packs may be less as well.

As the soils warm, snow molds will have less water and will produce less carbon dioxide, which may sound good in terms of global warming, but the trees in this system also depend on snow melt water and will ultimately die under extreme drought, thus leading to an overall decrease in carbon fixation by the system.

Table 6.2: Examples of Structural Changes during Growth at Low and High Temperature

Structural change	Examples	References
Increase in cell size	*Candida utilis*	Rose (1968); Olson and Nottingham (1980); Herbert (1986)
Decline in PLFA content in cellular membrane	Pure cultures of bacteria	Rose 1989 and Zogg *et al* 1997.
Filament formation;	*Escherichia coli*; *Pseudomonas putida*; *Salmonella enteritidis* PT4 strain E isolate	Shaw (1968), Jensen and Woolfolk (1985), Phillips *et al* (1998)
Mesosome deterioration	*Bacillus subtilis*	Neale and Chapman 1970
Formation of a double cell wall	*Bacillus subtilis*	Neale and Chapman 1970
lipase and proteinase production	*Pseudomonas* and certain other genera	Wouters *et al.*, 1999.
Red pigments at a lower temperature (25°C) compared with no red pigment produced at 37 °C	*Serratia marcescens*	Wouters *et al.*, 1999.
1000-fold increase in survival due to pre-treatment at 20 °C	*Streptococcus thermophilus*	Dufrenne *et al.*, 1997 and Gay and Cerf, 1997.

While rising temperatures may be reducing microbial carbon dioxide production, rising levels of carbon dioxide due to human activity can cause subtle but important shifts in the composition of microbial populations (Jim Sliwa, 2008). Ruess *et al.* (1999) investigated the effects of environmental manipulations simulating climate change on soil microorganisms and nematode populations. Soil temperature was enhanced by using passive greenhouses and the impact on soil organisms with and without NPK fertilizer addition was assessed. During temperature enhancement with or without fertilizer application led to a doubling of the population density, whereas fertilization alone caused an increase of about one third. The environmental manipulations resulted in a greater microbial biomass C and active fungal biomass in the elevated soil temperature. Increased density was also recorded for bacterial and fungal feeding nematodes at both sites. The results suggest that nematodes have an important impact on microbial biomass and turnover rates in the two subarctic systems. Elevated soil temperature apparently will lead to increased grazing on microorganisms, contributing to enhance net N and P mineralization rates and plant nutrient availability. However, biodiversity was generally affected negatively by the environmental manipulations.

Soil Microorganisms and Carbon

The world's soils contain 3.3 times more C than is contained in the atmosphere and 4.5 times more than the biotic pool (Lal, 2004). Whatever change occurs in climate will enhance the decomposition of this stored carbon, shifting soils from being carbon sinks to sources of atmospheric carbon dioxide and accelerates climate change.

Over the past two decades, experiments in pots, growth chambers and open-top chambers, and FACE (free air carbon dioxide enrichment) have demonstrated that enrichment of atmospheric CO_2 can substantially modify the soil environment, by increasing belowground C allocation, and changing water and nutrient availability. In this conceptual model, atmospheric CO_2 enrichment indirectly affects soil microbial biomass, community structure and activities by altering carbon, nutrient and water availability (Shujin Hu *et al.*, 1999) (Fig. 6.2).

Several studies show that increased temperatures accelerate rates of microbial decomposition, thereby increasing CO_2 emitted by soil respiration and producing a positive feedback to global warming (Allison *et al.*, 2010). In general, the response of soil microorganisms to warming remain uncertain that increased microbial activity in response to global warming will be sustained due to short term depletion of soil carbon or soil microorganisms may adopt to global warming.

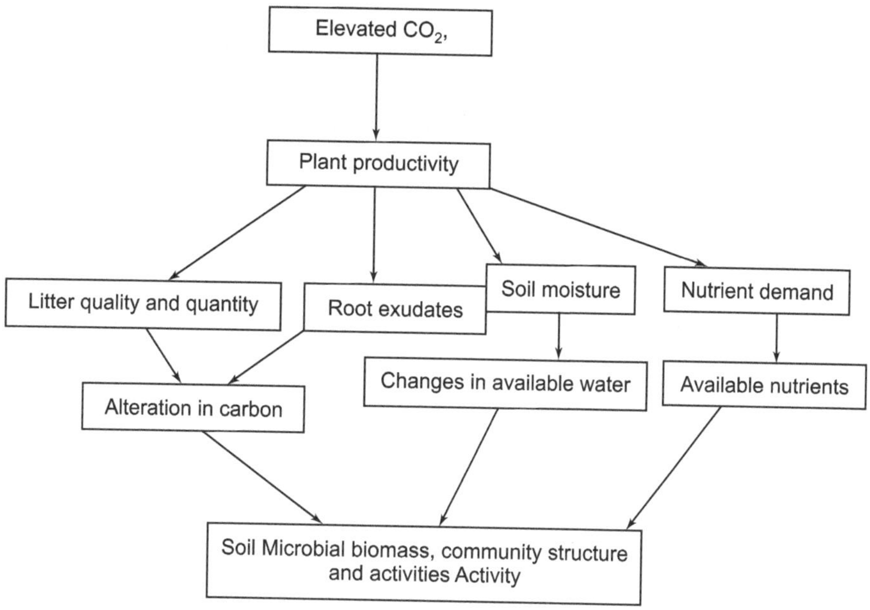

Fig. 6.2: Effect of elevated CO_2 on Soil Microorganisms

Impacts on microbial processes might feed back to elevated atmospheric (CO_2) directly by altering the rates of decomposition and CO_2 release, and/or indirectly by modifying nutrient transformations and transfer, plant community structure and further CO_2 uptake by plants (Paterson, 1997; Hodge, 1996 and Rouhier, 1994). Elevated CO_2concentration alters the relative availability of carbon (C) and nitrogen (N) for microbes over time, which affects microbial feedbacks to further plant growth (Fig. 6.3).

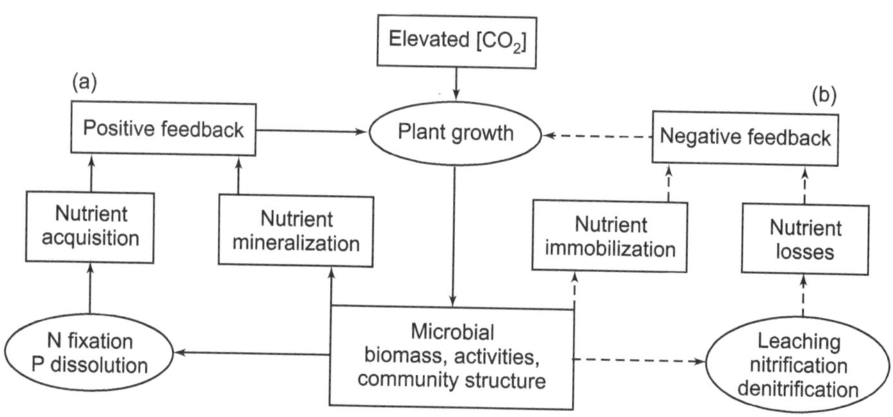

Fig. 6.3: Soil miroorganisms feed back to enhanced plant growth caused by elevated CO_2 concentration

(a) Positively, by promoting nutrient acquisition and facilitating nutrient mineralization (solid lines), (b) Negatively, by increasing nutrient immobilization and losses (broken lines)

When C is limiting to microbes, enhanced C inputs caused by elevated (CO_2) stimulate microbial activities and increase N availability for plant growth (a, unbroken lines). (b) As N accumulates in less labile pools, N deficiency limits microbial growth and activities, and retards N mineralization, negatively feeding back to plant growth (dashed lines). The dashed arrow from 'elevated (CO_2) to plant growth means that elevated (CO_2) does not have effects on plant growth because nutrient limitation constrains the plant response (Diaz, 1993 and Zak, 1993).

The rapid increase of carbon dioxide (CO_2) in the atmosphere over the last century has led to an increased global ecosystem C storage, at least temporarily, by stimulating photosynthesis (Hungate, 1997). However, the fate of this C and its effects on soil microbial communities are uncertain. Predicted changes in atmospheric CO_2 are small compared to the relatively high CO_2 concentrations in the pore space of active soils, so effects of elevated atmospheric CO_2 on soil microbes are generally mediated by plant root production and exudation (Rygiewicz, 1997).

In response to elevated CO_2, microbial biomass and activity have been observed to decrease, increase, or remain unchanged (Elhottova, 1997). No consistent effects of increased CO_2 on soil microbial community composition have yet emerged. CO_2-induced changes in microbial community composition have been detected in some cases, but none were found in others (Cotruto and Ine son, 1996).

Although rising atmospheric CO_2 is likely to affect soil fungi to a greater extent than bacteria, a number of experiments indicate there could be increases in total soil bacterial biomass in addition to functionally significant shifts in community composition (Drigo *et al.*, 2008). For example, the rhizosphere colonizers B*urkholdi*a and *Pseudomonas* were both stimulated by atmospheric CO_2 enrichment, whilst *Bacillus* species found primarily in bulk soil were not (Drigo *et al.*, 2009). Endosymbiotic N_2-fixing bacteria, such as rhizobia, also benefit from plant growth in high CO_2, and often, N_2-fixing plant species respond more strongly to atmospheric CO_2 enrichment than non-N-fixers (Rogers *et al.*, 2009). Increases in rhizosphere rhizobial populations (Schortemeyer *et al.*, 1996), population size of N-fixing organisms in bulk soil (Allen, 1990), increases in the size and number of root nodules (Serraj *et al.*, 1998), are all common effects of atmospheric CO_2 enrichment. Whilst stimulation of N fixation by CO_2 enrichment almost always occurs in managed plant systems that receive supplemental fertilization, the response of rhizobia in natural systems are sometimes dampened by multiple resource limitations (Groenigen *et al.*, 2006; Rogers *et al.*, 2009).

Changes in root deployment and C allocation patterns caused by CO_2 enrichment may lead to different outcomes over different time scales. For instance, effects of CO_2 enrichment (600 p.p.m.) on microbial biomass and community structure associated with perennial ryegrass (Lolium perenne) changed during the course of an 8-year FACE experiment. Exposure to CO_2 enrichment increased the population of *Pseudomonas* spp. After 3 years, but no effect of CO_2 enrichment was noted after 8 years (Marilley *et al.*, 1999, Tarnawski *et al.*, 2006). *Pseudomonas spp.* that secrete Fe-chelating siderophores were stimulated by exposure to long-term CO_2 enrichment. This is significant because the disease suppressive nature of many rhizobacteria is sometimes attributed to their ability to secrete siderophores. These molecules apparently complex with Fe3+, leading to inhibition of competing rhizosphere organisms that have a low affinity for iron. For example, siderophore production by rhizobacteria was linked to decreases in plant susceptibility to the fungal pathogens that cause rice blast disease (Naureen *et al.*, 2009) and *fusarium* wilt (de Boer *et al.*, 2003).

Soil Microorganisms and Methane

Methane is another important greenhouse gas and is 25 times more effective than CO_2 at trapping heat radiated from the Earth (Schlesinger and Andrews, 2000). Microbial methanogenesis is responsible for both natural and human-induced CH_4 emissions since methanogenic archaea reduce carbon into methane in anaerobic, carbon-rich environments such as ruminant livestock, rice paddies, landfills, and wetlands. Not all of the methane produced ends up in the atmosphere however, due to methanotrophic bacteria, which oxidize methane into CO_2 in the presence of oxygen. When methanogens in the soil produce methane faster than can be used by methanotrophs in higher up oxic soil layers, methane escapes into the atmosphere (Willey *et al.*, 2009). Methanotrophs are therefore important regulators of methane fluxes in the atmosphere, but their slow growth rate and firm attachment to soil particles makes them difficult to isolate. Further exploration of these methanotrophs' nature could potentially help to reduce methane emissions if they can be added to the topsoil of landfills, and capture some of the methane that would normally be released into the atmosphere.

Soil Microbes and Nitrogen

Ongoing climate change will lead to more extreme weather events, including severe drought periods and intense drying rewetting cycles. This will directly influence microbial nitrogen (N) turnover rates in soil by changing the water content and the oxygen partial pressure. In N-limited ecosystems strong competition between microorganisms and plants for N exists, which is determined mainly by abiotic factors , including soil temperature, oxygen partial pressure, pH and carbon (C) availability (Huang *et al* , 2007 and Hwang and Hanaki , 2000).

Drought decreases microbial activity and biomass due to osmotic regulation, limited diffusive transport of substrates and extracellular enzymes and decreased microbial motility (Voroney, 2007), additional Carbon limitation occurs due to reduced root biomass and root exudates (Gorissen *et al* 2004). Due to reduced plant performance, the competition for Nitrogen is reduced. Due to reduced soil moisture, O_2 content is increased which enhances nitrification, which is an aerobic process performed by autotrophic bacteria and archaea independent from labile C sources (Kowalchuk , 2001). Increased nitrification will lead to nitrate formation, which may leach to the ground water depending on soil type, reducing the available N pools in soil to a large extend.

High soil moisture leads to enhanced denitrification activities in combination with reduced oxygen levels (Fierer and Schimel, 2003, Pesaro *et al* 2004) and thus increased N losses from the ecosystem. Recent studies on the dynamics of microbes involved in N turnover under different environmental stress factors provide contradictory results. When investigating the influence of temperature and water content on bacterial, archaeal and denitrifying microbial communities, Stres *et al*. 2008, found no significant response of bacterial and denitrifier abundance and community structure, while archaeal communities were strongly influenced by temperature. In contrast, denitrifying communities in a pristine forest soil were highly affected by water content, and both archaeal ammonia oxidizers (AOA) and their bacterial counterpart (AOB) responded to different temperatures and water regimes (Szukics *et al* 2010). The nitrogen levels in the soil increased as temperatures rose, and nitrogen tends to suppress fungal decomposition rates.

In terrestrial ecosystems, the majority of soil N is present in organic macromolecules like chitin, proteins and nucleic acids (Schulten and Schnitzer (1997), Lipson and Na¨sholm (2001), which cannot be assimilated by plants directly (Paul and Clark (1996). Therefore, abundances of apr and chiA transcripts were used as proxy for soil N mineralizing microbes (*)*. For both apr and chiA transcript numbers a significant site effect was observed with lower transcripts under climate change conditions (increased soil temperature and decreased water availability) in average. It was surprising, as soil warming was shown to enhance biological processes like decomposition and N mineralization in general (Shaw and Harte (2001), Domisch *et al* (2006), Brankatschk *et al* 2011, Gschwendtner *et al* 2010, To ¨we *et al* 2010. N mineralization rate was more limited by low soil moisture than promoted by increased temperature (Emmett *et al* 2004, Beier *et al* 2008).

Climate change affects marine microorganisms also in number of ways. Evidences are accumulating on changes in composition, diversity, productivity, rate of metabolism and food web dynamics; and frequent occurrence of eutrophication, harmful blooms, diseases and coral bleaching in marine ecosystems (Vivekanandan, 2013). Climate change could increase the emission of greenhouse gases (NO, N_2O), but this effect might be only temporarily, because in September no difference between the denitrification (Anonymous, 2014). Total PLFA content, which reflects active microbial biomass (Vestal and White, 1989; Tunlid and White, 1992), declined from 95 pmol kg"1 at 5°C to 44 pmol kg"1 at 25°C. This decline in biomass probably resulted from greater metabolic stress at higher temperatures and is consistent with the changes we observed in PLFA profiles.

Mycorrhizal and N_2-fixing relationships are generally enhanced by CO_2 enrichment, but effects of warming are highly variable. Data suggest that energy flow through fungal pathways may be enhanced relative to bacterial pathways by both warming and atmospheric CO_2 enrichment (Pritchard, 2011). Applying emerging genetic techniques holds great promise for understanding how soil organisms will respond to global changes (Roesch *et al.*, 2007; Chakraborty *et al.*, 2008). *Dichanthelium lanuginosum* found in geothermal soils, an effect attributed to the presence of a thermotolerant virus present within the fungus (Redman *et al.*, 2002; Ma´rquez *et al.*, 2007). Gschwendtner *et al 2014* reported that the climate change influences activity pattern of microbial communities involved in denitrification processes to a different extend, which may impact emission rates of the greenhouse gas N_2O.

Soil Borne Pathogens and Climate

According to the IPCC (2007) report, climate change will alter patterns of infectious disease outbreaks in humans and animals. Soil pathogens are no exception: case studies support the claim that climate change is already changing patterns of infectious diseases caused by soil pathogens. For example, over the last 20 years, 67% of the 110 species of harlequin frogs (*Atelopus*) native to tropical regions in Latin America have gone extinct from chytridiomycosisthe, a lethal disease spread by the pathogenic chrytid fungus (*Batrachochytrium dendrobatidis*) (Willey *et al.*, 2009). However, as global warming progresses, *B. dendrobatidis* is able to expand its range due to increasing moisture and warmer temperatures at higher elevations (Muths *et al.*, 2008). This expansion exposes more amphibian communities in previously unaffected or minimally affected areas, specifically at higher elevations, to chytridiomycosisthe. As seen in the case of *Atelopus* harlequin frogs, the spread of soil pathogens due to climatic changes can significantly affect life at the macro scale and ultimately lead to species extinction.

It is currently unclear how rising atmospheric CO_2 will affect fungal and bacterial soil borne diseases because there are simply too few data on this topic. Both increases and decreases in soilborne diseases might be predicted based on documented effects of elevated CO_2 on plant and canopy processes. For instance, increased mycorrhizal symbioses, might improve resistance to soil borne, as well as other diseases. This idea was recently supported by Drigo et *al*. (2009), who found that the density of *Fusarium* spp., a genus that includes common root pathogens, was reduced in the rhizosphere of a mycorrhizal plant exposed to elevated CO_2. The authors suggested that this effect may have been caused by increased competitive ability of the mycorrhizal fungus relative to *Fusarium* under CO_2-enriched conditions. Alternatively, decreased *Fusarium* density may have also been caused by the positive effects of CO_2 enrichment on *Trichoderma*, a beneficial fungal genus well known for its ability to suppress plant-disease-causing fungi (Hagn *et al.*, 2007), or to the significant effect of CO_2 enrichment on bacterial-derived antibiotics also observed. In a recent study on FACE grown soybean, there was no effect of CO_2 or O_3 treatments on sudden death syndrome caused by the soil pathogen *F. virguliforme* (Eastburn *et al.*, 2010); it should be noted that foliar, not root, symptoms were used for diagnostic purposes in that study.

Furthermore, CO_2 enrichment could alleviate soil disease pressure through greater biosynthesis of carbon-based secondary metabolites, such as phenolics (Bezemer & Jones, 1998), or as a consequence of reduced root N concentrations (Thompson *et al.*, 1993). Tomato plants grown at high CO_2 concentrations (700 p.p.m.) were more tolerant of root rot caused by *Phytophthora parasitica*, an effect the authors attributed to increased transcription or post-translational turnover of pathogenesis-related proteins in conjunction with higher photosynthesis and water use efficiency (Jwa and Walling, 2001). On the other hand, root exudation might stimulate the growth of pathogens in the rhizosphere. Such an effect might explain the increase in cotton root infestation by *Rhizoctonia solani* when grown under FACE (Runion *et al.*, 1994). Detailed research studies have to be made to elucidate the likely impacts of elevated CO_2 on soil borne pathogens. It remains unclear how microbial metabolism is impacted by changes in temperature and moisture availability. This may be because microorganisms rely on many different types of metabolism that require various substrates. Some microbial taxa are able to shift their mode of metabolism based on environmental conditions. For example, many species of yeast are able to switch between aerobic and anaerobic metabolism. Other microorganisms rely on a single metabolic pathway and can regulate metabolic rates in response to their surroundings.

Conclusion

Impact of global climate change on soil microbial communities are potentially important, since microbes can control the responses of ecosystems through their effects on C and nutrient cycling. Microorganisms have the capacity to alter the climate. Even a tiny change in the amount of carbon in the soil (due to soil microbe activity) could really influence atmospheric carbon dioxide levels (Nicole Miller, 2007). Recently it has been recognised that marine microbes can also accelerate the pace of climate change by adding more greenhouse gases into seawater (Vivekanandan, 2013). In spite of their important role in the contemporary climate change, marine microorganisms have been neglected in discussions of climate science. Understanding the role of soil microbes as both contributors to and reactive components of climate change can help us to determine whether they can be used to curb emissions (Gschwendtner *et al* 2014).

In the current climate models not much importance was given for the role of soil and marine microbes in the release of green house gases into the atmosphere. The effects of climate change conditions on microbial communities and their functional traits are still poorly understood. The initiation of a new generation of climate-change experiments designed to study interactive effects of multiple climate-change factors, understanding the role of marine microorganisms may help us to reduce the emissions which in turn reduces the climate change.

REFERENCES

Allen L.H (1990) Plant Responses to Rising Carbon Dioxide and Potential Interactions with Air Pollutants. Journal of Environmental Quality 19, 15–34.,

Allison, S.D., Wallenstein, M.D., Bradford, M.A. (2010) Soil-carbon Response to Warming Dependent on Microbial Physiology. *Nature Geoscience* 3, 336-340.

Anonymous, (2014) Climate Change and Nitrogen Turnover in Forest Soils PLOS ONE | DOI:10.1371/journal.pone.0114278 December 2, 2014 15 / 20

Bardget, R.D (2011) Plant–Soil interactions in a Changing World. Biol. Reports, 3:16

Bardgett R.D, Freeman C, Ostle N.J. (2008) Microbial Contributions to Climate Change through Carbon-cycle Feedbacks. ISMEJ. 2:805–14. doi: 10.1038/ismej.2008.58.

Beier C, Emmett B.A, Penuelas J, Schmidt I.K, Tietema A, et al. (2008) Carbon and Nitrogen Cycles in European Ecosystems Respond differently to Global Warming. Sci Total Environ 407: 692–697.

Bezemer T.M, Jones T.H, (1998) Plant–insect Herbivore Interactions in Elevated Atmospheric CO2: Quantitative Analysis and Guild Effects. Oikos 82, 212–22.

Brankatschk R, To¨we S, Kleineidam K, Schloter M, Zeyer J (2011) Abundances and Potential Activities of Nitrogen Cycling Microbial Communities along a Chronosequence of a Glacier Forefield. ISME J 5: 1025–1037

Buyer.J.S , John R. Teasdale, Daniel P. Roberts, Inga A. Zasada, , Jude E. Maul (2010) Factors Affecting Soil Microbial Community Structure in Tomato Cropping Systems, Soil Biology and Biochemistry, 20 (5) : 831–841

Cavigelli, M.A., L.L. Lengnick, J.S. Buyer, D. Fravel, Z. Handoo, G. McCarty, P. Millner, L. Sikora, S. Wright, B. Vinyard and M. Rabenhorst. (2005) Landscape Level Variation in Soil Resources and Microbial Properties in a no-till corn field. Appl. Soil Ecol. 29: 99–123.

Chakraborty S, Luck J, Hollaway G et al. (2008). Impacts of Global Change on Diseases of Agricultural Crops and Forest Trees. CAB Reviews: Perspectives in Agriculture, Veterinary Science, Nutrition and Natural Resources 3, 1–15.

Christensen, J. H., Hewitson, B., Busuioc, A. et al.(2007) In: Climate Change 2007: The Physical Science Basis. Contribution of Working Group I to the Fourth Assessment Report of the Intergovernmental Panel on Climate Change. Solomon, S. et al. (eds.). Cambridge University Press: New York, USA.

Conrad. R. (1996). Soil Microorganisms as Controllers of Atmospheric Trace Gases (H_2, CO, CH_4, OCS, N_2O, and NO) Microbiological Reviews, Dec. 1996, p. 609–640

Cotrufo, M.F and P.Ineson. (1996). Elevated CO_2 Reduces Field Decomposition Rates of *Betula pendula* (Roth) Leaf Litter. Oecologia,106: 525–530.

de Boer M, Bom P, Kindt F *et al.*, (2003). Control of Fusarium Wilt of Radish by Combining Pseudomonas Putida Strains that have different disease-suppressive Mechanisms. Phytopathology 93, 626–32.

Diaz, S. (1993). Evidence of a Feedback Mechanism Limiting Plant Response to Elevated Carbon Dioxide. Nature, 364: 616–617.

Domisch T, Finer L, Laine J, Laiho R (2006) Decomposition and Nitrogen Dynamics of Litter in Peat Soils from Two Climatic Regions under different Temperature Regimes. Eur J Soil Biol 42: 74–81.

Dorrepaal E.S, Toet S, van Logtestijn R.S, Swart E, van de Weg M.J, Callaghan T.V, Aerts R. (2009) Carbon Respiration from Subsurface Peat Accelerated by Climate Warming in the Subarctic. Nature.: 460:616–9. doi: 10.1038/nature08216.

Drigo B, Kowalchuk G.A, van Veen J.A, (2008). Climate Change goes Underground: Effects of Elevated Atmospheric CO_2 on Microbial Community Structure and Activities in the Rhizosphere. Biology and Fertility of Soil 44, 667–79.

Drigo B, van Veen J.A, Kowalchuk G.A, (2009). Specific Rhizosphere Bacterial and Fungal Groups Respond differently to Elevated Atmospheric CO_2. The ISME Journal 3, 1204–17.

Dufrenne, J., E. Delfgou, W. Ritmeester and S. Notermans. (1997). The Effect of Previous Growth Conditions on the lag phase time of some Foodborne Pathogenic Microorganisms. Int. J. Food Microbiol., 34: 89–94.

Eastburn D.M, Degennaro M, Delucia E.H, Dermody O, McElrone A.J, (2010). Elevated Atmospheric Carbon Dioxide and Ozone Alter Soybean Diseases at SoyFACE. Global Change Biology 16, 320–30.

Elhottova, D. (1997). Rhizosphere Microflora of Winter Wheat Plants Cultivated under Elevated CO_2. Plant Soil, 197: 251–259.

Emmett BA, Beier C, Estiarte M, Tietema A, Kristensen HL, et al. (2004) The Response of Soil Processes to Climate Change: Results from Manipulation Studies of Shrublands Across An Environmental Gradient. Ecosystems 7: 625–637.

Fierer N, Schimel JP (2003) A Proposed Mechanism for the Pulse in Carbon Dioxide Production Commonly Observed following the Rapid Rewetting of a Dry Soil. Soil Sci Soc Am J 67: 798–805.

Gay, M and O. Cerf. (1997). Significance of Temperature and Preincubation Temperature on Survival of Listeria Monocytogenes at pH 4.8. Lett. Appl. Microbiol., 25: 257–60.

Gorissen A, Tietema A, Joosten NN, Estiarte M, Penuelas J, et al. (2004) Climate Change Affects Carbon Allocation to the Soil in Shrublands. Ecosystems 7: 650–661.

Granatstein .D and Bezdicek.D.(2003). Monitoring Soil Microbes – Invisible Helper. Tilth Producers Quarterly: 1-7.

Groenigen, K.L.V, Osenberg, C.W. and Hungate B.A. (2011). Increased Soil Emissions of Potent Greenhouse Gases under Increased Atmospheric CO_2. Nature 475: 214 – 216. (doi.10.1038/nature10176)

Gschwendtner S, Reichmann M, Mu¨ ller M, Radl V, Munch J, et al. (2010) Abundance of Bacterialenes Encoding for Proteases and Chitinases in the Rhizosphere of three different Potato Cultivars. Biol Fertil Soils 46: 649–652.

Gschwendtner, S. Javier Tejedor2, Carolin Bimueller, Michael Dannenmann2, Ingrid Ko¨ gel Knabner3, Michael Schloter, (2014). Climate Change Induces Shifts in Abundance and Activity Pattern of Bacteria and Archaea Catalyzing Major Transformation Steps in Nitrogen Turnoverin a Soil from a Mid-European Beech Forest (Retrived PLOS ONE | DOI:10.1371/journal.pone.0114278 December 2, 2014 1 / 20)

Hagn A, Wallisch S, Radl V, Munch J.C, Schloter M, (2007). A New Cultivation Independent Approach to Detect and Monitor Common Trichoderma Species in Soils. Journal of Microbiological Methods 69: 86–92.

Herbert RA. (1986). The Ecology and Physiology of Psychrophilic Microorganisms In: Herbert RA, Codd GA, editors. Microbes in Extreme Environments. London: The Society for General Microbiology, Academic Press. p 1–24 http://digitalcommons.mtu.edu/etds/755

Huang S, Pant H.K, Lu J (2007) Effects of Water Regimes on Nitrous Oxide Emission from Soils. Ecological Engineering 31: 9–15.

Hungate, B.A. (1997). The Fate of Carbon in Grasslands under Carbon Dioxide Enrichment. *Nature,* 388: 576–579.

Hodge, A. (1996). Impact of Elevated CO_2 on Mycorrhizal Associations and Implications for Plant Growth. *Biol.* Fertil. Soils, 23: 388–398.

Hwang S.J and Hanaki K (2000) Effects of Oxygen Concentration and Moisture Content of Refuse on Nitrification, Denitrification and Nitrous Oxide Production. Bioresource Technology 71: 159–165.

IPCC (2007) Intergovernmental Panel on Climate Change, Climate change 2007: Synthesis Report, A contribution of Working groups I, II and III to the Fourth Assessment Report of the IPCC (http://www.ipcc.ch/publications_and_data/publications_ipcc_fourth_assessment_report_synthesis_report.htm>)

Jensen R.H, Woolfolk C.A. (1985) Formation of Filaments by Pseudomonas Putida. Appl Env Microbiol 50:364–72.

Jim Sliwa. (2008). Climate Change could Impact Vital Functions of Microbes. American Society for Microbiology: 25-34.

Jwa N-S and Walling L.L, (2001) Influence of Elevated CO_2 Concentration on Disease Development in Tomato. New Phytologist 149, 509–18.

Killham K, Amato M, , Ladd J.N (1993) Effect of Substrate Location in Soil and Soil Pore-water Regime on Carbon Turnover. *Soil Biol Biochem* **25***:* 57–62.

Kirschner, A. K. T., A. Eiler, T. C. Zechmeister, B. Velimirov, A. Herzig, R. Mach and A. H.Farnleitner. (2002). Climate Change and Soil Microbes. Environmental Microbiol., 4(9): 546–555.

Kowalchuk G.A and Stephen J.R (2001) Ammonia-oxidizing bacteria: A Model for Molecular Microbial Ecology. Annu Rev Microbiol. 55: 485–529.

Kratz, C. and Jane, (2014) Impacts of Climate Change on Soil Microorganisms in Northern Hardwood Forests, Dissertation, Doctoral Research, Michigan Technological University

Lal R, (2004) Soil Carbon Sequestration to Mitigate Climate Change. Geoderma 123, 1–22.

Lipson D and Na¨sholm T (2001) The Unexpected Versatility of Plants: Organic Nitrogen use and Availability in Terrestrial Ecosystems. Oecologia 128: 305–316.

Marilley L, Hartwig U.A, Aragno.M, (1999). Influence of an Elevated Atmospheric CO_2 Content on Soil and Rhizosphere Bacterial Communities Beneath CO_2 Content on Soil and Rhizosphere Bacterial Communities Beneath Lolium Perenne and Trifolium repens under Field Conditions. Microbial Ecology 38, 39–49.

Ma´rquez L.M, Redman R.S, Rodriguez R.J, Roossinck M.J, (2007). A Virus in a Fungus in a Plant: Three-way Symbiosis required for Thermal Tolerance. Science 315, 513–5.

Meehl, G. A. (2007) : In: Climate Change 2007: The Physical Science Basis. Contribution of Working Group I to the Fourth Assessment Report of the Intergovernmental Panel on Climate Change. Solomon, S. et al. (eds.). Cambridge University Press: New York, New York, USA.

Muths, E., Pilliod, D.S., Livo, L.J. (2008). Distribution and Environmental Limitations of an Amphibian Pathogen in the Rocky Mountains, USA. *Biological Conservation* 141, 1484-1492.

Naureen Z, Price A.H, Hafeez F.Y, Roberts.M.R, (2009). Identification of Rice Blast Disease-Suppressing Bacterial Strains from the Rhizosphere of Rice grown in Pakistan. Crop Protection 28, 1052–60.

Neale E.K and Chapman G.B. (1970). Effect of Low Temperature on the Growth and Fine Structure of Bacillus Subtilis. J Bacteriol 104:518–28.

Nicole Miller (2007) Researcher Seeks 'Missing Piece' in Climate Change Models. UW-Madison News, Feb. 13.

Olson J.C and Nottingham P.M (1980) Temperature in Microbial Ecology of Foods Volume 1: Factors Affecting Life and Death of Microorganisms. International Commission on Microbiological Specifications for Foods. London: Academic Press. p 1–37.

Paul E.A and Clark F.E (1996) Ammonification and Nitrification. In: Paul EA, Clark FE, editors. Soil Microbiol Biochem. 2 ed. San Diego: Academic Press. pp. 182–183

Panikov, N.S. (1999). Understanding and Prediction of Soil Microbial Community Dynamics under Global Change. *Applied Soil Ecology* 11, 161-176.

Paterson, E. (1997). Effect of Elevated CO_2 on Rhizosphere Carbon Flow and Soil Microbial Processes. Glob. Change Biol., 3: 363–377.

Pendall E, Bridgham S, Hanson P.J *et al.*, (2004). Belowground Process Responses to Elevated CO_2 and Temperature: A Discussion of Observations, Measurement Methods, and Models. New Phytologist 162, 447–58.

Pesaro M, Nicollier G, Zeyer J, Widmer F (2004) Impact of Soil Drying-rewetting Stress Microbial Communities and Activities and on Degradation of two Crop Protection Products. Appl Environ Microbiol 70: 2577–2587.

Phillips L.E, Humphrey T.J, Lappin-Scott H.M. (1998). Chilling Invokes different Morphologies in two Salmonella Enteritidis PT4 Strains. J Appl Microbiol 84(5):820– 6.

Pritchard .S.G . (2011). Soil Organisms and Global Climate Change, Plant Pathology (2011) 60, 82–99 Doi: 10.1111/j.1365-3059.2010.02405.x

Redman R.S, Sheehan K.B, Stout R.G, Rodriguez R.J, Henson J.M, (2002). Thermotolerance Generated by Plant D Fungal Symbiosis. Science 298, 1581.

Roesch L.F.W, Fulthorpe R.R, Riva A *et al.*, (2007). Pyrosequencing Enumerates and Contrasts Soil Microbial Diversity. The ISME, Journal 1, 283–90.

Rogers A, Ainsworth E.A, Leakey A.D.B, (2009) .Will Elevated Carbon Dioxide Concentration Amplify the Benefits of Nitrogen Fixation Inlegumes? Plant Physiology 151, 1009–16.

Rouhier, H. (1994). Effect of Elevated CO_2 on Carbon and Nitrogen Distribution within a Tree (*Castanea sativa* Mill.) Soil System. Plant Soil, 162: 281–292.

Rose AH. (1968). Physiology of Microorganisms at Low Temperatures.J Appl Bact 31:182–4

Rose, A.H.(1989). Influence of the Environment on Lipid Composition. In C. Ratledge and S.G. Wilkinson (ed.) Microbial Lipids. VOl 2. Academic Press, London: 255-278.

Ruess Liliane, Michelsen Anders, Schmidt Inger and Jonasson Sven. (1999). Simulated Climate change Affecting Microorganisms, Nematode Density and Biodiversity in Subarctic Soils. Plant Soil, 212 (1): 63-73.

Runion G.B, Curl E.A, Rogers H.H, Backman P.A, Rodriguez- Ka´bana R, Helms B.E, (1994). Effects of free-air CO_2 Enrichment on Microbial Populations in the Rhizosphere and Phyllosphere of Cotton. Agricultural and Forest Meteorology 70, 117–30.

Rygiewicz, P.T. (1997). Lifetime and Temporal Occurrence of Ectomycorrhizae on Ponderosa Pine (*Pinus ponderosa* Laws) Seedlings Grown under Varied Atmospheric CO_2 and Nitrogen levels. *Plant Soil,* 189**:** 275–287.

Sadowsky, M.J and M. Schortemeyer. (1997). Soil Microbial Responses to Increased Concentrations of Atmospheric CO_2. Glob. Change Biol., 3**:** 217–224.

Schlesinger, W. H. and Andrews, J. A. (2000). Soil Respiration and the Global Carbon Cycle. *Biogeochemistry* 48, 7–20.

Schulten H.R, Schnitzer M (1997) The Chemistry of Soil Organic Nitrogen: A Review. Biol Fertil Soils 26: 1–15.

Schuur E.A.G, Vogel J.G, Crummer K.G, Lee H, Sickman J.O, Osterkamp T.E.(2011) The Effect of Permafrost thaw on Old Carbon Release and Net Carbon Exchange from Tundra. Nature. 2009;459:556–9. doi: 10.1038/nature08031

Schortemeyer M, Hartwig U, Hendry G, Sadowsky.M.J, (1996). Microbial Community changes in the Rhizospheres of White Clover and Perennial Ryegrass exposed to free Air Carbon Dioxide Enrichment (FACE). Soil Biology and Biochemistry 28, 1717–24.

Serraj R, Sinclair T.R, Allen L.H (1998). Soybean Nodulation and N2 Fixation Response to Drought under Carbon Dioxide Enrichment. Plant, Cell & Environment 21, 491–500.

Shaw M.K. (1968). Formation of Filaments and Synthesis of Macromolecules at Temperatures below the Minimum for Growth of Escherichia Coli. J Bacteriol 95:221–30.

Shaw M.R, Harte J (2001) Control of Litter Decomposition in a Subalpine Meadow- Sagebrush Steppe Ecotone under Climate Change. Ecol Appl 11: 1206–1223.

Shuijin Hu, Mary K Firestone and F. Stuart Chapin.(1999). Soil Microbial Feedbacks to Atmosphere CO_2 Enrichment. Tree, 14(11): 433-437.

Smith, K. A. et al. (2003) Exchange of Greenhouse Gases between Goil and Atmosphere: Interactions of Soil Physical Factors and Biological Processes. *Eur. J. Soil Sci.* 54, 779–791.

Stres.BTjaša Danevθiθ, Levin Pal, MirnaMrkonjić Fuka, Lara Resman, Simona Leskovec, Janez Hacin, David Stopar, Ivan Mahne, Ines Mandic-Mulec (2008) Influence of Temperature and Soil Water Content on Bacterial, Archaeal and Denitrifying Microbial Communities in Drained Fen Grassland Soil Microcosms. FEMS Microbiology Ecology. DOI: http://

dx.doi.org/10.1111/j.1574-6941.2008.00555.x 110-122 First published online: 1 October 2008

Szukics U, Abell G.C.J, Ho¨dl V, Mitter B, Sessitsch A, et al. (2010) Nitrifiers and Denitrifiers Respond Rapidly to Changed Moisture and Increasing Temperature in a Pristine Forest Soil. FEMS Microbiol Ecol 72: 395–406.

Tarnawski S, Hamelin J, Jossi M, Aragno M, Fromin N (2006). Phenotypic Structure of Pseudomonas Populations is Altered under Elevated pCO_2 in the Rhizosphere of Perennial Grasses. Soil Biology and Biochemistry 38, 1193–201.

Thompson G.B, Brown J.K,Woodward F.I (1993). The Effects of Host Carbon Dioxide, Nitrogen and Water Supply on the Infection of Wheat by Powdery Mildew and Aphids. Plant, Cell & Environment 16, 539–46.

Tunlid. A. and White, D.C.(1992). Biochemical Analysis of Biomass Community Structure, Nutrient Status and Metabolic Activity of Microbial Communities in Soil. In. J.Bollag and D. Slotsky(ed.) Soil Biochemistry. Marcel Dekker, New York.

To¨we S, Albert A, Kleineidam K, Brankatschk R, Du¨ mig A, et al. (2010) Abundance of Microbes involved in Nitrogen Transformation in the Rhizosphere of Leucanthemopsis Alpina (L.) Heywood Grown in Soils from Different Sites of the Damma Glacier Forefield. Microb Ecol 60: 762–770.

van Groenigen K.J, Six J, Hungate B.A, de Graaff.M.A, van Breemen N, van Kessel C, (2006). Element Interactions Limit Carbon Storage. Proceedings of the National Academy of Sciences, USA 103, 6571–4.

Vestal, J.R. and D.C.White, (1989). Lipid Analysis in Microbial Ecology. BioScience. 39: 535-541.

Vivekanandan. E. (2013). Role of Marine Microorganisms in Climate Change Retrived on 8.09.2015 (http://www.envismadrasuniv.org/nl20134-Role-of-marine-microorganisms-in-climate-change.html)

Voroney RP (2007) The Soil Habitat. In: Paul EA, Editor. Soil Microbiology, Ecology and Biochemistry. Oxford: Elsevier. pp. 25–49.

Willey, J.M., Sherwood, L.M., Woolverton, C.J. (2009) Prescott's Principles of Microbiology. McGraw-Hill, New York, NY: 2009.

Wouters, J.A., F.M. Rombouts, W.M. deVos, O.P. Kuipers and T. Abee. (1999). Cold Shock Proteins and Low Temperature Response of Streptococcus Thermophilus CNRZ302. Appl. Env. Microbiol., 65: 4436–42.

Zak, D.R. *et al.* (1993) Elevated Atmospheric CO_2 and Feedback between Carbon and Nitrogen Cycles. Plant Soil, 151: 105–117.

Zak, D. R., Pregitzer, K. S., King, J. S. & Holmes, W. E. (2000) Elevated Atmospheric CO_2, fine Roots and the Response of Soil Microorganisms: A Review and Hypothesis. *New Phytol.* 147,201–222

Zogg G. P.,* Zak. D. R., Ringelberg. D. B., Neil W. MacDonald, Kurt S. Pregitzer, and David C. White . (1997). Compositional and Functional Shifts in Microbial Communities Due to Soil Warming Soil Sci. Soc. Am. J. 61:475-481 .

Climate Change and Agro-Edaphic System **Pages 147–162**
Edited by: Dr. Alka Chauhan & Dr. Pawan Kumar 'Bharti'
ISBN: 978-93-86841-98-8
Edition: 2019
Published by: Discovery Publishing House Pvt. Ltd., New Delhi (India)

7 Climate Change and Indian Agriculture

[1]Alok Kumar Patra, [2]Pulak Kumar Patra and
[3]Ranjan Kumar Patra

ABSTRACT

Agriculture is the backbone of India's economy. Although there has been overall growth in agricultural production in the country over the years, there is also substantial variability about the trend. Weather variability is regarded as the primary cause of year-to-year fluctuations in yields. Despite technological advances, such as improved crop varieties, genetically modified organisms, and irrigation systems, weather is still a key factor in agricultural productivity, as well as soil properties and natural communities. Altering cropping seasons, increasing incidence of pests and diseases, rationing water supply, loss of agricultural biodiversity and limiting food supply are all evidences of climate change. These factors force farmers to adapt using meagre resources. A significant effect of global climate change is the altering of rainfall patterns, which affects agriculture in a big way. The adverse effects of climate change on agriculture have become a major course of concern in recent years. The length of the growing season and the type of crop grown are both affected by changes in temperature. Climate change will also modify the availability of water, which will have a profound effect on agricultural productivity.

To deal with effects of climate change, both adaptive measures and mitigation measures are to be taken. The impact of climate change on agriculture can be minimized through better preparedness, mitigation measures and improved response mechanisms. By issuing accurate forecasts and warnings in a form that is readily understood by the farming community can save the crops and farm animals from the risk of weather variability.

[1] Associate Professor (Agronomy), All India Coordinated Research Project on Integrated Farming Systems, Orissa University of Agriculture and Technology, Bhubaneswar-751003, Odisha, India

[2] Associate Professor, Department of Environmental Studies, Institute of Science, Visva-Bharati, Santiniketan-731235, West Bengal, India

[3] Professor (Soil Science & Agricultural Chemistry), College of agriculture, Orissa University of Agriculture and Technology, Bhubaneswar- 751003, Odisha, India

INTRODUCTION

Many aspects of the global climate are changing rapidly. Evidence for changes in the climate system abounds, from the top of the atmosphere to the depths of the oceans. The climate system is the highly complex system consisting of five major components; the atmosphere, the hydrosphere, the cryosphere, the land surface and the biosphere, and the interactions among them. The climate system evolves in time under the influence of its own internal dynamics and because of external forcings such as volcanic eruptions, solar variations and human-induced forcings such as the changing composition of the atmosphere and land-use.

The term 'climate variability' is often used to denote deviations of climatic statistics over a given period of time (*e.g.*, a month, season or year) from the long-term statistics relating to the corresponding calendar period. In this sense, climate variability is measured by those deviations, which are usually termed anomalies.

'Climate change' refers to a statistically significant variation in either the mean state of the climate or in its variability, persisting for an extended period (typically decades or longer). Climate change may be due to natural internal processes or external forcings, or due to persistent anthropogenic changes in the composition of the atmosphere or in land use. The United Nation's Framework Convention on Climate Change (UNFCCC) defines 'climate change' as 'a change of climate behaviour which is attributed directly or indirectly to human activity that alters the composition of the global atmosphere and which is in addition to natural climate variability observed over comparable time periods'. The UNFCCC thus makes a distinction between 'climate change' attributable to human activities altering the atmospheric composition, and 'climate variability' attributable to natural causes. Climate change is a long-term shift in weather conditions measured by changes in temperature, precipitation, wind, snow cover, and other indicators. It can involve both changes in average conditions and changes in variability, including, for example, changes in extreme conditions.

A key difference between climate variability and change is in persistence of 'anomalous' conditions. In other words, events that are used to be rare occur more frequently, or *vice versa*. Occasionally, an event or sequence of events occurs that has never been recorded before, such as the exceptional tsunami in the Indian Ocean in 2004 or hurricane season in the Atlantic in 2005. Yet even that could be a part of natural climate variability. If such a season does not recur within the next 30 years, by looking back it could be called as an exceptional year, but not a 'climate change'. Only a persistent series of unusual events taken in the context of regional climate parameters can suggest that a potential change in climate has occurred.

CAUSES OF CLIMATE VARIABILITY AND CHANGE

Climate change is a movement in the climate system because of internal changes within the climate system or in the interaction of its components, or because of changes in external forcing either by natural factors or anthropogenic activities (IPCC, 1996). Natural variability is a characteristic of the global climate and occurs on both long and short time scales.

Some external influences, such as changes in solar radiation and volcanism, occur naturally and contribute to the total natural variability of the climate system. Other external changes, such as the change in composition of the atmosphere that began with the industrial revolution, are the result of human activity. The influence of solar irradiance changes and volcanic eruptions has been very small relative to the influence of human emissions of greenhouse gases since the beginning of the industrial revolution. The build-up of greenhouse gases in the atmosphere is the primary cause for concern about climate change now and into the immediate future.

The causes of climate change can broadly be divided into two categories, natural and human causes (Patra, 2012). The natural variability and the climate fluctuations of the climate system have always been part of the earth's history; however, there have been changes in concentrations of greenhouse gases in the atmosphere growing at an unprecedented rate and magnitude.

Natural Causes

The earth's climate can be affected by natural factors, such as volcanic eruptions, ocean current, the earth's orbital changes and solar variations.

1. **Volcanic eruptions:** When a volcano erupts it throws out large volumes of sulphur dioxide, water vapour, dust and ash into the atmosphere. Large volumes of gases and ash can influence climatic patterns for years by increasing planetary reflectivity causing atmospheric cooling. Tiny particles called aerosols are produced by volcanoes. Because they reflect solar energy back into space they have a cooling effect on the world. Volcanic eruptions are episodic and have relatively short-term effects on climate.
2. **Ocean current:** The oceans are a major component of the climate system. Ocean currents move vast amounts of heat across the planet. Winds push horizontally against the sea surface and drive ocean current patterns. Interactions between the ocean and atmosphere can also produce phenomena such as *El Nino* which occurs every 2 to 6 years. The oceans play an important role in determining the atmospheric concentration of CO_2. Changes in ocean circulation may affect the climate through the movement of CO_2 into or out of the atmosphere.
3. **Earth's orbital changes:** The earth makes one full orbit around the sun each year. It is tilted at an angle of 23.5° to the perpendicular plane of

its orbital path. Changes in the tilt of the earth can lead to small but climatically important changes in the strength of the seasons; more tilt means warmer summers and colder winters; less tilt means cooler summers and milder winters. Slow changes in the earth's orbit lead to small but climatically important changes in the strength of the seasons over tens of thousands of years.

4. **Solar variations:** The sun is the source of energy for the earth's climate system. Although the sun's energy output appears constant from an everyday point of view, small changes over an extended period of time can lead to climate changes. As the sun is the fundamental source of energy that is instrumental in our climate system it would be reasonable to assume that changes in the sun's energy output would cause the climate to change. Current global warming however cannot be explained solely by solar variations.

Human Causes

Climate change can also be caused by human activities, such as the burning of fossil fuels and the conversion of land for forestry and agriculture. Since the beginning of the industrial revolution in the 19th century, these human influences on the climate system have increased substantially. Carbon dioxide is the most important greenhouse gas in the atmosphere. Changes in land use pattern, deforestation, land clearing, agriculture, and other activities have all led to a rise in the emission of carbon dioxide. Methane is another important greenhouse gas in the atmosphere. It is released from animals such as dairy cows, goats, pigs, buffaloes, *etc*. Methane is also emitted during the process of oil drilling, coal mining, leaking gas pipelines, landfills and waste dumps. It is this human-induced enhancement of the greenhouse effect that is of concern because ongoing emissions of greenhouse gases have the potential to warm the planet to levels that have never been experienced in the history of human civilization. This change in the climate parameter, also known as global warming, has occurred faster than any other climatic change recorded by humans. Such climate change could have far-reaching and/or unpredictable environmental, social, and economic consequences.

Greenhouse gases: The earth has a natural greenhouse effect where certain gases, known as greenhouse gases, in the atmosphere allow the sunlight to enter and absorb the heat radiation. Because these gases absorb the heat, they keep the average surface temperature on earth around 14° C. Without the natural greenhouse effect, the earth's average surface temperature would be around –19° C. Since the industrial revolution, human activity has increased the amount of greenhouse gases in the atmosphere. The increased amount of gases which absorb heat, has directly lead to retention of more heat in the atmosphere and thus an increase in global average surface temperatures. This change in temperature is known as global warming. The increase in temperature is also leading to other effects on the climate system. Together these effects are known as anthropogenic climate change. The three main causes of the increase in greenhouse gases observed over the past 250 years have been fossil fuels, land use and agriculture (IPCC, 2006).

The principal greenhouse gases (GHGs) include carbon dioxide, methane, **nitrous oxide and chlorofluorocarbons (CFCs). Carbon dioxide constitutes** only a small part of the atmosphere, but it is one of the most important GHGs. CO_2 is released naturally into the atmosphere through volcanic eruptions and animal respiration but it is also released through human activities such as deforestation and the burning of fossil fuels for energy. CO_2 also spends a long time in the atmosphere increasing its impact. **Methane,** the second most important GHG, is produced both naturally and through human activities. The most significant sources of methane come from the decomposition of organic matter under anaerobic conditions. Another large source is from the digestion of ruminants. Methane is a stronger GHG than CO_2 because it can absorb more heat; however it is much less abundant in the atmosphere. **Nitrous oxide,** a very powerful greenhouse gas is released during the production and use of organic fertilisers. It is also produced when burning fossil fuels. **Chlorofluorocarbons are the** manmade compounds which are mainly used in refrigerants and air conditioners.

Since the beginning of the 20th century industrial activity grew 40-fold, and the emissions of greenhouse gases grew 10-fold. The amount of CO_2 in the air increased from some 280 parts per million by volume (ppmv) at the beginning of the century to 389 ppmv at the end of 2010. It is predicted that the level will be 450 ppmv in 2050 resulting in increase in temperature by 1.8 to 3° C. The amount of CO_2 varies throughout the year as the result of the annual cycles of photosynthesis and oxidation. Similarly, methane rose from a preindustrial atmospheric concentration of around 700 parts per billion by volume (ppbv) to about 1789 ppbv by 2007. The change in major green house gases since the industrial revolution is presented in the table 7.1.

Table 7.1: Change on Major Greenhouse Gases since the Industrial Revolution

Gas	Pre-1750 tropospheric concentration	Recent tropospheric concentration (2012)	Increased radiative forcing (W/m^2)
Carbon dioxide (ppm)	280	395.4	1.88
Methane (ppb)	722	1893	0.49
Nitrous oxide (ppb)	270	326	0.17
Tropospheric ozone (ppb)	237	337	0.40

(**Source**: IPCC, 2013)

Aerosols in the atmosphere: Atmospheric aerosols are able to alter climate in two important ways; they scatter and absorb solar and infrared radiation and may change the microphysical and chemical properties of clouds and possibly their lifetime and extent. The scattering of solar radiation acts to cool the planet, while absorption of solar radiation by aerosols warms the air directly instead of allowing sunlight to be absorbed by the surface of the earth. Human activity contributes to the amount of aerosols in the atmosphere in several ways. Dust is often a bi-product of agricultural processes. Biomass burning and industrial processes produce a wide variety of aerosols depending on the type of raw materials and products. Exhaust emission from transports generates pollutants that are either aerosols from the outset, or are converted by chemical reactions in the atmosphere to form aerosols.

Land use change: Land-use changes (*e.g.*, cutting down forests to create farmland) have led to changes in the amount of sunlight reflected from the ground back into space (the surface albedo). The scale of these changes is estimated to be about one-fifth of the forcing on the global climate due to changes in emissions of greenhouse gases. The largest effect of deforestation is estimated to be at high latitudes where the albedo of snow-covered land, previously forested, has increased. This is because snow on trees reflects only about half of the sunlight falling on it, whereas snow-covered open ground reflects about two-thirds. Another contributing cause of climate change is when agriculture alters the earth's land cover, which can change its ability to absorb or reflect heat and light. Land use change such as deforestation and desertification, together with use of fossil fuels, are the major anthropogenic sources of carbon dioxide release into the atmosphere.

Deforestation: The rainforests form part of a delicate ecosystem that has taken millions of years to evolve. Rainforests every year help to absorb almost 20% of manmade CO_2 emissions; therefore, deforestation can be classed as a major contributor to the causes of climate change. Cutting down rainforests faster than they can be replaced has a devastating effect on the carbon emission cycle producing an extra 17% of greenhouse gases. Deforestation by means of cutting down and burning these tropical rainforests usually pave the way for agriculture and industry which often produce even more CO_2. Fossil fuels release carbon dioxide into the atmosphere contributing to global warming and climate change. Forest alleviates this change by converting carbon dioxide to carbohydrate during photosynthesis. The world's forests contain about 125 per cent of the carbon found in the atmosphere. This carbon is stored in the form of wood and vegetation through 'carbon sequestration'. Trees possess about 20 per cent carbon by weight and biomass of forest acts as a 'carbon sink'. The soil organic matter produced by the decomposition of dead plant material also acts as a carbon store.

CLIMATE CHANGE SCENARIO IN INDIA

Climate change in India may pose additional stresses on ecological and socioeconomic systems that already face tremendous pressures from rapid urbanisation, industrialisation and economic development. India Meteorological Department (IMD) maintains a well distributed network of more than 500 stations in the country for more than a century. Meteorological data collected from these stations from 1901 to 2009 was analysed and the trend in change of climate parameters in India was published (Attri and Tyagi, 2010).

Temperature

The annual mean temperature for the country as a whole has risen by 0.56° C over a period of 1901-2009. It may be mentioned that annual mean temperature has been generally above normal (normal based on period, 1961-1990) since 1990. This warming is primarily due to rise in maximum temperature across the country, over larger parts of the data set. However, since 1990, minimum temperature is steadily rising and rate of its rise is slightly more than that of maximum temperature. Spatial pattern of trends in the mean annual temperature shows significant increasing trend over most parts of the country except over parts of Rajasthan, Gujarat and Bihar, where significant decreasing trends were observed. Season wise, maximum rise in mean temperature was observed during the post-monsoon season (0.77° C) followed by winter season (0.70° C), pre-monsoon season (0.64° C) and monsoon season (0.33° C).

Precipitation

The country as a whole does not show any significant trend with respect to the all India annual and monsoon rainfall for the period 1901-2009. Similarly rainfall for the country as whole for the same period for individual monsoon months also does not show any significant trend. However, during the winter season, rainfall is decreasing in almost all the subdivisions except in Himachal Pradesh, Jharkhand, Nagaland, Manipur, Mizoram and Tripura. Rainfall is decreasing over most parts of the central India during the pre-monsoon season. However during the post-monsoon season, rainfall is increasing for most of the sub-divisions.

Extreme Rainfall Events

A large amount of the variability in rainfall is related to the occurrence of extreme rainfall events. Number of heavy rainfall events is increasing almost over the entire landmass. Also the frequency and intensity of extreme events defined as one-day maximum precipitation shows increasing trend everywhere except some northern parts of the country. Country's highest observed one day point rainfall (156.3 cm) and also world's highest 2-day point rainfall (249.3 cm) occurred in Cherrapunji in the year 1995 (IMD, 2006). The exceptionally heavy rainfall of 944 mm over Mumbai on 26th July, 2005 was very unprecedented in nature, which led to many more studies on frequency and variability of heavy rainfall events.

GENERAL EFFECTS OF CLIMATE CHANGE

Climate is changing naturally at its own pace since the beginning of evolution of the earth. But presently it has gained momentum due to inadvertent anthropogenic disturbances. Today, climate change is a global concern. The earth is facing one of the greatest environmental, economic and social threats through climate change. Stronger and more frequent typhoons, warmer nights, and longer and hotter days are some of the most common evidences of climate change. The general consequences of climate change are discussed below.

1. **Ecological imbalance:** Climate change can make summer months warmer or cold months cooler than usual. These changes in temperature can cause animals to migrate to more suitable places or force them to adapt with adverse effects on their physical conditions. Some may even die and become extinct because of their inability to adapt to extreme environmental conditions. Biodiversity is thus at more risk now than ever because of climate change.
2. **Extreme climate variability:** Climate variability refers to short term changes in climate such as longer dry or rainy season, intense heat during summer, more or scanty rains during rainy months.
3. **Increasing temperature:** Global warming is the biggest threat being faced by mankind today. It refers to the observed and projected increase in the earth's average temperature due to natural or anthropogenic causes. The measured average atmospheric temperature near the earth's surface rose by 0.74° C during the last 100 years, 1906-2005 (IPCC, 2007). Cold days, cold nights and frost have become less frequent and hot days, hot nights and heat waves more frequent. Diurnal temperature range has also decreased. It is estimated that average annual temperature will rise by 1.8 to 4° C within the next 100 years. Gases created through industrial and agricultural practices increase the heat-reflecting potential of the atmosphere, thereby raising the planet's average temperature.
4. **Limited food supply:** Climate change can alter the schedule and duration of cropping seasons. Farmers can become confused as to when they should plant crops, thereby affecting length of cropping season, time of harvest and food supply. Water shortage during dry months can also affect crop growth and overall food production.
5. **Increased occurrence of pests and diseases:** Climate change can affect the life cycle of pests by increasing their population at a different time. Farmers may be unaware of or caught unprepared for these changes. Diseases can also become prevalent based on the environmental conditions resulting from climate change.

6. **More powerful typhoons:** Global warming increases ocean temperature and rate of evaporation. As water vapour in the atmosphere increases, the typhoons carry more rains. Climate change, through global warming has increased the frequency and intensity of typhoons over the years.
7. **Rise in sea levels:** Increasing global temperature causes glaciers and polar icecaps to melt, thereby making sea levels rise. If sea levels continue to increase, more land could be submerged under water permanently. The IPCC estimates that sea levels rose 17 cm in 20th century and it may further increase by 18-59 cm by the year 2100.
8. **Glacier retreat and disappearance:** The continued retreat of glaciers will have a number of different quantitative impacts. In the areas that are heavily dependent on water runoff from glaciers that melt during the summer months, a continuation of the current retreat will eventually deplete the glacial ice and substantially reduce or eliminate runoff. A reduction in runoff will affect the ability to irrigate crops and will reduce summer stream flows necessary to keep dams and reservoirs replenished. Approximately 2.4 billion people live in the drainage basin of the Himalayan rivers. India, China, Pakistan, Afghanistan, Bangladesh, Nepal and Myanmar could experience floods followed by severe droughts in coming decades. In India alone, the Ganges provides water for drinking and farming for more than 500 million people.

EFFECT OF CLIMATE CHANGE ON AGRICULTURE

Agriculture is the largest human activity in the world which depends on climatic parameters. Climate change and agriculture are interrelated processes, both of which take place on a global scale. Despite technological advances, such as improved crop varieties, genetically modified organisms, and irrigation systems, weather is still a key factor in agricultural productivity, as well as soil properties and natural communities. The effect of climate change on agriculture is related to variabilities in local climates rather than in global climate patterns. The growth, development and reproductive processes in both plants and animals are also temperature dependent. All these physiological processes show their maximum activity, hence good productivity, only at their optimum temperature. A genotype gives good yield only under suitable climatic conditions and other management practices. For each plant variety, there is an optimal temperature for vegetative growth, with growth dropping off as temperature increases or decreases. Similarly, there is a range of temperatures at which a plant will produce seed. Outside of this range, the plant will not reproduce. More than 50% differences in yield are due to climatic variations. Thus climate change has a profound effect on agricultural practices.

Most significant feature of the Indian-subcontinent climate is its monsoon circulation. The south-west monsoon contributes about 80% of the total annual rainfall in a major part of the region. Although the summer monsoon rainfall exhibits a remarkable stability over time - as evidenced by past data of more than a century, displays a variety of temporal and spatial variations. While a large part of the seasonal anomalies in the monsoon is accounted by the inter-annual variability, decadal and longer term changes manifest themselves as changing frequencies of extreme anomalies (Gupta *et al.*, 2009).

Altering cropping seasons, increasing incidence of pests and diseases, rationing water supply, loss of agricultural biodiversity and limiting food supply are all evidences of climate change. These factors force farmers to adapt using meagre resources. A significant effect of global climate change is the altering of rainfall patterns, which certainly affects agriculture. Extended drought can cause the failure of small and marginal farms with resultant economic, political and social disruption.

Impact of Climate Change on Crop

Climate change projections made up to 2100 for India, indicate an overall increase in temperature by 2-4°C coupled with increase in precipitation, especially during the monsoon period. The available evidence shows significant drop in yields of important cereal crops like rice and wheat under climate change conditions (Mall *et al.*, 2006).

Changes in temperature, amount of carbon dioxide (CO_2), and the frequency and intensity of extreme weather could have significant impacts on crop yields. Many weeds, pests and fungi thrive under warmer temperatures, wetter climates, and increased CO_2 levels.

Warmer temperatures may make many crops grow more quickly, but warmer temperatures could also reduce yields. Crops tend to grow faster in warmer conditions. However, for some crops, faster growth reduces the length of time available for seeds to grow and mature. In the case of an annual crop, the duration between sowing and harvesting will shorten. The shortening of such a cycle could have an adverse effect on productivity because senescence would occur sooner. Thus, yield potential of the crops may not be fully exploited. In some areas, warming may benefit the types of crops that are typically planted there. However, if warming exceeds a crop's optimum temperature, yields can decline. Increase in temperature also increases crop respiration rate and alters partitioning of photosynthates to economic products.

Higher CO_2 levels can increase yields. The yields for some crops, like wheat and soybeans, could increase by 30% or more under a doubling of CO_2 concentrations. However, some factors may counteract these potential increases in yield. For example, if temperature exceeds a crop's optimal level or if sufficient water and nutrients are not available, yield increases may be reduced or reversed.

More extreme temperature and precipitation can prevent crops from growing. Extreme events, especially floods and droughts, can harm crops and reduce yields. Dealing with drought could become a challenge in areas where summer temperatures are projected to increase and precipitation is projected to decrease. As water supplies are reduced, it may be more difficult to meet water demands. Extreme climate conditions may affect quality of fruits, vegetables, tea, coffee, aromatic and medicinal plants.

Decrease in stratospheric ozone may increase biologically dangerous ultraviolet radiation on earth's surface. Ultra violet radiation may damage nucleic acids creating long term effects. Excess ultraviolet radiation can affect plant physiology either directly or indirectly through changed pollinator behaviour and cause massive amounts of mutations. Tropospheric ozone causes foliar injury. This may reduce productivity of many crops.

More detailed analysis of rice yields by the International Rice Research Institute forecasts 20% reduction in yields over the region per degree (in Celsius) rise in temperature. Rice becomes sterile if exposed to temperatures above 35° C for more than one hour during flowering and consequently produces no grain.

Impact of Climate Change on Soil Health

The warmer atmospheric temperature observed over the past decades is expected to lead to a more vigorous hydrological cycle, including more extreme rainfall events. Erosion and soil degradation is more likely to occur, creating sedimentation in streams and reservoirs. Soil fertility would also be affected by global warming. The increase in the temperature would induce a greater rate in the N mineralisation but there will be more volatilisation and denitrification loss. High soil temperature reduces soil organic matter both in quantity and quality. This may also decrease microbial population reducing soil productivity and nutrient cycling. Excess rainfall causes waterlogging, soil salinity problems and salt water ingression in coastal areas.

Impact of Climate Change on Water Resources

Climate change will modify rainfall, evaporation, runoff and soil moisture storage. In some areas, more frequent heavy downpours may cause localised flooding. Increased evaporation from the soil and accelerated transpiration in the plants will cause moisture stress. Thus, crops will need frequent irrigation. The water resources will come under increasing pressure and could become seasonally scarce as a result of regional changes in water supply due to changes in precipitation or snow and glacier melt. Climate change affects the availability of fresh water for irrigation. The over draft and non-replenishment of groundwater will lower the groundwater level permanently.

Impact of Climate Change on Pest

Global warming would cause an increase in rainfall in some areas, which would lead to an increase of atmospheric humidity and the duration of the wet seasons. Combined with higher temperature, these could favour the development of fungal diseases. Similarly, because of higher temperature and humidity, there could be an increased pressure from insects and disease vectors. An increase in temperature may accelerate the growth and multiplication of insect pests. The polycyclic diseases become epidemic with climate change. The geographical range of insects is expanded with increased risk of infestation.

Impact of Climate Change on Livestock

Risk of climate variability affects dairy, meat and wool production, mainly arising from its impact on grassland and rangeland productivity. Heat distress suffered by animals reduces the rate of animal feed intake and results in poor growth performance (Rowlinson, 2008). Climate change affects feed production and nutrition of livestock. There will be less fodder production due to increased water scarcity. Rise in temperature causes more lignifications of plant tissues reducing its digestibility. Global warming increases the requirements for water, shelter and energy to meet the projected milk demands.

Drought may threaten pasture and feed supplies. Drought also reduces the amount of quality forage available to grazing livestock. Some areas could experience longer, more intense droughts, resulting from higher summer temperature and reduced precipitation. For animals that rely on grain, changes in crop production due to drought could also become a problem. Heat waves, which are projected to increase under climate change, could directly threaten livestock. Heat stress affects animals both directly and indirectly. Over time, heat stress can increase vulnerability to disease, reduce fertility, and reduce milk production.

Climate change may increase the prevalence of parasites and diseases that affect livestock. In areas with increased rainfall, moisture-reliant pathogens could thrive. Vector borne diseases may have more impacts on livestock. Increases in carbon dioxide may increase the productivity of pastures and plants on which livestock feed, but may also decrease their quality.

Impact of Climate Change on Fisheries

Fishery enterprises already face multiple stresses, including overfishing and water pollution. Climate change may worsen these stresses. In particular, temperature changes could lead to significant impacts. Increased water temperature affects fish breeding, migration and harvest. Many marine species have certain temperature ranges at which they can survive. Increased temperature and tropical cyclonic conditions affect capture, production and marketing cost of marine fish. Many aquatic species migrate towards colder areas of streams, lakes or ocean to avoid warm water. However, moving into new areas may put these species into competition with other species over food and other resources. Changes in temperature and seasons could affect the timing of reproduction and migration. Many steps within an aquatic animal's lifecycle are controlled by temperature and the changing of the seasons. Some diseases that affect aquatic life may become more prevalent in warm water.

In addition to warming, the world's oceans are gradually becoming more acidic due to increases in atmospheric carbon dioxide. Increasing acidity could harm shellfish by weakening their shells, which are created from calcium and are vulnerable to increasing acidity. Acidification may also threaten the structures of sensitive ecosystems upon which some fish and shellfish rely. The effects of climate change on agriculture by 2050 as predicted by Ministry of Agriculture, Fisheries and Food, Govt. of United Kingdom are presented in table 7.2.

Table 7.2: Predicted Effects of Climate Change on Agriculture by 2050

Climatic element	Expected changes by 2050	Confidence in prediction	Effects on agriculture
CO_2	Increase from 360 ppm to 450 - 600 ppm	Very high	Good for crops; increased photosynthesis; reduced water use
Sea level rise	Rise by 10 -15 cm	Very high	Loss of land, coastal erosion, flooding, salinisation of groundwater
Temperature	Rise by 1-2° C; winters warming more than summers; increased frequency of heat waves	High	Faster, shorter, earlier growing seasons, range moving north and to higher altitudes, heat stress risk, increased evapotranspiration
Precipitation	Seasonal changes by ± 10%	Low	Impacts on drought risk , soil workability, water logging, irrigation supply, transpiration
Storminess	Increased wind speeds, more intense rainfall events	Very low	Lodging, soil erosion, reduced infiltration of rainfall
Variability	Increases across most climatic variables; predictions uncertain	Very low	Changing risk of damaging events (heat waves, frost, droughts, floods) which effect crops and timing of farm operations

(**Source:** MAFF, 2000)

MEASURES ADDRESSING THE EFFECT OF CLIMATE CHANGE ON AGRICULTURE

The adverse effects of climate change on agriculture have become a major course of concern in recent years. The length of the growing season and the type of crop grown are both affected by changes in temperature. Climate change will also modify the availability of water, which will have a profound effect on agricultural productivity. To deal with effects of climate change, both adaptive measures and mitigation measures are to be taken.

Adaptation Strategies

As agricultural production increases, resource constraints, particularly water, will become tighter. Agriculture globally accounts for about 70% of the world's freshwater withdrawals. Climate change is expected to alter the seasonal timing of rainfall and snow pack melt resulting in a higher incidence and severity of floods and droughts. Both rainfed and irrigated agriculture need to be managed more sustainably to reduce production risks. The greater uncertainty from climate change can be best addressed through contingent planning. Adaptation through such measures as crop and livestock insurance, social safety nets, and research on and dissemination of flood, heat and drought resistant crops, including conservation of traditional plant varieties with those characteristics can be facilitated.

Adaptive approaches to minimise the adverse effects of climate change on agriculture include initiating reforestation and afforestation activities, developing water harvesting techniques, improving irrigation efficiency, conserving soil moisture through appropriate tillage methods. Another adaptation strategy taken by farmers is crop diversification and changing planting dates that has proven to be one of the most popular farm level responses to climate variability and change. Improved livestock management practices like providing better housing and shade, change to heat tolerant breeds, change in stocking rate, altered grazing and rotation of pasture, *etc.* may prove to be beneficial. Early warning systems and protection measures for natural disasters like droughts, floods, tropical cyclones, *etc.* should be developed.

Mitigation Technologies

IPCC (2007) defines mitigation as the technological change and substitution that reduce resource inputs and emissions per unit of output. Significant mitigation can be achieved through improved cropland and grazing land management, restoration of degraded lands, and land use change like agroforestry to increase soil carbon storage. Emissions from livestock production can be reduced through improved nutrition and better management of manure. Improved land management through mulching, minimum/zero tillage, intensive cropping, growing legumes, green manuring, crop residues management, improved nutrient management, improved composting including vermicomposting can be undertaken to mitigate the climate change impact on agriculture. A large proportion of the mitigation potential of agriculture arises from soil carbon sequestration, which has strong synergies with sustainable agriculture and generally reduces vulnerability to climate change. Improved rice cultivation techniques can reduce methane gas emissions. Improved nitrogen fertiliser application techniques can also reduce N_2O emissions. Suitable energy crops should be encouraged to replace fossil fuel use.

A study was undertaken by the International Crops Research Institute for the Semi-Arid Tropics to find science based, pro-poor approaches and techniques that would enable Asia's agricultural systems to cope with climate change, while benefitting poor and vulnerable farmers. The study's recommendations ranged from improving the use of climate information in local planning and strengthening weather based agroadvisory services, to stimulating diversification of rural household incomes and providing incentives to farmers to adopt natural resource conservation measures to enhance forest cover, replenish groundwater and use renewable energy. Other mitigation measures include change in crop management practices, crop insurance, *etc.*

1. The crops and varieties which can withstand water logging conditions for a fairly long period should be preferred in the flood and cyclone prone areas. At present varieties for various crops, particularly for rice many varieties are available which are tolerant to flood conditions. Awareness should be created among the farmers of flood prone areas and adequate seeds of these varieties should also be ascertained.
2. In areas of perennial waterlogging where even rice cultivation is difficult, aquatic crops with economic importance such as water chestnut can be introduced with fish farming. Colocasia can also be cultivated in flood prone waterlogged areas.
3. The contingent crop plans should be prepared for post flood and cyclone areas. Short duration pulses and vegetable crops should be encouraged and package of practices for these crops should be standardized for difficult situations.
4. In lowlands under high rainfall region and flood prone areas, land modification such as raised and sunken bed technique can be practiced. Trenches of 5-8 metre width and 1.2-1.5 metre depth with 10 metre or suitable length can be opened at a spacing of 10-15 metre in-between two trenches. The excavated soil is put on the space between two trenches to prepare raised beds. Vegetables and short duration fruit crops can be grown on the raised beds while trenches are utilized for fish farming. In dry season irrigation can be provided to the crops on the raised beds from the trenches.
5. In flood prone and waterlogged areas, the practice of bio-drainage using *Casuarina* and *Eucalyptus* plantations would act as a viable flood resilient system. Crops can be grown on the tree alleys. This increases land productivity.

CONCLUSION

Climate and weather is a basic input considered the most vital in agricultural production system since it affects the agricultural planning in a big way starting from land preparation to harvesting, processing and transportation. Thus, climate may be considered as the most critical factor determining the sustainability of agricultural systems. But climate variability and climate extremes are already having impacts on agricultural production systems. During the last few decades climate change has threatened the Indian food security in a big way. However, risks associated with climate change can be reduced through timely preparedness, coupled with appropriate mitigation actions and programmes. Short to medium range weather forecasts and early warning systems can be useful ele-ments for the agricultural decision-making process, leading to reduced risks and increased opportunities. Immediate attention should be given to contingency crop planning and integrated cyclone and flood management strategies for reducing the extent of damage. The projected extent of climate change and its effect on agriculture is a top priority item, which deserves due attention of planners, policy makers, scientists, extension workers and all other interested in development of agriculture. There is also a need for intensifying research activity on this important agenda.

REFERENCES

Attri, S.D. and Tyagi, A. (2010): Climate Profile of India. India Meteorological Department, Ministry of Earth Sciences, Government of India, New Delhi, pp: 122.

Gupta, A.K., Nair, S.S. and Sehgal, V.K. (2009): Hydro-meteorological Disasters and Climate Change: Conceptual Issues and Data Needs for Integrating Adaptation into Environment - Development Framework. *e-Journal Earth Science India* 2(2): 117-132.

IMD. (2006): Trends in Precipitation Extremes over India. *NCC Research Report No. 3/2006.*

IPCC. (1996): Climate Change 1995: The Science of Climate Change. Contribution of Group I to the Second Assessment Report on the Intergovernmental Panel on Climate Change. Cambridge University Press, U.K.

IPCC. (2007): Climate Change 2007: The Physical Science Basis. Cambridge University Press, U.K.

IPCC. (2013): *Climate Change 2013: The Physical Science Basis. Contribution of Working Group I to the Fifth Assessment Report of the Intergovernmental Panel on Climate Change.* Cambridge University Press, Cambridge, U.K.

MAFF. (2000): Climate Change and Agriculture in the United Kingdom. Ministry of Agriculture, Fisheries and Food, London, U.K.

Mall, R.K., Singh, R., Gupta, A. Srinivasan, G. and Rathore, L.S. (2006): Impact of Climate Change on Indian Agriculture: A Review. *Climatic Change*, 78: 445-478.

Patra, P.K. (2012): A Text Book on Climatology. Kalyani Publishers, Ludhiana, pp: 255.

Rowlinson, P. (2008): Adapting Livestock Production Systems to Climate Change – Temperate Zones. Livestock and Global Change Conference Proceedings, May 2008, Tunisia.

Climate Change and Agro-Edaphic System **Pages 163–167**
Edited by: Dr. Alka Chauhan & Dr. Pawan Kumar 'Bharti'
ISBN: 978-93-86841-98-8
Edition: 2019
Published by: Discovery Publishing House Pvt. Ltd., New Delhi (India)

8

Phytoplankton to Combat Global Warming

[1]Noor El Deen AIE

ABSTRACT

The phytoplankton is a marvelous discovery that may change our life completely. That one-cell plant which grows in the water of our seas and oceans is likely to give us a perfect solution for global warming, green house gases and the CO_2 continuous concentration in our ecological system. It could be a magical solution to absorb CO_2 and produce O_2 and food for us. Scientists all over the world for the last 10 years have been performing experiments to produce the phytoplankton. Its growth needs some ecological factors i.e. air velocity, humidity, sun light, temperature and others. These factors are combined together in Egypt and exactly in Al Qattara Depression. But it seems that phytoplankton will give a great push to these projects. Phytoplankton will draw the prosperous future of Egypt on almost all fields.

Keywords: Project- Phytoplankton-Global warming- Al Qattara- Solution.

INTRODUCTION

Global warming has been worsening because of carbon dioxide increasing rates as a result of deforestation, fossil fuel burning, the increasing green house effects and heat trapping gases. The Oceans are constantly absorbing large quantities of carbon dioxide (100 Giga Ton) which are converted into vitamins, amino acids, oxygen and other important elements useful for marine and human life. This process of absorbing carbon dioxide , occurs in two ways the dissolution way and the biological way. Dissolution method physically and chemically dissolves atmospheric carbon dioxide in the surface seawater. Compared to other atmospheric gases such as oxygen and nitrogen, carbon dioxide dissolves very well in water. The lower the sea temperature and the higher the atmospheric pressure, the greater the dissolution.Many trials were devoted to study how terrestrial plants, aquatic seaweeds and sea grasses (Xu and Baldocchi, 2003) and phytoplankton can be used to mitigate the dramatic

[1] Department of hydrobiology, Veterinary Division, National research Center, Egypt.

increase in atmospheric carbon dioxide (Suker *et al*, 2004). The partial pressure of carbon dioxide in the seawater decreases through serial processes executed by organisms in the surface seawater, and an equivalent amount of carbon dioxide can then be dissolved from the atmosphere. Clarifying the mechanisms of the carbon cycle in the oceans, which function as the main absorption buffer of carbon dioxide, is a very important theme in forecasting the future global environment. For that reason, it is necessary to understand the movement of the phytoplankton in the oceans, and to quantify how primary production fluctuates. In addition, phytoplankton will provide a standard tool for measuring ocean productivity since it feeds many fish species such as sardines and tuna through the food chain (Zimmerman *et al*, 1997). Marine phytoplankton are known as the oceans fundamental food web. Marine phytoplankton consists of a big variety of single cell plants found in the surface-upper zone of aquatic system. Phytoplankton have ability to transform inorganic minerals and sea water, natural warmth, and the Earth's sun light and carbon dioxide into usable vitamins, proteins, amino acids and carbohydrate, in essence creating food for the global ecosystem. Marine phytoplankton nourish the cells completely. Because of photosynthesis our diverse marine biology ocean plants take in both sea and the sun and produce nutrients. Phytoplankton contains almost every element you need for sustaining life: contains nine essential amino acids: essential fatty acids including omega3 and 6, vitamins A,B,C,D and minerals (Boyed *et al*, 2000). This study will be conducted to measure the oligotrophic carbon dioxide in sea floor. One of the main goals of the present research is to know the percentage of increase of fish production with iron fertilization in experimental fish ponds. It seems that phytoplankton is our newest gift from God to solve the problems we made out of our own hands.

BACKGROUND

The policy of the Ministry of Electricity and Energy in Egypt is to increase the utilization of all natural resources for energy production, especially the hydro-potential as the most important source (e.g. the Aswan hydro-electrical station with an installed capacity of 2400 MW). Theoretically, a big project concerning the utilization of Qattara Depression for this purpose was designed many years ago. Qattara Depression is located in the western desert in Egypt, about 134 m below sea level at its lowest point. At zero level, the surface area of the depression is about 19,500 km^2 representing 1/15 of the area of Egypt, whereas at filling of 60m below sea level the surface area of the depression is about 12,100 km^2 with water volume of 209.3 km^3. The depression is planned to be connected to the Mediterranean Sea either through tunnels or open canal. The discharged water will be regulated by water turbines thus utilize the difference between sea level and the depression for power production. A preliminary intake for the water canal was chosen at El Sirra area located 15 km west of El Dabaa. After the establishment of the project, the maximum annual energy forecast is about 15400 TWH. It can be noted that the surface of the foreseen formed lake at level of 60 m below sea level will be 12,100 km^2 and volume of water will amount to 209,3 cubic kilometers Ministry Electricity and Energy in Egypt (1972). Depending on our finding concerning the net primary production (C sequestration) of phytoplankton at the expected water intake of the project is 355g $m^{-3}year^{-1}$. At filling of 60m below sea level the surface area of the depression is about 12,100 km^2 with water volume of 209.3 km^3. It is predicted that the total C sequestered by phytoplankton per year, according to this water volume, is about $700x10^5$ tons of carbon which mean 70 million tons of carbon dioxide will be removed from the atmosphere. If we know that the annual increase of atmospheric carbon dioxide amount to 3.2 Giga ton, Qattara Depression will be responsible for removing of about 1.5% of this increase Medhat.K.,et al 2009. In Chesapeake Bay, in the temperate eastern region of US, Harding et al 2002 observed a late winter minimum, average, of 325 mg C m^{-2} d^{-1}, with rising temperature they observed a summer maximum, average, of 1500 mg C m^{-2} d^{-1}. In general they observed a 2-3 fold increase in net primary production during summer compared with late winter-early spring. Similar results were reported by Smith & Kemp 1995 . Our measures of phytoplankton net primary production were at temperature of 17°C, mid winter, and oligo-mesotrophic conditions of nutrient concentrations. In agreement with Harding et al 2002 and Smith, & Kemp, 1995 rising temperature during summer will increase the net primary production in Qattara Depression 2-3 fold which means an increase from 1.5 to 3-4.5% in the annual removing of the atmospheric carbon dioxide increased per year. In the same time, nutrient enrichment in oligo-mesotrophic conditions may enhance the net primary production to levels that make Qattara Depression remove more than 5% of the annual increase of CO_2. Chen Y. L. (2005) Studied the effect of nutrient enrichment in south China Sea and indicated that while N enrichment enhanced phytoplankton growth all year round, P enrichment only occasionally increased production. In all enrichments, whenever N was supplemented, either singly or in combination with other nutrients, phytoplankton production was greatly enhanced. The primary production for the +N treatment measured was 7.82 $mgCm^{-3}$ h^{-1}. It was 9.22 $mgCm^{-3}$ h^{-1} for the +NP treatment. These values are approximately 5–10 times greater than the control (1.66 $mgCm^{-3}$ h^{-1}) or the +P enrichment (0.89 $mgCm^{-3}$ h^{-1}). These results in combination with those of Veldhuis et al 1997, may support our hypothesis that using Qattara Depression as aquaculture may remove more than 5% of the annual increase of CO_2 in the atmosphere.

In conclusion, using the projected Qattara Depression for hydropower generation as aquaculture may be useful in sequestration carbon dioxide and combat global warming.

REFERENCES

American Public Health Association (APHA) 1992. Standard Methods of the Examination of Water and Waste Water. 17th edition, AWWA, WPCF, 1015P.

Boyd, P.W., Watson, A.J., Law, C.S., Abraham, E.R., Trull, T., Murdoch, R., Bakker, D.C.E., Bowie, A.R., Buesseler, K.O., Chang, H., Charette, M.A., Croot, P., Downing, K., Frew, R.D., Gall, M., Hadfield, M., Hall, J.A., Harvey, M., Jameson, G., La Roche, J., Liddicoat, M.I., Ling, R., Maldonado, M., McKay, R.M., Nodder, S.D., Pickmere, S., Pridmore, R., Rintoul, S., Safi, K., Sutton, P., Strzepek, R., Tanneberger, K., Turner, S.M., Waite, A., Zeldis, J., 2000. A mesoscale phytoplankton bloom in the polar Southern Ocean stimulated by iron fertilization. Nature 407, 695–702.

Bozeca Y., Bakkerb C.E., Hartmannc C., Thomasa H., Richard G.J. Bellerbyd D., Riebesellc U., Watsonb J., Hein J.W..2005. The CO2 System in a Redfield Context during an Iron Enrichment Experiment in the Southern Ocean. Marine Chemistry 95: 89– 105.

Charles, D., Knowles, C., and Davis, R. (2002). Protocols for the Analysis of Algal Samples Collected as Part of the U.S. Geological Survey National Water-Quality Assessment Program. Patrick Center for Environmental Research Report No. 02-06, The Academy of Natural Science, Philadelphia . http://diatoms.acnasci.org/nawqa/.

Chen Y. L. (2005). Spatial and Seasonal Variations of Nitrate-based new Production and Primary Production in the South China Sea Deep-Sea Research, 52 (1): 319–340.

Denman K (1996) Marine Biotic Responses to Environmental Change and Feedbacks to Climate. In: Houghton JT, Meira Filho LG, Callader BA, Harris N, Kattenberg A, Maskell K (eds) Climate Change 1995: The Science of Climate Change. Cambridge University Press, New York.

Dillard, G.E., 1991. Freshwater Algae of the Southeastern, United States, By J. Krammer, Berlin, Stuttgart.

Ehleringer JR, Cerling TE, Flanagan LB (2001) Global Change and the Linkages between Physiological Ecology and Ecosystem Ecology. In: Press MC, Huntley NJ, Levin S (eds) Ecology: Achievement and Challenge. Blackwell Science, Williston, VT.

Harding L. W., Jr, Malloneea M. E. and Perryc E. S. (2002). Toward a Predictive Understanding of Primary Productivity in a Temperate, Partially Stratified Estuary. Estuarine, Coastal and Shelf Science 55, 437–463.

James, Carmelo 1997. Identification of Marine Phytoplankton, Academic Press, Harcourt Brace & Company, New York.

Keeling CD (1997) Climate Change and Carbon Dioxide: An Introduction. Proc Natl Acad Sci USA 94:8273–8274.

Kleypas JA, Buddemeier RW, Archer D, Gattuso JP, Langdon C, Opdyke BN (1999) Geochemical Consequences of Increased Atmospheric Carbon Dioxide on Coral Reefs. Science 284: 118–120.

Krammer, K. and H. Lange-Bertalot., 1986. Bacillariophyceae. Teil: Naviculaceae. Susswasserflora von Mitteleuropa, 2/1:1-876. Gustav Fisher Verlag, Stuttgart, Germany.

Marker, A.F., Crowther, C.A., and Gunin, R.J. (1980). Methanol and Acetone as Solvents for Estimating Chlorophyll-a and Phaeopigments by Spectrophotometer. Arch. Hydrobiol. Beih. Ergebn. Limnol., 14: 52 – 69.

Manabe S, Stouffer RJ (1994) Multiple-century Response of a Coupled Ocean-atmosphere Model to an Increase of Atmospheric Carbon Dioxide. J Clim 7:5–23.

Ministry Electricity and Energy in Egypt (1972). Qattara Depression. 48pp.

Medhat.K.,Mona, S. Z.,Mohamad,S. A. and Noor El Deen,A. I.(2009). Predicated Study of Carbon Sequestration by Phytoplankton in South Coast of Mediterranean Sea Opposite the Projected Canal Connected to Qattara Depression under press.

Nusch, E.A. (1980). Comparison of different Methods for chl. and Phaeopigments Determination. Arch. Hydrobiol. Beih. Ergebn. Limnol., 14: 14 – 36.

O'Neill BC, Oppenheimer M (2002) Dangerous Climate Impacts and the Kyoto Protocol. Science 296:1971–1972.

Sarmiento JL, Hughes TMC, Stouffer RJ, Manabe S (1998) Simulated Response of the Ocean Carbon Cycle to Anthropogenic Climate Warming. Nature 393:245–249.

Suyker, A.E., Verma, S.B., Burba, G.G., Arkebauer, T.J., Walters, D.T., Hubbard, K.G., 2004. Growing Season Carbon Dioxide Exchange in Irrigated and Rainfed Maize. Agric. For. Meteorol. 124, 1–13.

Starmach, K., 1968. Flora Slodkonda Polaki Toms. pp. 594.

Strickland, J. D. and Parsons T. R. (1965). A Manual of Sea Water Analysis "2nd Edition Fisheries Research". Board of Canada, Ottawa.

Smith, E. M. & Kemp, W. M. 1995 Seasonal and Regional Variations in Plankton Community Production and Respiration for Chesapeake Bay. Marine Ecology Progress Series 116, 217–231.

Trenberth K (1996). The Climate System: An Overview. In: Houghton JT, Meira Filho LG, Callader BA, Harris N, Kattenberg A, Maskell K (eds) Climate Change 1995: The Science of Climate Change. Cambridge University Press, New York.

Tikkanen, T., 1986. Kasviplanktonopas. Suomen Luonnonsuojelun Tuki Oy (Italia.), Helsinki. pp. 278.

Utermohl, H., 1958. Zur Vervollkommung der Quantitativen Phytoplankton-methodik. Internationale Vereinigung fur Theoretische 'and Angewandte Limnologi, 9: 1-38.

Vollenweider, R. A. (1996). A Manual Method for Measuring Primary Production in Environment. IBP. Handbook No. 12. Oxford and Edinburgh, 213 pp.

Veldhuis, M.J.W., Kraay, G.W., Van Bleijswijk, J.D.L., Baars, M.A., 1997. Seasonal and Spatial Variability in Phytoplankton Biomass, Productivity and Growth in the Northwestern Indian Ocean: The Southwest and Northeast Monsoon, 1992–1993. Deep-Sea Research I 44, 425–449.

Xu, L., Baldocchi, D.D., 2003. Seasonal Variation in Carbon Dioxide Exchange over a Mediterranean Annual Grassland in California. Agric. For. Meteorol. 123, 79–96.

Zeebe RE, Wolf-Gladrow D (2001) CO2 in Seawater: Equilibrium, Kinetics, Isotopes. Elsevier, New York.

Zimmerman RC, Kohrs DG, Steller DL, Alberte RS (1997) Impacts of CO2-enrichment on Productivity and Light Requirements of Seagrass. Plant Physiol 115:599–607.

Climate Change and Agro-Edaphic System **Pages 168–181**
Edited by: Dr. Alka Chauhan & Dr. Pawan Kumar 'Bharti'
ISBN: 978-93-86841-98-8
Edition: 2019
Published by: Discovery Publishing House Pvt. Ltd., New Delhi (India)

9

Soil-Plant-Water Interactions in Varying Ecosystems

Current Interactions and Future Predictions under Changed Climatic Conditions

[1]Wenjun Ji, [2,3]Asim Biswas

INTRODUCTION

With the ever increasing population demand, maintaining and improving food security is critical in the twenty first century (Farsund, *et al.*, 2015). However, to maintain and improve food security around the world, the governing criterion is soil security (Flora, 2015). Soil security, which is analogous to food security, depends on how the community invests in its natural and built capitals. And with the current scenario of changing climate, the new and increasingly impacting environmental stresses affecting theagricultural communities extensively (Flora, 2015). As the changing climate exert intense pressure on our natural resources, meeting the food demand requires better and optimum management of our natural resources including soil as it provides the basis of plant growth and development.

Earth's only true autotrophs are green plants (Hillel, 2004). Green plants are able to create new living matter from inorganic material including water (Hillel, 2004). In fact, around 90% of plants' structural mass is water (Hillel, 2004). Therefore, water is a necessity for the survival of plant life and by extension, all life. The source of water that all plants utilize is mostly from soil. Therefore, it is critical that soil water be available to plants and equally critical to understand water uptake mechanisms. This paper will review the current body of knowledge surrounding soil-plant-water interactions, how these interactions differ in different ecosystems and how the plant-soil-water interactions could change under climate change conditions. It is predicted that all the ecosystems studied, grasslands, deserts, permafrost and forests, will

1 Department of Bioresource Engineering, McGill University, 2111 Lakeshore Road, Ste-Anne-de-Bellevue, QC H9X 3V9, Canada
2 Department of Natural Resource Sciences, McGill University, 2111 Lakeshore Road, Ste-Anne-de-Bellevue, QC H9X 3V9, Canada
3 School of Environmental Sciences, University of Guelph, 50 Stone Road East, Guelph, ON N1G 2W1, Canada

all undergo a change in their soil-plant-water interactions with the changing climate.

Understanding the current soil-water uptake mechanisms of today's ecosystems is essential. The planet is warming at an alarming rate. From 1880 to 2012 there has already been an increase of almost 1 degree Celsius (IPCC, 2013). Desertification and deforestation are predicted to be two major consequences of climate change, along with ecosystems migrating northwards as the temperature rises (IPCC, 2013). An overall increase in precipitation is predicted under climate change conditions, but there will also be much harsher droughts in certain areas (IPCC, 2013). As aforementioned we need plants to survive. This review will serve as a baseline for the future. Since climate change will have a significant effect on soil hydrology and soil-water availability to plants,it's important to understand the different ecosystems ongoingin order to more accurately predict how soil-water availability will change as the ecosystems change under warming conditions and perhaps find solutions to the already predicted unfavourable outcomes (Farkas *et al.*, 2014).

SOIL WATER AND ITS MOVEMENT

Soil Water

Water in the soil exists in three zones, the root, the vadose, the phreatic zones. These zones are controlled by the hydrological cycle (Brady and Weil, 2008). The phreatic zone is a saturated region in the soil where the hydrostatic pressure is dominant in the total water potential. Due to seasonal variations, the groundwater fluctuates with plant uptake and climatic events. Depending on the site's location, the groundwater could be very shallow or could be tens of meters deep from the soil's surface (Scott, 2000). The vadose zone, ranges up to near saturation due to capillary rise (Scott, 2000). Through the action of surface tension, which is discussed later, capillarity occurs within pore spaces which are modelled as thin, continuous, uniform columns. The height of the capillary rise is inversely proportional to the radius of the pore. Therefore, the smaller the radius (i.e. micropores), the higher the capillary fringe extends to the soil's surface (Scott, 2000; Brady and Weil, 2008). The root zone is where plant roots extract water during the process of transpiration. The general rooting behavior of plants tends towards a greater rooting densities near the soil's surface, thus water is extracted more readily near the surface rather than from the vadose zone. The time of year and climatic events act at providing a zone that ranges from unsaturated to saturated (Scott, 2000).

Water content and water potential are two key criteria to first understand how water moves within the soil. Water content is simply the amount of water that is in the soil; either gravimetrically or volumetrically measured (Kirkham, 2005). Soil water potential is "the difference in energy level of water from one site or one condition to another determines the direction and rate of water movement in soils and plants (Brady and Weil, 2008)." The total water potential of a soil is mainly comprised of the matric, gravitational, solute, and hydrostatic potentials (Brady and Weil, 2008; Kirkham, 2005; Scott, 2000).

Water is held in the soil by adhesive and cohesive forces. The fundamental principle of adhesive and cohesive forces is hydrogen bonding. Hydrogen bonding occurs when the positive dipole hydrogen on the water molecule is attracted to the negative dipole oxygen of another molecule. Cohesion is therefore the attraction of water molecules to one another and adhesion is the attraction of water molecules to (a) surface(s), in this case, soil surface(s). These two forces allow the soil to retain water, control its movement and make it available to use. Surface tension is a result of these two forces. This property is affiliated with an air-liquid interface and results in the attraction of water molecules to one another which is greater than the air interface above, causing a U-shaped curvature of the water. The U-shaped curvature results from adhesion through hydrogen bonding to the negatively charged soil surfaces and as the distance from the soil surface increases, cohesive forces dominate. So, surface tension controls capillarity, which controls how water will move and be retained in the soil (Brady and Weil, 2008; Scott, 2000).

Changes in soil water can occur from climatic events such as continual precipitation resulting in a satiation of soil pore space to long periods without precipitation producing highly adsorbed, unavailable water to the plant. Based on a general scenario, the soil gets moisten by precipitation/water table fluctuation and dries by solar radiation, wind, and evaporation. The fluctuation in soil is due to capillarity but the changes that occur within the soil's pore space is another mechanism called hysteresis. Hysteresis is the relation of soil water potential and soil water content with regard to desorption and sorption of water on the soil surfaces (Brady and Weil, 2008). Soil pore space is not constant in the soil as all soils have different textures and structures. This inconsistency in pore geometry creates an inherent assumption for capillarity. The hysteresis is affected by four known factors including, entrapped air, swelling and shrinking, contact angle effect and the geometric non-uniformity of individual pores. For example, if an arbitrary pore is initially saturated, desorption depends on the narrow radii of three dimensional connecting channels and sorption depends on the maximum diameter of the large pores. Therefore, as long as the water content remains unchanged with decreasing matric suction for a narrow radius, the pore will remain wet. If the matric potential is slightly less than the matric suction of a larger pore, the pore will suddenly empty and depict a difference in the water content (Scott, 2000). Therefore, the occurrence of hysteresis is important to consider of how water fluctuates in the soil and thus how it moves (Kirkham, 2005).

Soil Water Movement

Depending on the plant, spatial distribution and size of the root system will vary in the extraction pattern. Two following models are being considered, water extraction by the root system and by a single root. The root system models, created by Molz in 1971 and Nimah and Hanks in 1973, assess the flow of water from a differential volume at a certain rate. The three variable processes are controlled by the soil profile depth, the volumetric soil water content and the time during the growing season (Scott, 2000). Transpiration is assumed to be equivalent to the cumulative water extracted by the root system in the soil profile and also assumed to be the actual evapotranspiration rate under low soil evaporation conditions as most water extracted is transpired. It has been studied that the soil water depletion curve depends on climate, soil physical and chemical characteristics and water extraction rate. The issues with the macroscopic model are the average matric and osmotic potential is used and does not account for a decrease in water potential in the plant. Also the changes in concentration of salts at the soil-root interface are not accounted for (Scott, 2000). The single root model created by Gardner in 1960, is microscopically based and depicts the root system's individual roots are an array of parallel, hollow cylinders (Scott, 2000). The flow of water is said to be two dimensional and follows the cylindrical coordinate version of Darcy's Law, where the variables are the volumetric water content, time, radial distance from the root center, and soil water diffusivity. With using this model, it was found to exhibit little water potential gradients in the area around the roots until the soil reaches a more negative matric potential. It was found that an unsaturated hydraulic conductivity of less than 10-8 mm d^{-1} impedes water movement from the soil to the roots. One of the disadvantages of this model is the inadequate values of hydraulic conductivity attained, as it has been noted that the best conductivity is the rhizosphere hydraulic conductivity rather than the soil hydraulic conductivity (Kirkham, 2005; Scott, 2000). Other, more recent models have been parameterized, using soil water contents to estimate evapotranspiration and root water uptake profiles (Guderle and Hildebrandt, 2014) and complex root water uptake models (Bechmann *et al.*, 2014).

Gardner's equation (single root model) has been applied in different scenarios; the effect of wet and dry soil, the effect of root diameter, the effect of water uptake and the effect of root distribution on wilting (Kirkham, 2005). The effect of wet soils yielded a constant water uptake into plant roots at a matric potential of 5 bar, whereas at 15 bar there was a lower hydraulic conductivity closer to the root. The effect of root radius was not important as increasing root diameter can decrease the change in matric potential from bulk soil to the soil-root interface. The effect of water uptake with roots showed that at very short distances from the root there is little difference between suction, until the soil becomes very dry. Therefore, Gardner assumed that the roots are at the same potential as the surrounding soil (Kirkham, 2005). Lastly, the more extensive the root system, the lower rate of water uptake per unit length of root occurs. Therefore the flux of water into a root is a function of transpiration and the extent of the root system. To provide an example of the effect of root distribution on wilting is that at low water uptakes, the wilting negative pressure of the soil is very close to the suction in the plant roots (Kirkham, 2005). Root water uptake rates were comparative to the root length, root densities and the water potential in the soil. Although, the main issue with this model does not consider root connectivity (Couvreur *et al.*, 2014).

SOIL WATER UPTAKE BY PLANTS AND MOVEMENT IN PLANTS

Structure and Function of Roots

Roots are the most necessary part of the plant in terms of the uptake of soil-water. Below is a figure from Hillel demonstrating the different parts of a root.

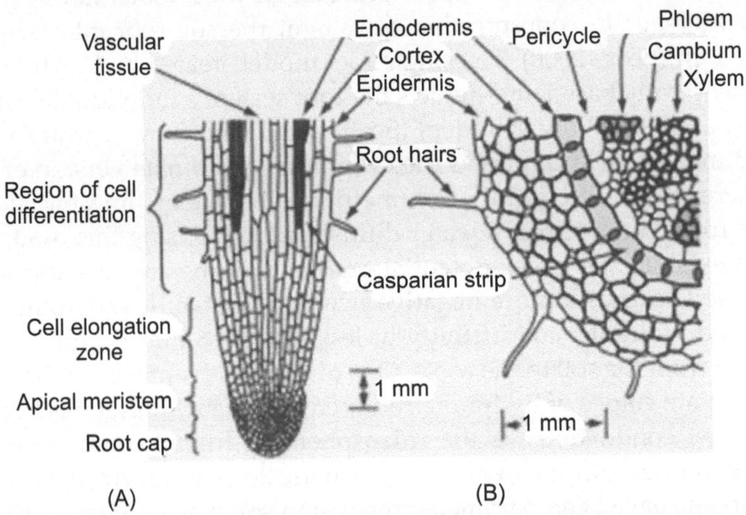

Fig. 9.1: (a) Longitudinal section of a root. (b) Cross section of a root. (Hillel, 2004)

The root cap acts as a lubricant, clearing a path for the root to grow (Hillel, 2004). The root hairs, as seen in Fig. 9.1. Act as the soil-water and nutrient uptake system. The root hairs increase the surface area of the root (Hillel, 2004). This allows for the plant to increase its interaction with the soil and uptake more soil-water (Hillel, 2004).

In a study conducted by Yu *et al.*, maize plants in natural wet and dry soil were observed to study the effect of vertical root distribution. In term of a plant's ability to cope with water storage, it was found that the depth of the most densely rooted soil layer was more important than the reach of the deepest single root (Yu *et al.*, 2007).

Soil-Root Interface

As briefly mentioned, the soil has a certain water potential and this is the main reason how water can move within the soil; high to low gradients. If a plant absorbs water from the soil, the plant must have a lower potential. This is the same reasoning as water moves up the stem and into the leaves and finally to the atmosphere; as elevation in the plant increases the potential becomes more negative (Brady and Weil, 2008). For example, Brady and Weil (2008) illustrated how water moves up a tree; the soil is at-50 kPa, the root potential is -70 kPa, up to -500 kPa in the leaves and finally reaching the atmosphere at -20,000 kPa. The driving force of the sap is then proportional to the transpiration flux from the leaves (Kim *et al.*, 2014).

A root has been imaged as an inverse animal intestinal epithelium with two functions, selective uptake and acting as a diffusion barrier. The two key components of a root's cross section are the epidermis and endodermis. The epidermis and root hairs are in contact with the soil, serving as the selective uptake center, whereas within the root the stele (comprised of the vascular bundles or xylem and phloem) is surrounded by the endodermis. The endodermis forms a barrier to allow the diffusion of solutes and ions from the epidermal layer. There are three pathways that water and nutrients can use to enter into the plant; the apoplastic pathway, the symplastic pathway, and a combination of the two (Barberon and Geldner, 2014).

The function of the apoplastic route is based on mass flow and diffusion mechanisms. The water and nutrients move toward the stele through intercellular spaces, which is called the apoplast. Diffusion rates are based on an ionic gradient from the soil environment and the apoplast. Cations from the soil solution can accumulate in the apoplast and anions are rejected due to the galacturonic monomers of pectin (negatively charged); cations of significant concentration can be found in the root apoplast, particularly aluminum, iron and silicon. Before the stele lies the endodermal cells and the Casparian strip. This strip blocks the passive flow of solutes and water in the apoplast. Therefore, the apoplastic pathway ends when the water and nutrients hit the Casparian strip, so the nutrients and water can only migrate into the xylem poles through the endodermal symplast (Barberon and Geldner, 2014).

The symplastic pathway is involved with cell to cell transport by a process called plasmodesmata. Due to the nature of plant cells having cell walls, intercellular communication is difficult. However, with plasmodesmata, channels are formed providing cytoplasmic continuity between each cell. A factor of plasmodesmata permeability is callose which restricts the channel's aperture to promote or inhibit cell to cell interaction; callose is then a modulator of nutrients. The plasma membrane is the barrier between the soil and the root surfaces and is the primary selective surface for nutrients and water to enter this pathway. Although not well understood, once the nutrients have entered the cell, their mobility is controlled by chelation factors with other macromolecules (Barberon and Geldner, 2014).

Water Transportation in the Plant

Soil-water that has been up taken by plants also acts as a solvent for nutrient and ion transport within the plant (Hillel, 2004). Most of the water in a plant can be found in cell vacuoles, under positive pressure (Hillel, 2004). This positive pressure caused by the water ensures the cells are turgid, and therefore gives rigidity to the entire plant (Hillel, 2004).

The vascular system of a plant connects the roots to the stems and leaves (Hillel, 2004). This vascular system is made up of two main components, the xylem and the phloem. Horizontal flows to the xylem within roots can be measured relatively easily (Holbrook & Zwieniecki, 2005). The xylem vessels transport water, minerals and organic compound from the soil to the upper parts of the plant (Hillel, 2004). The organic compounds in xylem transport are metabolized in the roots (Hillel, 2004). Xylem cells are hollow, being devoid of protoplasm, and have perforated plates allowing them to form continuous tubes throughout one another (Hillel, 2004). The aqueous solution absorbed by the roots flows up through the xylem in the direction of decreasing hydraulic pressure (Hillel, 2004). This leads the solution up through the stem, through the petiole and into the leaf veins (Hillel, 2004). The phloem vessels distribute the organic compounds synthesized in the leaves throughout other areas of the plant (Hillel, 2004).

Once the water is in the xylem, plant physiologists term the theory of water movement as cohesion-tension theory. Among the persistent challenges this theory has received, the cohesion-tension theory acts as the main driving force in how water moves up the plant to the tension that is exhibited by the leaves through transpiration. This increasingly negative pressure with an increase in elevation causes water to move up through the xylem wicks, acting as fine, capillary networks. The cohesion of the dipolar molecules is what gives water its high tensile strength which maintains the water connectivity throughout the plant's vasculature (Kim *et al.*, 2014).

Water adheres to the cellulosic fibrillar tubes and other hydrophilic components in the xylem. According to the conservation of energy, thus the conservation of mass, as one molecule of water evaporates from the air spaces in the leaf structure, cohesive forces dominate and an ascending force (tension) pulls another water molecule up to takes the other's place. The mechanism of this ascending force is created by surface tension in the air-water interface in the substomatal chambers in the leaves. This surface tension has been assumed for the past 30 years to be transferred a continual column of water to the roots (Kim *et al.*, 2014).

Photosynthesis and Transpiration

Plants are the foundation for life on earth. Water serves as a hydrogen donor in plants, and is a building block for the creation of carbohydrates (Ehlers & Goss, 2003). Specifically, they allow for the synthesis of basic sugars through a chemical reaction between soil-water, carbon dioxide, and sunlight energy known as potosynthesis (Hillel, 2004). The following chemical reaction describes this process;

$$6CO_2 + 6H_2O + \text{sunlight energy} \rightarrow C_6H_{12}O_6 + 6O_2 \text{ (Hillel, 2004)}$$

As one can see, water is a main reactant for this reaction. Therefore without soil-water, the essential building block for food chains would be non-existent since water is the main metabolic agent in the life of a plant (Hillel, 2004).It is also a source of hydrogen atoms for the reduction of carbon dioxide as well as a product of respiration (Hillel, 2004).

In dry conditionsonly a small portion of water is used for photosynthesis (Hillel, 2004). Most soil-water up taken by plants, often over 98%, is lost via the process of transpiration (Hillel, 2004). Transpiration occurs due to the necessity of absorbing carbon dioxide into the plant (Hillel, 2004). Transpiration creates a loss of water through the plant leaves. Water deficits can be damaging and/ or fatal to a plant (Hillel, 2004). Mesophytes, plants that are neither adapted to extremely wet or dry conditions, are extremely susceptible to massive water loss due to transpiration (Palta&Lee-Stadelmann, 1983).

Within the leaf structure, there are air spaces and the connecting organ to the air-leaf interface is a stomata. Stomata regulate the gas exchanges from the leaf aerenchymal cells and the atmosphere (Takahashi and Kinoshita, 2014). Stoma function as pressure regulators which limits pressure by controlling the flow rate and the stoma limit the plant water potential with soil water and the evaporative demand by managing transpiration. Being modelled as a pressure regulator, this prevents the plant from becoming damaged by cavitation due to the low potential exhibited in the tree (Sperry *et al.*, 2002). With a reduction in the atmospheric pressure (more negative potential), the hydraulic balance in the plant shifts to a demand which in turn decreases the water balance in the leaf; stomata regulate this decrease in potential by opening or closing the aperture. The guard cells, which control the aperture opening of the stomata, are mediated to changes in the osmotic pressure (Buckley, 2005). Therefore, depending on the type of plant and the amount of solutes within the guard cells, the guard cells can stay closed to reduce the chance for further dehydration, thus is a protection mechanism against drought. Since the atmosphere is at a far lower potential than in the leaf (Brady and Weil, 2008), the movement of water through the stomatal aperture is toward the free atmosphere.

Turgidity

Water plays a crucial and irreplaceable role in the process of cell division and expansion, or essentially plant growth (Hillel, 2004). The cell wall, consisting of mainly cellulose, and the cytoplasm within the cell, are generally permeable to water (Hillel, 2004). Water therefore either diffuses or flows in and out of the cell (Hillel, 2004). Another component of the plant cell, between the cell wall and the cytoplasm, is the plasmalemma (Hillel, 2004). This membrane is selectively permeable and can help restrict and select what enters the cell (Hillel, 2004). The vacuoles, or the largest cellular component by volume, are also surrounded by a membrane; the tonoplast.The tonoplast selectively conveys molecules through itself by means of active transport (Hillel, 2004).

Cell expansion occurs when internal cellular pressure, or turgor, stretches the cell's elastic walls (Hillel, 2004). Plant cells have maximum turgor when the plant cell is filled with the maximum amount of water it can hold (Ehlers & Goss, 2003). When a plant requires hydration, or is under moisture stress, its cells are not fully turgid (Hillel, 2004). The plant cell acts as a small, very efficient,osmometer(Palta & Lee-Stadelmann, 1983). The osmotic potential of cell water, due to the sugars and salts dissolved in it, is negative with respect to that of pure water, and will draw water into the vacuole through that gradient (Hillel, 2004).

The aperture, or closure, of the stomatason the leaves is light and CO_2 dependant (Hillel, 2004). Stomatas can close in the dark or when CO_2 concentrations are high (Hillel, 2004). Stomatas are also influenced by the turgidity of the cell (Hillel, 2004). When the cell is more turgid (increased hydration) they bulge and dilate the space between them, and when they are less turgid (decreased hydration) they collapse against each other (Hillel, 2004).

SOIL WATER INTERACTIONS AMONGST DIFFERENT ECOSYSTEMS

Now that the mechanisms behind soil-water uptake have been explored, we can look at how this uptake is influenced by the different soils and ecosystems. In this section we will explore grassland, forest, desert, and permafrost ecosystems and how resistant plants are to deficiencies in their regular soil-water uptake. With these observations we will be able to predictions whether these ecosystem will experience a change in soil-plant-water interactions.

Plant Soil Interactions in Grasslands

Grassland ecosystems encompass a broad spectrum of plant-soil interactions (Burke *et al.,* 1998). The key constraints to plant growth, including water, nutrients, and light, vary drastically both spatially and temporally in grasslands (Burke *et al.,* 1998). For example, in semi-arid to arid grasslands there is strong coupling between the structure of plant communities and the spatial distribution of soil resources, such as water (Burke *et al.,* 1998).

An experiment was conducted in the mountain grasslands of the Alps to determine the response of CO_2 and H_2O exchange to natural fluctuations in soil-water content (Brilli *et al.,* 2011). Observations were taken over a nine-year period, from 2001-2009 (Brilli *et al.,* 2011). Net ecosystem CO_2exchange was measured with the Eddy covariance method and gross primary production was calculated(Brilli *et al.,* 2011). A laboratory drought experiment was also used to assess the physiological performance of certain species under the stress of a water shortage (Brilli *et al.,* 2011). Leaf gas exchange measurements were collected for the laboratory experiment (Brilli *et al.,* 2011). The methods included encasing the species in a cuvette that was flushed with synthetic air (Brilli *et al.,* 2011).

It was found that over the 9-year period the occurrences of dry periods did not lead to substantial reductions in CO_2 exchange or evapotranspiration (Brilli *et al.,* 2011). The laboratory experiments conducted by Brilli et al. showed similar results. The experiment results showed that the species they tested were insensitive to progressive drying (Brilli *et al.,* 2011).The species reached very low soil-water content of less than 0.01 m^3/m^{-3} nevertheless CO_2 and H_2O exchange recovered fully after rehydration (Brilli *et al.,* 2011). These low soil moisture conditions were never reached in the field (Brilli *et al.,* 2011).Brilli et al. concluded that the mountain grassland species are well adapted to surviving short extreme droughts with low soil moisture.

Since the grassland productivity will not be impaired by soil-water shortage Brilli et al predict that the water spending strategy of the mountain grassland species will continue to contribute to a net cooling affect on the climate. They do state, however, that if critically low soil-water content is reached, there will be a swift and dramatic decline in the ecosystem's CO_2 evapotranspiration and assimilation (Brilli *et al.,* 2011). Therefore, at least for the foreseeable future, potential reduction of soil- water content under climate change conditions will not have a severe effect on mountain grasslands vegetation and the area will continue to contribute to cooling the planet.

Plant Soil interactions in Deserts

In the desert ecosystems are dominated by shrubbery and the distribution of soil properties, such as nutrients and water, are strongly affected by the vegetation (Schlesinger &Pilmanis, 1998). Therefore it is important to understand the mechanism behind how the soil influences water transport and drought resistance in the desert. Sperry and Hacke explored in their experiment how soil texture influences plant-water relations in the Great Basin desert of North America.Sperry and Hacke hypothesized that finer soil textures in arid climates would be more negatively associated with plant and soil water potentials during drought, have a greater resistance of xylem to cavitation (the process of essentially boiling a liquid so it changes to vapour phase only via changing the pressure), and would have more shallow root systems than in coarser soil. To test these hypotheses eight species, varied in rooting depth and phenology, were compared growing in sand versus loam soil (Sperry & Hacke, 2002).

It was found that xylem pressures for the species on the loam site were more negative than the sand site, despite greater precipitation (Sperry & Hacke, 2002). The loam site also had more cavitation in the roots and shallower rooting than the sand site (Sperry & Hacke, 2002).There was lower gas exchange in the loam versus sand sites due to transpiration being negatively correlated to xylem conductivity (Sperry & Hacke, 2002). The loam site also showed more leaf drop and branch mortality overall compared to the sandy soil site (Sperry & Hacke, 2002). Sperry and Hacke concluded that the differences in cavitation resistance of roots between the desert species potentially contributed to differences in the sensitivity of gas exchange to soil drought (Sperry & Hacke, 2002). Therefore sandy soils arebetter suited for the desert species in terms of deeper rooting, resistivity to cavitation, and water-uptake during droughts.

If, under warming conditions, the deserts were to get hotter and experience longer droughts, it can be predicted, from the experiments conducted by Sperry and Hacke, that the plants in the sandy soil texture would have better access to soil water, and thus be more prepared to survive. The texture of the sand allows for the plants to root deeper and is better suited for water uptake during droughts (Sperry & Hacke, 2002).

Permafrost

Soil-water content can alter soil thermal properties, which in turn strongly affects permafrost dynamics (Fan *et al.,* 2011). The movement of liquid water was found to play a large role in permafrost heat transport (Fan *et al.,* 2011). Fan et al found that soil temperature during the growing season was overestimated by 2–4 °C if the movement of water was not taken into account. Since the thermal properties of soil are so dependant on the transport of water, in drier sites the permafrost will have a reduced vulnerability to thawing under warming conditions (Fan *et al.,* 2011).

Therefore, under warming conditions such as climate change, sites with more moisture availability will induce faster permafrost melt. This melting of the permafrost will free up more soil-water for plant water uptake, allowing more plants to grow in previously-frozen locations. Although the increase in soil-water availability for plants may seem like it would contribute to a net cooling effect, permafrost itself is a carbon sink storing a seventh of the world's carbon (Schiermeier, 2001). Therefore even though there would be more soil-water availability for plants, the massive out pouring of carbon would still most likely result in the permafrost area becoming a carbon source and contributing to the warming effect.

Forests

In a mathematical model of the future run by Farkas et al. the soil-water balance was examined on a daily time step in 30–year long subperiods. The reference period was 1981-2010, REF, the near-future period was 2021–2050, and the 2071–2100 period was considered as the far future (Farkas *et al.*, 2014). The metrics used for the mathematical model were as follows: gross and net rainfall, potential evapotranspiration, actual evapotranspiration, potential evaporation, actual evaporation, potential transpiration, actual transpiration, and deep percolation or the net amount of water leaving the profile (Farkas *et al.*, 2014). In terms of forests Farkas et al. found that of arable land, forested land, and grassland, it was forested lands that are projected to have the highest number of days with soil moisture deficits. Forest soil-water content deficits were highest in both the upper 50 cm soil layer and the whole soil profile, which could be as high as 61% of days below optimal soil-water content range (Farkas *et al.*, 2014).Farkas et al. concluded that the effect of climate change on the soil-water regime is determined by soil type and vegetation cover (Farkas *et al.*, 2014). It was suggested that further exploration between the relation of soil, land cover, and climate be conducted (Farkas *et al.*, 2014).

Data from research conducted by Carlson et al on plant-soil-water relationships of silvopastoral systems near Coravillis Oregon confirmed that grazing of the understory vegetation may reduce water stress of trees during dry periods by reducing transpirational water use by the forage plants (Carlson *et al.*, 1994). It was also found by Warren et al. that roots of trees conduct hydraulic redistribution most efficiently in dry conditions. Perhaps a combination of grazing and hydraulic redistribution could be employed to increase available soil moisture in the future.

CONCLUSION AND RECOMMENDATIONS FOR FUTURE AREAS OF INTEREST

Understanding the main processes of soil-water uptake in plants is necessary to allow for full comprehensive evaluation of plant-soil-water interactions. In this review photosynthesis and transpiration processes, structure and function of roots, water transport and turgidity were explored. Furthermore recent studies in soil-water up take by plants were analyzed to determine how different ecosystems water uptake mechanisms will react to climate change conditions.

It can be concluded that in the mountain grasslands the water spending strategy of the vegetation will continue to contribute to a net cooling affect on the climate in the future. In the deserts, the sandy soils will be better adapted to maintain plant life under extreme drought conditions of climate change and in the permafrost area, sites with moist soil water availability will thaw faster allowing for vegetation to move in. Finally in a mathematical model prediction of the future under climate change conditions it was found that forests will undergo substantial soil water deficits.

In all four ecosystems researched, the soil-plant-water interactions will change under climate change and warming conditions. To be able to predict these changes will be of utmost importance to finding ways to mitigate the effect of climate change and preserve the cooling effects of these ecosystems. Future areas of research should include wetlands, as they are the largest source of primary productivity. Long-term observations of trends should be analyzed and extrapolated into the future. These proposed studies will contribute to a knowledge base of what to expect and provide a baseline for mitigation and ecosystem remediation efforts.

REFERENCES

Barberon, M., and N. Geldner. 2014. Radial Transport of Nutrients: The Plant Root as a Polarized Epithelium. *Plant Physiology* 166:528-537.

Bechmann, M., C. Schneider, A. Carminati, D. Vetterlein, S. Attinger, and A. Hildebrandt. 2014. Parameterizing Complex Water Root Uptake Models - The Arrangement of Root Hydraulic Properties within the Root Architecture Affects Dynamics and Efficiency of Root Water Uptake. *Hydrol. Earth Sys. Sci. Discuss.* 11:757-805.

Brady, N. C. and R. Weil. 2008. The Nature and Properties of Soils. Pearson Prentice Hall, Upper Saddle River, New Jersey.

Brilli F., Hortnagl L., Hammerle A., Haslwanter A., Hansel A., Loreto F., and G. Wohlfahrt. 2011. Leaf and Ecosystem Response to Soil Water Availability in Mountain Grasslands. Agricultural and Forest Meteorology. 151 (12): 1731-1740.

Buckley, T. N. 2005. The Control of Stomata by Water Balance. *New Phytologist* 168:275-292.

Burke I. C., Lauenroth W. K., Vinton M. A., Hook P.B, Kelly R. H., Epstein H.E., Aguiar M.R., et al. 1998. Plant-Soil Interactions in Temperate Grasslands. Biogeochemistry. 42 (1-2): 121-143.

Carlson, D. H., Sharrow S.H., Emmingham W.H., and D. P. Lavender. 1994. Plant-soil-water relations in Forestry and Silvopastoral Systems in Oregon. Agroforestry Systems : An International Journal Incorporating Agroforestry Forum. 25 (1): 1-12.

Couvreur, V., J. Vanderborght, L. Beff, and M. Javaux. 2014. Horizontal Soil Water Potential Heterogeneity: Simplyfing Approaches for Crop Water Dynamics Models. *Hydrol. Earth Sys. Sci.* 18:1723-1743.

Ehlers W. and M. J. Goss. 2003. Water Dynamics in Plant Production. Wallingford, Oxon, UK: CABI Pub. http://dx.doi.org/10.1079/9780851996943.0000.

Fan, Z., Neff J. C., Harden J. W., Zhang T., Veldhuis H., Czimczik C.I, Winston G.C, and J.A. O'Donnell. 2011. Water and Heat Transport in Boreal Soils: Implications for Soil Response to Climate Change. Science of the Total Environment. 409 (10): 1836-1842.

Farkas C., Gyorgyi G., Zsoìfia B., Horel A., Hagyoì A., Dobor L., Kaìsa I., and E. Toìth. 2014. Impact of Expected Climate Change on Soil Water Regime under different Vegetation Conditions. Biologia : Botany, Zoology and Cellular and Molecular Biology. 69 (11): 1510-1519.

Farsund, A. A., C. Daugbjerg, and O. Langhelle. 2015. Food Security and Trade: Reconciling Discourses in the Food and Agriculture Organization and the World Trade Organization. *Food Sec.* 7:383-391.

Flora, C. B. 2015. Community, Climate Change, and Sustainable Intensification: Why Gender is Important. In: Lal, R. *et al.*, editors, Sustainable Intensification to Advance Food Security and Enhance Climate Resilience in Africa. Switzerland. p. 515-532. doi: 10.1007/978-3-319-09360-4.

Guderle, M., and A. Hildebrandt. 2014. Using Measured Soil Water Content to Estimate Evapotranspiration and Root Water Uptake Profiles - A Comparative Study. *Hydrol. Earth Sys. Sci. Discuss.* 11:10859-10902.

Hillel, D. 2004. Introduction to Environmental Soil Physics. Amsterdam: Elsevier Academic Press. http://www.engineeringvillage.com/controller/servlet/OpenURL?genre=book&isbn=9780123486554.

Holbrook, N. M., and M. A. Zwieniecki. 2005. Vascular Transport in Plants. Burlington, MA: Elsevier Academic Press. http://www.engineeringvillage.com/controller/servlet/OpenURL?genre=book&isbn=9780120884575.

IPCC. 2013. Climate Change 2013: The Physical Science Basis. Intergovernmental Panel on Climate Change.

Karlen, D. L., C. A. Ditzler, and S. S. Andrews. 2003. Soil Quality: Why and How? *Geoderma* 114:145-156.

Kim, H. K., J. Park, I. Hwang. 2014. Investigating Water Transport through the Xylem Network in Vascular Plants. *Journal of Experimental Botany* 65(7):1895-1904.

Kirkham, M. B. 2005. Principles of Soil and Plant Water Relations. Academic Press, Waltham, Massachusetts. ISBN: 978-0-12-409751-3.

Palta, J. P. and O. Y. Lee-Stadelmann. 1983. Vacuolated Plant Cells as Ideal Osmometer: Reversibility and Limits of Plasmolysis, and Estimation of Protoplasm Volume in Control and Water-stress-tolerant Cells. Plant, Cell & Environment. 6 (8): 601-610.

Scherer, T. F., D. Franzen, and L. Cihacek. 2013. Soil, Water and Plant Characteristics Important to Irrigation. Rep. AE1675. North Dakota State University, Fargo, North Dakota.

Schiermeier Q. 2001. Fears Grow over Melting Permafrost. Nature. 409 (6822).

Schlesinger W. H., and A. M. Pilmanis. 1998. Plant-soil Interactions in Deserts. Biogeochemistry. 42 (1-2): 169-187.

Scott, H. D. 2000. Soil Physics: Agricultural and Environmental Applications. Iowa State University Press, Ames, Iowa.

Sperry J. S, and U. G Hacke. 2002. Desert Shrub Water Relations with Respect to Soil Characteristics and Plant Functional Type. Functional Ecology. 16 (3): 367-378.

Sperry, J. S., U. G. Hacke, R. Oren, and J. P. Comstock. 2002. Water Deficits and Hydraulic Limits to Leaf Water Supply. *Plant, Cell and Environment* 25:251-263.

Takahashi, Y., and T. Kinoshita. 2014. Stomatal Function has an Element of Hysteresis. *New Phytologist* 205:455-457.

Wang, X., D. K. Thompson, G. A. Marshall, C. Tymstra, R. Carr, M. D. Flannigan. 2015. Increasing Frequency of Extreme Fire Weather in Canada with Climate Change. *Climate Change*: 1-14. doi: 10.1007/s10584-015-1375-5.

Warren J. M., Meinzer F.C., Brooks J. R., Domec J-C., and R. Coulombe. 2007. Hydraulic Redistribution of Soil Water in two old-growth Coniferous Forests: Quantifying Patterns and Controls. New Phytologist. 173 (4): 753-765.

Yadav, S., M. Irfan, S. Hayat. 2011. Causes of Salinity and Plant Manifestations to Salt Stress: A Review. *J. Environ. Biol.* 32:667-685.

Yu, G-R., Jie Z., Nakayama K., and Y. Jin. 2007. Root Water Uptake and Profile Soil Water as Affected by Vertical Root Distribution. Plant Ecology: An International Journal. 189 (1): 15-30.

Climate Change and Agro-Edaphic System **Pages 182–188**
Edited by: **Dr. Alka Chauhan & Dr. Pawan Kumar 'Bharti'**
ISBN: 978-93-86841-98-8
Edition: **2019**
Published by: **Discovery Publishing House Pvt. Ltd., New Delhi (India)**

10

Egyptian Contribution to a Solution of Global Warming by Aquaculture in Qattara Depression

a Simulation Study

[1]A.I. Noor El Deen, Mona S. Zaki, [2]M. Khafagy and [3]M.S. Abd El Karim

ABSTRACT

This study was conducted to study how the development of inland oligotrophic marine ecosystem in Qattara Depression may act to mitigate the increase in the atmospheric carbon dioxide. Three sites with different nutrient concentrations were chosen at the Mediterranean Egyptian coast to study the phytoplankton composition, biomass and productivity. Site 1 was highest in nutrient concentration but least in water transparency, whereas site 2 was moderate in nutrient concentrations but highest in water transparency. Both gross and net production have a climax at site 2 with values reached up to 793.9 and 355.9 gC/m /year, respectively. The net primary production (C sequestration) of phytoplankton at the expected water intake of the project is 355g m 3 year 1. At filling of Qattara Depression at 60m below sea level the water volume will be 209.3 km3, the total C sequestered by phytoplankton per year is about 700 × 105 tons of carbon, which is about 1.5% of the annual increase of atmospheric carbon dioxide worldwide. Rising temperature during summer and nutrients enrichment in Qattara Depression may increase sequestration of carbon dioxide up to 5% of total annual carbon increase in earth atmosphere.

Keywords: Global warming Phytoplankton Primary productivity and Qattara Depression.

INTRODUCTION

The policy of the Ministry of Electricity and Energy in Egypt is to increase the utilization of all natural resources for energy production, especially the hydro-potential as the most important source (e.g. the Aswan hydro-electrical station

[1] National Research Centre, Cairo, Egypt
[2] National Cancer Institute, Cairo University, Cairo, Egypt
[3] National Institute of Oceanography and Fisheries, Cairo, Egypt

with an installed capacity of 2400 MW). Theoretically, a big project concerning the utilization of Qattara Depression for this purpose was designed many years ago. Qattara Depression is located in the western desert in Egypt, about 134 m below sea level at its lowest point. At zero level, the surface area of the depression is about 19,500 km^2 representing 1/15 of the area of Egypt, whereas at filling of 60m below sea level the surface area of the depression is about 12,100 km^2 with water volume of 209.3 km^3. The depression is planned to be connected to the Mediterranean Sea either through tunnels or open canal. The discharged water will be regulated by water turbines thus utilize the difference between sea level and the depression for power production. A preliminary intake for the water canal was chosen at El Sirra area located 15 km west of El Dabaa. After the establishment of the project, the maximum annual energy forecast is about 15400 TWH. It can be noted that the surface of the foreseen formed lake at level of 60 m below sea level will be 12,100 km^2 and volume of water will amount to 209,3 cubic kilometers.

Anthropogenic activity has increased the carbon dioxide concentration of the atmosphere by 30% from pre-industrial concentrations averaging 270 ppm. Carbon dioxide concentrations are expected to rise to 450 ppm by 2065 and to 650 ppm by 2100. These CO_2 ncreases may have dramatic impacts on global climate, lobal carbon cycles, ocean circulation, biotic diversity and marine ecosystem function. Elevated atmospheric CO_2 will also increase the dissolved aqueous CO_2 concentration [CO_2 (aq)] in seawater and decrease pH. The resulting drop in seawater pH may cause widespread decline of carbonate accretion systems such as coral reefs.

Plants are known to sequester atmospheric carbon dioxide through photosynthesis resulted in the key stones of life (food and oxygen). One way to mitigate the increase in the atmospheric carbon dioxide (CO_2) concentration is to increase the carbon (C) uptake (or C sequestration) in different plant life forms. In this direction, many trials were devoted to study how terrestrial plants, aquatic seaweeds and sea grasses and phytoplankton can be used to mitigate the dramatic increase in atmospheric carbon dioxide.

This study was conducted to investigate how the development of inland oligotrophic marine ecosystem in Qattara Depression may act to mitigate the increase in the atmospheric carbon dioxide.

MATERIALS AND METHODS

Sampling Sites: Three different sites with three different trophies were selected at the south coast of Mediterranean Sea at Egypt. The locations of the three sites were presented in Table 10.1.

Water Sampling: Subsurface water samples were collected by a polyvinyl chloride, Van Dorn bottle. The Dissolved Oxygen was performed by azide modification whereas; different nutrient concentrations were determined using colorimetric techniques. GF/F filter papers were used for chlorophyll-a (chl-a) measurements, the filters were socked in 10 ml hot ethanol according to. Phytoplankton samples were fixed with Lugol's solution enumerated and counted using the inverted microscope method. Identification of the main phytoplanktonic groups was made with reference of: Cyanoprokaryotes;, Bacillariophyceae; Chlorococcales. For diatoms identification for the species level, subsamples were oxidized by concentrated nitric acid and mounted in Naphrax medium. Primary production was determined by oxygen light-dark bottles method. Water samples were collected in 300-ml glass BOD bottles. Triplicates light bottles (LB) and dark bottles (DB) were incubated in the field at 50 cm below the water surface. Oxygen concentration was measured (Winkler's method) at the beginning of the experiment as initial bottles (IB). After the incubation, LB and DB.

Table 10.1: Latitude and Longitude of the Selected Sites

Sites	Location	Latitude	Longitude
1.	East of Alexandria City	9,32'36°31	"51,51'56°28
2.	West of Alexandria City	40,27'8°31	"10,74'49°29
3.	El-Alamein City	"21,22'50°30	"51,51'56°28

RESULTS

The different nutrient concentrations showed a significant decrease westward (Figure 1). The maximum concentrations of NO_2, NO_3, NH_4, PO_4, TP (µg/l) and silicate (mg/l) (19.7, 66.2, 105.6, 51.5, 147.8 and 3.5, respectively) were detected at site 1. On the other side, the minimum values of these nutrients 3.0, 39.7, 46.6, 14.6, 43.7 and 2.8, respectively, were measured at site 3. The spatial variation of the different nutrient concentrations were highly significant ($P>0.005$) except for silicate; where its variation was non-significant ($P= 0.08$).

The phytoplankton representation by both biomass and cell density was a mirror image to the eutrophication status represented by the nutrient concentrations. Biomass (chlorophyll a) and cell density were greatly decreased westward from site 1 to site 3 (Figure 10.2). The highest phytoplankton chlorophyll a of 18.6 µg/l was measured at site 1, whereas the least biomass value 2.3µg/l was found at site 3. The phytoplankton cell density peaked at site 1 (8326 cell × 10^3/l) whereas the density was minimum at site 3 (897.2 cell × 10^3/l).

The gross and net productions pattern at the area of investigation differ from the eutrophic status of the area of study. Both gross and net production have a climax at site 2 with values reached to 793.9 and 355.9 gC/m^3/year, respectively. The net production was least at site 3 with value of 109.5 gC/m^3/year, (Figure 10.3).

DISCUSSION

Depending on our finding concerning the net primary production (C sequestration) of phytoplankton at the expected water intake of the project is 355g m^3 year. It is predicted that the total C sequestered by phytoplankton per year, according to this water volume, is about 700 × 10^5 tons of carbon which mean 70 million tons of carbon dioxide will be removed from the atmosphere. If we know that the annual increase of atmospheric carbon dioxide amount to 3.2 Giga ton, Qattara Depression will be responsible for removing of about 1.5% of this increase.

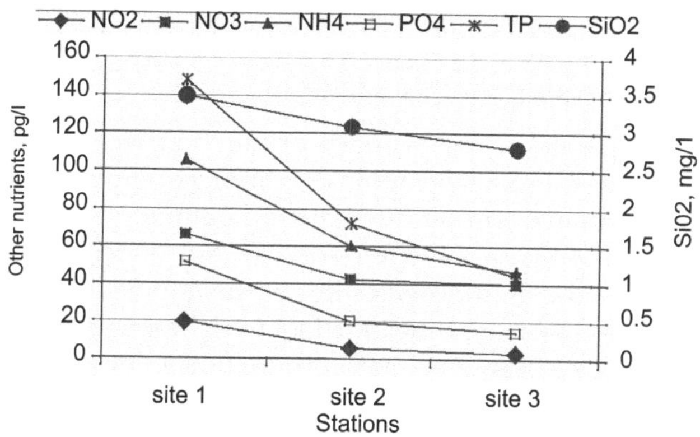

Fig. 10.1: Different nutrient concentrations at different sites

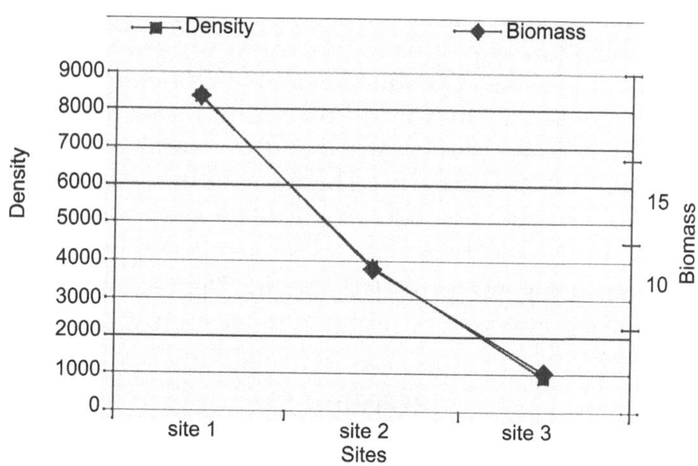

Fig. 10.2: Phytoplankton population density (no of cells × 10_3l^1) biomass (μg l^1)

In Chesapeake Bay, in the temperate easternr egion of US, observed a late winter minimum, average, of 32.5 mg Cm2d, with rising temperature they observed a summer maximum, average, of 1500 mg Cm2 d1. In general they observed a 2-3 fold increase in net primary production during summer compared with late winter-early spring. Similar results were reported by. Our

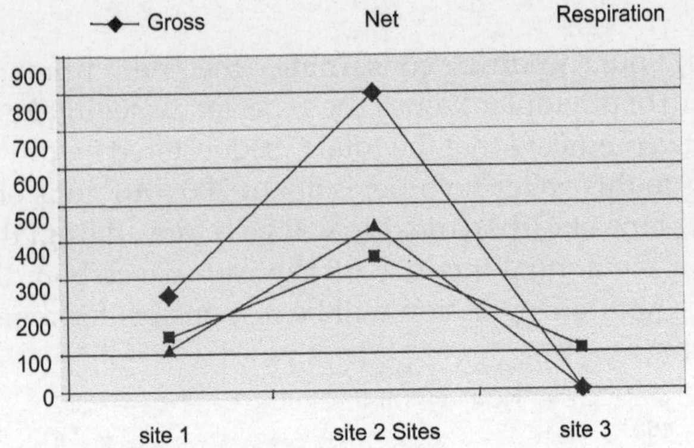

Fig. 10.3: Gross, net production and respiration (gC/m³/year) at the studied area

measures of phytoplankton net primary production were at temperature of 17°C, mid winter and oligomesotrophic conditions of nutrient concentrations. In agreement with rising temperature during summer will increase the net primary production in Qattara Depression 2-3 fold which means an increase from 1.5 to 3-4.5% in the annual removing of the atmospheric carbon dioxide increased per year. In the same time, nutrient enrichment in oligo-mesotrophic conditions may enhance the net primary production to levels that make Qattara Depression remove more than 5% of the annual increase of CO_2. Studied the effect of nutrient enrichment in South China Sea and indicated that while N enrichment enhanced phytoplan enrichment only occasionally increased production. In all 20 enrichments, whenever N was supplemented, either singly or in combination with other nutrients, phytoplankton production was greatly enhanced. The primary production for the +N treatment measured was 7.82 mgCm^3 h^1. It was 9.22 mgCm^3 h^1 for the +NP treatment. These values 5 are approximately 5-10 times greater than the control (1.66 mg Cm^3 h^1) or the +P enrichment (0.89 mg Cm^3 0 h^1). These results in combination with those of may support our hypothesis that using Qattara Depression as aquaculture may remove more than 5% of the annual increase of CO_2 in the atmosphere.

In conclusion, using the projected Qattara Depression for hydropower generation as aquaculture may be useful in sequestration carbon dioxide and combat global warming.

REFERENCES

American Public Health Association (APHA), 1992. Standard Methods of the Examination of Water and Wastewater. 17th edition, AWWA, WPCF, pp. 1015.

Boyd, P.W., A.J. Watson, C. S. Law, E.R. Abraham, T. Trull, R. Murdoch, D.C.E. Bakker, A.R. Bowie, K.O. Buesseler, H. Chang, M.A. Charette, P. Croot, K. Downing, R.D. Frew, M. Gall, M. Hadfield, J.A. Hall, M. Harvey, G. Jameson, J. La Roche, M.I. Liddicoat, R. Ling, M. Maldonado, R.M. McKay, S.D. Nodder, S. Pickmere, R. Pridmore, S. Rintoul, K. Safi, P. Sutton, R. Strzepek, K. Tanneberger, S.M. Turner, A. Waite and J. Zeldis, 2000. A Mesoscale Phytoplankton Bloom in the Polar Southern Ocean Stimulated by Iron Fertilization. Nature, 407: 695-702.

Bozeca, Y., C.E. Bakkerb, C. Hartmannc, H. Thomasa, G.J. Richard, D. Bellerbyd, U. Riebesellc, J. Watsonb and J.W. Hein, 2005. The CO2 System in a Redfield Context during an iron Enrichment Experiment in the Southern Ocean. Marine Chemistry, 95: 89-105.

Carmelo, J., 1997. Identification of Marine Phytoplankton, Academic Press, Harcourt Brace and Company, New York.

Charles, D., C. Knowles and R. Davis, 2002. Protocols for the Analysis of Algal Samples Collected as part of the U.S. Geological Survey National Water-Quality Assessment Program. Patrick Center for Environmental Research Report No. 02-06, The Academy of Natural Science, Philadelphia.

Chen, Y.L., 2005. Spatial and Seasonal Variations of Nitrate-based New Production and Primary Production in the South China Sea Deep-Sea Research, 52: 319-340.

Denman, K., 1996. Marine Biotic Responses to Environmental Change and Feedbacks to Climate. In: J.T. Houghton, L.G. Meira Filho, B.A. Callader, N. Harris, A. Kattenberg and K. Maskell, (eds) Climate change 1995: The Science of Climate Change. Cambridge University Press, New York.

Dillard, G.E., 1991. Freshwater Algae of the Southeastern, United States, By; J. Krammer, Berlin, Stuttgart, Germany.

Ehleringer, J.R., T.E. Cerling and L.B. Flanagan, 2001. Global Change and the Linkages between Physiological Ecology and Ecosystem Ecology. In: M.C. Press, N.J. Huntley and S. Levin, (eds) Ecology: Achievement and Challenge. Blackwell Science, Williston, VT.

Harding, L.W., Jr, M.E. Malloneea and E.S. Perryc, 2002. Toward a Predictive Understanding of Primary Productivity in a Temperate, Partially Stratified Estuary. Estuarine, Coastal and Shelf Science, 55: 437-463.

Keeling, C.D., 1997. Climate Change and Carbon Dioxide: An Introduction. Proc Natl Acad Sci USA 94: 8273-8274.

Kleypas, J.A., R.W. Buddemeier, D. Archer, J.P. Gattuso, C. Langdon and B.N. Opdyke, 1999. Geochemical Consequences of increased Atmospheric Carbon Dioxide on Coral Reefs. Science, 284: 118-120.

Krammer, K. and H. Lange-Bertalot, 1986. Bacillariophyceae. Teil: Naviculaceae. Susswasserflora von Mitteleuropa, 2/1: 1-876. Gustav Fisher Verlag, Stuttgart, Germany.

Manabe, S and R.J. Stouffer, 1994. Multiple-century Response of a Coupled Ocean-atmosphere Model to an increase of atmospheric carbon dioxide. J. Clim., 7: 5-23.

Marker, A.F., C.A. Crowther and R.J. Gunin, 1980. Methanol and Acetone as Solvents for Estimating Chlorophyll-a and phaeopigments by Spectrophotometer. Arch. Hydrobiol. Beih. Ergebn. Limnol., 14: 52-69.

Ministry Electricity and Energy in Egypt (1972). Qattara Depression, pp. 48.

Nusch, E.A., 1980. Comparison of different Methods for chl. and Phaeopigments Determination. Arch. Hydrobiol. Beih. Ergebn. Limnol., 14: 14-36.

O'Neill, B.C. and M. Oppenheimer, 2002. Dangerous climate impacts and the Kyoto Protocol. Science, 296: 1971-1972.

Sarmiento, J.L., T.M.C. Hughes, R.J. Stouffer and S. Manabe, 1998. Simulated Response of the Ocean Carbon Cycle to Anthropogenic Climate Warming. Nature, 393: 245-249.

Smith, E.M. and W.M. Kemp, 1995. Seasonal and Regional Variations in Plankton Community Production and Respiration for Chesapeake Bay. Marine Ecology Progress Series, 116: 217-231.

Starmach, K., 1968. Flora Slodkonda Polaki Toms., pp. 594.

Strickland, J.D. and T.R. Parsons, 1965. A Manual of Sea Water Analysis "2nd edition Fisheries Research". Board of Canada, Ottawa.

Suyker, A.E., S.B. Verma, G.G. Burba, T.J. Arkebauer, D.T. Walters and K.G. Hubbard, 2004. Growing Season Carbon Dioxide Exchange in Irrigated and Rainfed Maize. Agric. For. Meteorol., 124: 1-13.

Tikkanen, T., 1986. Kasviplanktonopas. Suomen Luonnonsuojelun Tuki Oy (Italia.), Helsinki, pp. 278.

Trenberth, K., 1996. The Climate System: An Overview. In: J.T. Houghton, L.G. Meira Filho, B.A.Callader, N. Harris, A. Kattenberg and K. Maskell, (eds). Climate Change 1995: The Science of Climate Change. Cambridge University Press, New York.

Utermohl, H., 1958. Zur Vervollkommung der Quantitativen Phytoplankton-methodik. Internationale Vereinigung fur Theoretische and Angewandte Limnologi, 9: 1-38.

Veldhuis, M.J.W., G.W. Kraay, J.D.L. Van Bleijswijk and M.A. Baars, 1997. Seasonal and Spatial Variability in Phytoplankton Biomass, Productivity and Growth in the Northwestern Indian Ocean: the Southwest and Northeast Monsoon, 1992–1993. Deep-Sea Research, 44: 425-449.

Vollenweider, R.A., 1996. A Manual Method for Measuring Primary Production in Environment. IBP. Handbook No. 12. Oxford and Edinburgh, pp. 213.

Xu, L. and D.D. Baldocchi, 2003. Seasonal Variation in Carbon Dioxide Exchange over a Mediterranean Annual Grassland in California. Agric. For. Meteorol., 123: 79-96.

Zeebe, R.E. and D. Wolf-Gladrow, 2001. CO2 in Seawater: Equilibrium, Kinetics, Isotopes. Elsevier, New York.

Zimmerman, R.C., D.G. Kohrs, D.L. Steller and R.S. Alberte, 1997. Impacts of CO2- enrichment on Productivity and Light Requirements of Seagrass. Plant Physiol., 115: 599-607.

Index

A

Actinobacillus suis, 87
AIE, Noor El Deen, 163
Air pollution and climatic changes, 74-102
  air pollution, 77-79
  climate change and air pollution: an analysis of the causative agents of air pollution and their subsequent effects, 81-82
  effects of climatic changes due to air pollution with special reference to plants, animals and human beings, 83
  energy related strategies, 91
  general regulations for air quality control, 90-91
  implications for air quality management, 89-90
  interactions between climate and air pollution, 76-77
  introduction, 74-76
  on animals, 85-87
  – humans, 83-85
  – plants, 87-89
  plants as phytoremediator of air pollutants, 91-93
  pollutant categories, 79-81
  reactive nitrogen, 82
  research and management needs, 93
  sulphur dioxide and sulphur deposition, 82-83
Andhra Pradesh, 69
Anthropogenic Global Warming Theory (AGWT), 103
Arctic circle, 2
Atelopus, 139
Atlantic Multidecadal Oscillation (AMO), 122
Azolla pinnata, 92
Azotobacter, 129

B

Bacillus species, 136
Bangladesh, 69
Bara Shigri Glacier, 35
Bhandari, B.S., 74
Bharti, Pawan Kumar, 1
Biswas, Asim, 168
Brahmacharimayum, Jesmita, 20

C

Casuarinas, 161
CDM, 39
CFCs, 14
Chesapeake Bay, 185
Chhota Shigri, 35
Clean Development Mechanism (CDM), 16, 38
Climate change, 1-19, 20-49, 74-102, 103-126, 127-146, 147-162
Climate change and Indian agriculture, 147-162
  causes of climate variability and change, 149
    human causes, 150-153
      aerosols in the atmosphere, 152
      deforestation, 152
      greenhouse gases, 150-151
      land use change, 152
    natural causes, 149-150
      earth orbital changes, 149-150
      ocean current, 149
      solar variations, 150
      volcanic eruptions, 149
  climate change scenario in India, 153
    extreme rainfall events, 153-154
    precipitation, 153

temperature, 153
effects of climate change on agriculture, 155-156
impact of climate change on
crop, 156-157
fisheries, 158-159
livestock, 158
pest, 158
soil health, 157
water resources, 157
general effects of climate change, 154-155
ecological imbalance, 154
extreme climate variability, 154
glacier retreat and disappearance, 155
increased occurrence of pests and diseases, 154
increasing temperature, 154
limited food supply, 154
more powerful typhoons, 155
rise in sea levels, 155
introduction, 148
measures addressing the effect of climate change on agriculture, 159-160
adaptation strategies, 160
mitigation technologies, 160-161
Climate change and its causes, 103-126
ACRIM vs. PMOD satellite total solar irradiance controversy, 115-117
astronomical origin of the climate oscillations, 120-123
climate sensitivity uncertainty to CO_2 increase, 107-110
– meaning of recent paleoclimatic temperature reconstructions, 110-112
introduction, 103-105
IPCC pro-anthropogenic warming bias, 105-107
large 60 year cycle in the temperature record, 117-120
phenomenological solar signature since 1600, 112-114
problems with the global surface temperature record, 117
Climate change scenario in India and evidences in the Indian Himalayan region, 20-49
adaptation and mitigation strategies, 36
CDM in Indian agricultural sector, 38-39
India stand on CDM projects, 38
role in climate change mitigation, 37-38
– of Paris agreement, 36-37
status of ratification, 38
climate change adaptation strategies for the Indian Himalayan region, 41
National Action Plan on Climate Change (NAPCC), 41
national missions, 41-42
climate change and global warming, 21-22
– – impacts on agriculture and food security, 31-34
– – impacts on extreme events
cold waves and heat waves, 28-29
cyclones, 24
floods and droughts, 26-27
fog, 27-28
forest fires, 29-30
sea level rise, 24-26
– – – – glaciers and water sources, 34-36
– – in the Indian himalayan region (IHR), 22-23
discussion, 23
climate change impacts in IHR, 23
climate change impacts on extreme events, 23-30
introduction, 21
sustainable approach at an individual level, 42-43
– development goals (SDGs), 39-40

Climate Resilient Agriculture, 33
Coleopteran, 33
Coping Capabilities in Facing Natural Disasters, 68

D

Deen, A.I. Noor El, 182
Dhevagi, P., 127
DNA, 10

E

Egyptian contribution to a solution of global warming by aquaculture in Qattara depression, 182-188
introduction, 182-183
materials and methods, 183-184
sampling sites, 183
water sampling, 183-184
results, 184
discussion, 185-186
Environmental Protection Agency, 82
Eucalyptus, 161
European Union, 59

F

Famine and Pandemics, 17
Fusarium, 140

G

GDP, 38, 65
GHGs, 7, 31, 37
Global Forest Resource Assessment, 30
Global warming, 4, 17, 163
Green Climate Fund (GCF), 40
Green House Effect, 17
Green Revolution, 67
GWP, 4

H

HCFCs, 14
HIV/AIDS, 56

I

Increasing human activities and climate change, 1-19
anthropogenic activities, 4
atmosphere, 2-3
consequences, 10
air quality, 12-14
health problems, 10-11
local weather, 12
temperature variation, 11-12
global environmental issues, 4
climate change, 7-8
global warming, 4-5
green house effect, 5-6
ozone depletion, 8-10
industrialization, 3-4
introduction, 1-2
legal initiatives, 14
Kyoto protocol, 15-16
montreal protocol, 14-15
India Meteorological Department (IMD), 153
Indian agriculture, 147-162
Indian Himalayan region, 20-49
Intergovernmental panel of climate change with special reference to health, 50-73
adaptation solutions, 61
drought and desertification, 62
sea level rising/floods/water nuisance, 61-62
brief history of international agreements on climate change, 52-53
causes of global climate change, 54-55
climate events, 63-72
– system, 52
– variability and climate change, 51-52
consequences of global climate change, 55
economic consequences, 56-57
natural consequences, 55-56
defining weather and climate, 51
greenhouse effect, 53-54
– gases, 54
heat, 62-63

introduction, 50-51
method, 59
mitigation solutions, 59-61
potential health impacts of climate change, 57-58
since greenhouse gases make up such a small percentage of the atmosphere, why do changes in their concentrations have such a big effect on climate, 54
why global warming is the wrong term, 52

IPCC, 21, 25

J

Ji, Wengun, 168

K

Karim, M.S. Abd El, 182
Khafagy, M., 182
Kharif crops, 32
Kumar, Prasann, 50, 103
Kyoto Protocol, 37

M

Maurya, Shalini Singh, 20
Mediterranean sea at Egypt, 183
Melting of Glaciers, 17
Millennium Development Goals (MDGs), 39

N

NASA Jet Propulsion Laboratory, 8
National Fire Prevention, 30
National Mission for a Green India, 42
National Mission for Enhanced Energy Efficiency, 41
National Mission for Sustainable Agriculture, 42
National Mission for Sustaining the Himalayan Ecosystem, 41
National Mission on Strategic Knowledge for Climate Change, 42
National Mission on Sustainable Habitat, 41
National Solar mission, 41
National Water Mission, 41
Nationally Determined Contribution (NDC), 37
Natural Disaster Management Division, 68
Navneet, Akash, 74
Nepal, 69
NMVOCs, 90
NOAA, 22
North Indian Ocean, 24, 25

O

ODS, 14
Ozone Depletion, 17

P

Pacific Decadal Oscillation (PDO), 122
Pacific oceans, 64
Paris Agreement, 37
Pathak, Shweta, 50, 103
Patra, Alok Kumar, 147
Patra, Pulak Kumar, 147
Patra, Ranjan Kumar, 147
Phaseolus, 33
Phytophthora parasitica, 140
Phytoplankton to combat global warming, 163-167
introduction, 163-164
Pine trees, 43
Ponniah, C., 127
Pseudomonas, 136

Q

Qattara depression, 182-188

R

Rabi crops, 32
Reduce, Reuse and Recycle (3 Rs), 43
Regional Meteorological Centres (RMCs), 24
Rhizoctonia solani, 140
River Chenab, 35

S

Saichen glacier, 35
Sharma, Bhavika, 20
Soil microorganisms and climate change, 127-146

factors affecting soil microorganisms, 128-131
introduction, 127-128
soil borne pathogens and climate, 139-140
– microbes and climate change, 132-134
– microbes and nitrogen, 137-139
– microorganisms and carbon, 134-137
– microorganisms and methane, 137
types of soil microorganisms, 128
Soil-plant-water interactions in varying ecosystems, 168-181
introduction, 168-169
recommendations for future areas of interest, 179
soil water and its movement, 169
soil water, 169-170
– – movement, 171-172
soil water interactions amongst different ecosystems, 176
forests, 179
permafrost, 178
plant soil interactions in
deserts, 177-178
grasslands, 176-177
soil water uptake by plants and movement in plants, 172
photosynthesis and transpiration, 175
soil-root interface, 173-174
structure and function of roots, 172
turgidity, 176
water transportation in the plant, 174
SSTs, 64
Streptococcus suis, 87
Submergence of Coastal Nations, 17
Sustainable Development Goals (SDGs), 39

U

UNEP, 58, 103
UNFCCC, 15, 21, 36
United Nations, 39
Uttar Pradesh, 28

V

VOCs, 4, 13

W

WMO, 58, 103
World Health Organization, 7
World Meteorological Organization, 23, 24

Z

Zaki, Mona S., 182
Zea mays, 92
Zinnia anguistifolia, 92